Taylor Woodrow

International Commodity Trading

WILEY TRADING SERIES

The Elliott Wave Principle: Key to Market Behavior
Robert R. Prechter

Dynamic Technical Analysis
Philippe Cahen

Encyclopedia of Chart Patterns
Thomas N. Bulkowski

The Psychology of Finance
Lars Tvede

Integrated Technical Analysis
Ian Copsey

Financial Markets Tick by Tick: Insights in Financial Markets Microstructure
Pierre Lequeux

Technical Market Indicators: Analysis and Performance
Richard J. Bauer and Julie R. Dahlquist

Trading to Win: The Psychology of Mastering the Markets
Ari Kiev

Pricing Convertible Bonds
Kevin Connolly

At the Crest of the Tidal Wave: A Forecast for the Great Bear Market
Robert R. Prechter

INTERNATIONAL COMMODITY TRADING

Physical and Derivative Markets

Ephraim Clark, Jean-Baptiste Lesourd, and René Thiéblemont

John Wiley & Sons, Ltd
Chichester • New York • Weinheim • Brisbane • Singapore • Toronto

Other Wiley Editorial Offices

John Wiley & Sons, Inc., 605 Third Avenue,
New York, NY 10158-0012, USA

Wiley-VCH GmbH, Pappelallee 3,
D-69469 Weinheim, Germany

John Wiley & Sons Australia, Ltd, 33 Park Road, Milton,
Queensland 4064, Australia

John Wiley & Sons (Asia) Pte Ltd, 2 Clementi Loop #02-01,
Jin Xing Distripark, Singapore 129809

John Wiley & Sons (Canada) Ltd, 22 Worcester Road,
Rexdale, Ontario, M9W 1L1, Canada

Library of Congress Cataloging-in-Publication Data

Clark, Ephraim.
    International commodity trading : physical and derivative markets/Ephraim Clark,
    Jean-Baptiste Lesourd, and René Thiéblemont.
        p.cm. — (Wiley trade series)
    Includes bibliographical references and index.
    ISBN 0-471-855210-4 (alk. paper)
    1. Commodity exchanges. 2. International trade. I. Lesourd, Jean-Baptiste. II.
    Thiéblemont, René. III. Title. IV. Series.
    HG6046 .C5735 2001
    332.63'28–dc21   00-068505

British Library Cataloguing in Publication Data

A catalogue record for this book is available from the British Library

ISBN 0 471 85210 4
Typeset in 10/12pt Times by Laser Words, Madras, India
Printed and bound in Great Britain by Bookcraft Bath Ltd, Midsomer Norton, Somerset
This book is printed on acid-free paper responsibly manufactured from sustainable forestry,
in which at least two trees are planted for each one used for paper production.

Contents

Preface

This book is devoted to the international markets for basic commodities and to the international trade that takes place on these markets, together with their implications for corporate management and corporate finance. These problems are interesting problems, which are quite important in today's world. This is because international commodity markets are global markets for essential resources, just like capital, which is traded on international capital markets. The ongoing evolution of international commodity markets is indeed a fascinating aspect of globalisation, inasmuch as many basic commodities are traded globally on international physical markets, often associated with efficient and global futures markets.

Buying and selling basic commodities necessarily requires some knowledge of the specific mechanisms applying to these markets. In this book, we are concerned with the various techniques, including quantitative techniques, associated with the management of market operations involving basic commodities. Besides an understanding of the economics of basic commodity markets, this includes the development and understanding of the specific topics regarding the risks, and the management of these risks, that are encountered when buying, selling or trading basic commodities. To this end, we present and analyse the various kinds of commodity markets with special emphasis on the negotiation of commodity contracts. We also develop the simple hedging instruments available on the organised futures and options exchanges as well as the more advanced or 'exotic' instruments, such as swaps, caps and floors as applied to commodities, available on the over-the-counter (OTC) markets. We then go into the different techniques for forecasting commodity prices and end up with an in-depth analysis of the activities of the various actors operating on commodity spot and derivative markets.

In summary, then, we are concerned generally with the *trading of commodities*, whether it means physical trading or trading on derivative markets. The book is divided into two main parts. The first part of the book is devoted to the various markets. It includes the description of the main features of international *physical* commodity markets (spot markets or forward markets) and of the associated derivative markets (organised futures and option markets, as well as OTC futures and options markets), which are used for hedging against price risks. We aim to give the practical insights with the necessary theoretical developments, especially when we deal with the new techniques and instruments in the constantly evolving OTC derivative markets.

The second part deals with the analysis, in terms of *management*, of the various *actors* on the international commodity markets, their actions, and the interplay among them. It begins with a discussion of the management of information concerning commodity markets and of forecasting techniques that may be used on them. It then outlines the general features of the management of selling and purchasing physical commodities, and of related positions on derivative instruments, with a discussion of their importance for corporate finance and in a global economy. Finally, it goes into the negotiation of (physical) commodity contracts. Throughout the second part of the book, we are interested in the actors involved in the physical trading of basic commodities: producers (mining companies, agroindustrial companies, and primary energy producers), industrial users (the food and beverage industry, other transformation industries such as the tyre industry, the mechanical and electrical appliances industries, the secondary energy industries), and physical commodity trading companies (such as Cargill, Dreyfus, Johnson Matthey, Engelhard, etc.) who act as intermediaries between other physical actors. We are also interested in actors involved in the trading on futures and derivative markets for commodities, which often are the same as the above physical actors, but are also closely linked to financial actors such as banks and other financial institutions and intermediaries.

Foreword

With the almost universal move to free market economies, the need for guidance and education on the management of financial affairs and particularly the management of risk, has grown accordingly. This is especially true in the case of commodities, where the underlying risks of adverse price movements in the value of raw materials, combined with increased volatility, can have dramatic effects for financial institutions and in some cases national economies. *International Commodity Trading: Physical and Derivative Markets* is an excellent addition to the library of anyone entering this field of activity, as well as those already involved in the market place, be they financial strategists, economists or students. It gives a brief but useful introduction to the various international markets and the instruments they trade. This is followed by a well developed explanation of various hedging, commercial and actor strategies.

Ephraim Clark, Jean-Baptiste Lesourd and René Thiéblemont have done an excellent job in producing this very useful study which I highly recommend to any current or potential participant in the field of commodity trading.

Raymond Sampson
(London Metal Exchange)

Acknowledgements

One of the characteristic features of this work is to provide an in-depth analysis of physical commodity markets and of physical commodity trading practices and of their relationships with commodity derivative markets.

The authors wish to thank all professionals and companies who contributed to their work in providing useful and first-hand information to them. In particular, they gratefully acknowledge the very helpful support of the following persons: Jacques Emler (Tradigrain, Farmland Group), and Patrick Felix (Sugar Division, Tradigrain, Farmland Group); Jean Lerbret, Honorary President of the French Chartering and Shipbrokers Association; Olivier Matringe (United Nations); Bogdan Rascanu (Société Générale de Surveillance).

The remarks and suggestions of three anonymous referees concerning previous outlines and previous versions of the text, which contributed significantly to improving our work, are also gratefully acknowledged.

1
Physical commodity markets: an overview

1.1 INTRODUCTION

1.1.1 Basic Commodities

Production, in the economic sense of the term, is the transformation of *scarce* productive inputs (also called production factors, such as skilled and non-skilled labour, land and other natural resources, durable and consumable intermediate goods, services, etc.), into other scarce goods or services that are useful to satisfy human needs. Production (at least in the case of so-called private goods or services) is often carried out through the business firm, which coordinates *buying* inputs on markets, combining and transforming these inputs into suitable products, that are *sold* on other markets. In market economies, firms have a strong incentive to carry out activities that will generate some *profit*, or net revenue, which is the difference between the income derived from the sale of the products, and the costs of the inputs used for production.

One way to increase profits is of course to *minimise costs*. In practice, many costs are fixed, at least in the short run. This is the case of the costs of durable intermediate goods (also called fixed capital), and, in many cases, of labour, of many services and of public goods. There is, however, a class of productive inputs on which firms may act through *purchasing management*: these are non-durable intermediate goods, including, in particular, *raw materials or basic commodities, half-products, and parts*. These play an important role in business management, because their costs are *controllable* costs, often the *only* short-run controllable costs. Basic commodities are important within this class of non-durable intermediate goods, because of several of their features:

1. For reasons that will be discussed later, the prices for basic commodities are *flexible*, that is, they go *up* and *down* in terms of both nominal and real prices.

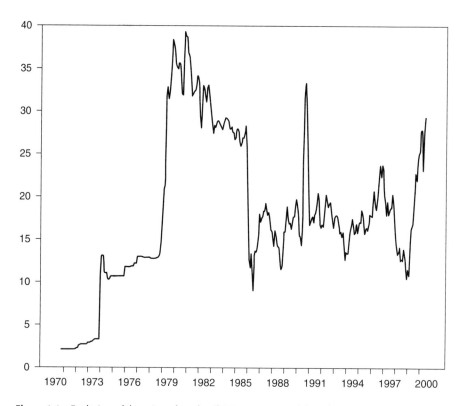

Figure 1.1   Evolution of the price of crude oil (1970–2000, US$/barrel)

We can see, for example, in Figure 1.1 that the price of crude oil has been up to a nominal spot price of $35 (quarterly average, last quarter of 1980), down to $11 (quarterly average, third quarter of 1986). It has later averaged about $18 between 1993 and 1997, going down to about $12 at the end of 1998 only to go back up to the range of $25–30 by early 2000.

2. Basic commodities are goods whose *quality* may be easily controlled and that are readily obtained in *standard* qualities.
3. Basic commodities are very often *traded internationally*, on *organised markets*.

Natural resources (land, water, forests, mines . . .) are productive inputs which may be used for the production of basic commodities or so-called raw materials, which, in this case, might also be termed natural commodities. These natural commodities are goods which are obtained in the first step of transformation from natural resources and which are inputs for further steps of production and are generally not directly of use for final consumption. Natural commodities may therefore be defined as *non-durable intermediate inputs* (to be distinguished from durable intermediate inputs or capital goods) that are directly produced, or

produced after one or at most two steps of transformation, from nat
More elaborate intermediate inputs are called *half-products*. Mos¹
these commodities are the object of international trade, and are c
organised spot and futures markets.

1.1.2 Beyond Basic Commodities: The General Commodity Concept

Beyond basic commodities, the concept of a *commodity* (from the Latin *commodus*, which means convenient) tends to be a rather general one. Any intermediate good which is useful to production and has constant and standard qualities may be called a commodity. Electronic chips used in the smart-card industry, other components for the electronic industry, and in particular, for the computer assembly industry, and even services such as freight and shipping, may be considered as commodities, and may be traded on organised international markets, which can be either spot or futures markets.

Historically, besides financial assets, agricultural commodities were the first to be traded on organised markets. Since then, trading on organised markets has progressively expanded to many kinds of industrial intermediate goods. Natural media, such as agricultural land, forests, rivers, seas, the atmosphere, etc. may or may not be scarce resources, although most of them are scarce, subject to property rights and market allocation. They are often transformed by human activity. In the latter case, they are economic natural resources and are sold and bought, or rented, on markets.

Raw materials, also called primary commodities, are *intermediate goods* produced from natural resources after one or two agricultural or industrial transformation steps (in the economic sense of the term).

Examples: A metal such as copper ore is mined from the earth and is considered a natural resource. Mining is the first transformation step. Smelting is the second, which yields the final metal. Wheat grain is obtained from agricultural land after one step of transformation, harvesting.

A commodity is, however, a much more general concept than a raw material. Clearly, at first sight at least, a commodity may be defined as follows: 'An intermediate good with a standard quality, which can be traded on competitive and liquid global international physical markets.'

The fact that commodity markets are defined as 'competitive and liquid' has several implications. Liquidity requires that the market be cleared at all times, with total supply being equal to total demand, an objective that is quite difficult to attain in a global market which is competitive with many suppliers and many buyers. Hence the importance of intermediaries on these physical markets, whose activity is *trading*, that is, buying the product, stocking it, and reselling it at a profit, often with high economic risks. This is the traditional activity of *traders*, who were usually individuals before the Industrial Revolution, but nowadays are more likely to be companies[1] because of the high risks and the huge capital backing these risks entail. This is a feature of the commodity markets, which is shared by financial intermediaries such as banks and insurance companies.

Throughout this book, we stress the importance of the activity of these intermediaries, the *trading companies* and the *merchants*, on the physical commodity markets. Trading companies or merchants are defined as active market intermediaries that contribute to making supply meet demand by being either buyers or sellers. In other words, traders, trading companies and merchants will buy goods in order to resell them profitably. They may, in the course of their activity, also hold inventories. On the other hand, *brokers* are market intermediaries (individuals or firms) that contribute to making supply meet demand without actually buying or selling themselves. They only furnish a service that helps potential buyers and sellers to come together and are less important than trading companies and merchants on the physical commodity markets. Brokers are, however, important on derivative markets for commodities where there are also traders who will buy commodity derivatives in order to resell them profitably. While brokers charge a price, called a commission, for their services, trading companies make their income from the differences between their selling price and their buying price called a *spread*.

A second implication of liquidity on these markets is that supply and demand are subject to continuous fluctuations due to various seasonal imbalances and changing circumstances. Thus, the discrepancy between supply and demand may become negative at times, with supply exceeding demand, thus pushing prices downward, or positive at other times, with demand exceeding supply and thus pushing prices upward. This means that commodity prices are flexible and may vary at any time. Such a situation provides incentives for holding speculative stocks and all the actors on the physical markets, including producers, traders, and purchasers, may from time to time hold speculative inventories that they buy when prices are low in the hope of reselling them when prices are higher. This price volatility also provides the grounds for establishing derivative markets, which, as we will show in Chapters 2–4, can be used as tools for hedging, or protecting oneself against adverse price movements. They can also be used for speculation, which involves purely financial positions on futures or options markets as opposed to holding physical inventories.

Clearly, the markets for many raw materials, such as crude oil, common non-ferrous metals, precious metals (gold, silver, platinum, etc.) and a number of agricultural commodities such as wheat, corn, cotton, coffee and cocoa share most, if not all, of the characteristics of our definitions of commodities. Other markets and, in particular, smaller markets, or markets for commodities with

---

[1] There still are individuals commonly called traders, who do trading on markets, but they are generally employed by trading companies or financial institutions.

numerous or complex quality characteristics, may be less in line with the definition. However, the commodity concept can be extended beyond raw materials to services with less or no material basis and which are not storable and may not be considered as assets, such as freight, as well as to currencies and financial assets. In this respect, currencies, and especially currencies that are used in international trade, may be thought of as commodities. In the financial industries, such as banks, investment funds, pension funds, and insurance companies, financial instruments such as money market deposits, bonds, shares, and in general all sorts of financial assets may be thought of as commodities, and are often considered as such. These financial instruments are traded on global spot markets and on the markets for the derivative instruments related to them.

In this book, we focus on non-financial commodities and the characteristics that distinguish them from purely financial commodities. However, outside of the boundaries of basic commodities, most of which are traditional raw materials, the number of intermediate goods which undergo what we might call 'commoditisation' is expanding almost daily in a very innovative and global economic environment. Goods that were once traded only on monopolistic or local markets according to rigid constraints now share some, if not all, of the features that we have associated with commodities. They are increasingly traded in standardised qualities on competitive and efficient international markets with flexible spot markets that create the need for hedging instruments, including derivative products such as organised futures and options.

There are a number of examples of goods that are being 'commoditised' in this sense. A first example is electricity, which, some 20 years ago, was traded on national and regional markets. At that time, it was often produced by either regulated private utility companies (a typical situation in the USA), or public monopolies (a typical situation in a number of Western European countries such as the UK, France, and Germany, as well as in some Canadian provinces, such as Quebec and Ontario). The first step was a strong push towards privatisation and deregulation. Various countries such as the UK, Germany, the Scandinavian countries, South Korea, and, of course, a number of countries in transition such as Poland, the Czech Republic, and others have totally or partially privatised their electricity utilities. The second step, which is more recent, and dates back from the last decade of the twentieth century, has been 'commoditisation' of electricity in some regions of the world, especially in the USA, where spot and futures markets are now operating in several states or regions, such as California (electricity is thus quoted on the NYMEX/COMEX), and in Europe, with the interesting case of the spot and futures markets for electricity that recently developed in the Nordic countries of Denmark, Finland, Norway, and Sweden.

A second, and more recent example of 'commoditisation' concerns telecommunication services, which also underwent a strong and almost universal movement towards privatisation, both partial or total, of operators that used to be public and government-operated throughout the world, except in some countries such as the USA. In a second and more recent stage, which started in the last years of the twentieth century, the markets for telecommunication services that were once thought of as natural monopolies have been deregulated. In this field, an informal, but global and efficient spot market for telephone time appeared as recently as 1998 with the development of specialised trading activities in telephone time. About 100 billion minutes of telephone time were exchanged on this global spot market in 1999 and informal forward and futures markets for telephone time are also developing steadily.

1.1.3   The Economic Status of Commodities

In many industries, basic commodities are essential resources, such as labour, capital and materials. Their management as an autonomous set of techniques is thus no less essential than labour and human resource management or financial management. It is even equal in rank with them in some 'heavy' industries, such as some metallurgical industries, cement industries, oil and heavy chemical industries as well as in services such as air transportation. Most, if not all, of these commodities are the object of international trade and are often traded on organised spot and futures markets.

1.1.4   Commodities, and Management

Another important feature of inputs such as raw materials, natural commodities and energy is that they are *technical* objects. The efficient use of inputs such as energy and materials is therefore first a technical problem because for many years, engineers have been concerned with such an efficient use through *technical innovations* (for instance, in the case of fuels). It is, however, clear that some management techniques lend themselves to significant improvements in terms of efficient management of this category of costs. These management and financial techniques are also an extremely innovative field. Some examples of financial innovations, which rest on developments in economics and the management and behavioural sciences rather than in the physical sciences, are to be found, for instance, in the theory of finance and derivative pricing. The ubiquitous Black and Scholes option pricing formula is a case in point. The development of various new OTC derivatives, including 'exotic' or second-generation options, is also a field in which a number of recent innovations have been introduced, especially since the beginning of the 1990s. These have actually been of practical use for basic commodity management problems. These management techniques appear as very general tools that may be used whatever the particular production or commodities to which they are applied.

The management of basic commodities concerns firms that purchase commodities as inputs. It concerns those firms of sectors that produce the commodities themselves, such as agriculture and mining. Traders, as purchasers and suppliers, are concerned with both sides of their markets.

1.1.5 Examples of Commodities

Examples of commodities include:

1. Energy commodities: primary energies (crude oil, coal, natural gas, nuclear fuels); secondary energies: electricity, refined oil products (residual oil, various fuel oils, heating oil, diesel fuel, gasoline (US), petrol (UK), jet kerosene, lique-fied petroleum gas (LPG)). Half-products such as petrochemicals (ethylene, naphtha, etc.) may also be included with energy commodities in a broad sense.
2. Mineral commodities: ores and other minerals; ferrous metals: iron, cast iron, steel and steel products (rolled products, flat products, wires, bars, and beams); common non-ferrous metals (aluminium, copper, lead, nickel, tin, zinc); other special non-ferrous metals (chromium, molybdenum, titanium, tantalum, vana-dium, etc.); precious metals (gold, silver, platinum, palladium and other plat-inum group metals); asbestos, diamonds, phosphates; some half-products such as cement may be added to this list.
3. Agricultural food products: Cereals (wheat, corn, rice, etc.), beverages (cocoa, coffee, tea), fruit (apples, bananas, dates, grapes, olives, oranges), meats (beef, lamb, pork, poultry), oils (soya-bean oil, olive oil, groundnut oil, etc.), sugar (white and brown), potatoes, wine, etc.
4. Textiles (cotton, jute, wool, etc.)
5. Rubber, timber, etc.
6. Seafood products (various species of fish, crabmeat, shrimps, lobster, etc.).

To this list, one may add, according to our previous discussion, commodi-ties which are not raw materials, including immaterial services such as freight, telephone time, etc.

The rest of this chapter will therefore be organised as follows. In the next section, we will outline the characteristics of physical commodity markets, including market structure and market organisation. In the subsequent section, we present and analyse the economics of physical commodity markets and their links with corresponding derivative markets. A chapter conclusion will discuss the essential and specific features of these commodity markets and of commodity trading.

1.2 THE CHARACTERISTICS OF PHYSICAL COMMODITY MARKETS

1.2.1 General Considerations

Today's commodity markets involve a large number of commodities as we have defined them: energy commodities such as crude oil and refined oil products, natural gas, coal and electricity, mineral commodities such as ferrous and non-ferrous metals, diamonds, all agricultural commodities, and services.[2] These markets are global and truly international and are becoming increasingly competitive. Furthermore, the trading techniques that are used by actors operating on these markets are often highly innovative. Innovations in the trading techniques are both innovations in communication techniques that stem from developments of the computer, telecommunication, and network technologies, and from innovations concerning financial instruments, such as exotic options and other new financial instruments.

Although today's commodity markets have become very innovative and complex, they may still be analysed in terms of a number of basic market characteristics:

1. *Market structure*: Are these markets fully competitive, or are they subject to more or less imperfect competition, which range from monopolies or cartels at one end, to various sorts of oligopolies at the other end?
2. *Market organisation*: Are these markets centralised markets, such as auction markets or centralised exchanges, or decentralised markets, including over-the-counter (OTC) markets, or markets with posted prices?
3. *Physical markets and derivative markets*: Are these markets *physical markets*, on which the physical commodity is traded, or *derivative markets*, which are financial markets on which paper representing a physical underlying commodity is traded? In the case of physical markets, are these markets *spot or cash markets*, with contracts providing for immediate delivery (and payment), or *forward* markets, with contracts providing for a delayed physical delivery (and payment)?

As far as *derivative markets* are concerned, they may technically be equivalent to forward markets in some cases, with the possibility of physical delivery in the form of warehouse receipts representing rights to the physical commodity. This is the case of the London Metal Exchange (LME), for example, on which commodity receipts for immediate or delayed delivery from inventories of the six metals traded may be issued as the result of the transaction. However, most derivative markets are *futures markets*, an expression which refers to organised financial markets with the possibility of either delayed physical delivery in the form of a warehouse receipt, or financial offsetting of the contract at any time before the delivery date. Futures markets also imply that the contract is quoted daily with daily settlements called marking-to-market that we will discuss in Chapter 2. A further refinement of futures markets is that futures contracts may either be firm or optional. These are usually referred to simply as options

---

[2] Markets for financial commodities, which, as we mentioned in the introduction, are outside the scope of this book, also share many of the characteristics of the markets for physical commodities and non-financial service commodities.

contracts. In all cases, the possibility of physical delivery at the delivery date ensures that the futures price will converge to the spot price because any profitable and riskless arbitrage between the spot market, and the futures market with physical delivery is excluded. Similarly, the value of an option will converge to a value closely related to the difference between the spot price at the time of delivery and the exercise price, which is its intrinsic value.

1.2.2 Market Structure

Market structure refers to the degree of concentration of the market, or, in economic terms, to its characteristics in terms of *competition*. International or global commodity markets may take several forms, according to several classifications that will be given below. They may be more or less close to the attributes of so-called *competitive* and *informationally efficient* markets.

A competitive market can be defined as being exempt of any monopolistic, oligopolistic or monopsonistic power. This implies that no agent trading on a market can influence prices significantly because the individual quantities traded by one agent are negligible with respect to the aggregate quantities. This implies that there are a large number of traders on both the supply and the demand sides of a competitive market and that each of these traders is a price-taker.

Market efficiency, which differs from competitiveness, is another feature of markets. Fama (1970, 1991) developed this concept in the context of financial markets, but it applies to any market. One often refers to *informational efficiency*, or simply *efficiency* defined as the fact that any new information concerning the market is immediately reflected in current prices. According to Fama, there are three versions of efficiency, depending on what sort of information is taken into account:

1. In the *weak* version of efficiency, all information reflected in past prices is also reflected in today's prices.
2. In the *semi-strong* version of efficiency, all publicly available information is also reflected in present prices.
3. Finally, in the *strong* version of efficiency, all available information, whether public or not, is reflected in present prices.

Whether or not a market is competitive refers to the degree of competition that exists on the market, and, according to the definition, this depends on the number of actors operating on the market. Monopolistic or oligopolistic markets are in general not competitive and may not be efficient either, although monopoly or oligopoly does not necessarily preclude efficiency. The same is true of cartelised markets in which a group of dominant producers acts in very much the same way as a monopolist. Nowadays, monopolistic or cartelised commodity markets tend to be the exception. This is the case, for example, of the international diamond market, on which the dominant actor is De Beers, the well-known South African company. In the past, however, there have been a number of commodity markets on which there was a dominant producer, or a dominant group of producers, who imposed a posted price or whose price became a reference price in national or international contracts. This was the case of the international oil market between 1973 and 1982 when the international posted price was the OPEC price. Before 1973, it was the price set by the seven biggest international companies (called the *seven sisters*) and, prior to 1911 it was set by Rockefeller's Standard Oil Company in the USA.[3]

This was also the case of some other markets, such as the aluminium market, on which the reference price was, until about 1980, the price set up by Alcoa, as Alcoa was the largest American and international producer at that time. Since 1978, even though Alcoa still remains a major actor, the market for aluminium has become a much more competitive market with at least four or five major actors. Alcoa, Reynolds, Alcan, Algroup (ex-Alusuisse), and Pechiney, among others. The turning point of the evolution of the aluminium market towards a competitive market was when aluminium became quoted on the LME in 1978, so that LME prices, whether spot or futures, became the reference prices for commercial contracts in the international trade of aluminium.

Many physical commodity markets, if not most, have become competitive markets or have evolved from monopoly markets or from cartelised markets towards at least some degree of competitiveness. They might not be perfectly competitive in the theoretical sense of the term, but there are at least several large companies operating on the supply side of these markets.

The problem of *informational efficiency* in the case of industrial or physical commodities differs much, in practice, from what is observed on organised financial markets, such as stock markets. Most stock exchanges are subject to regulations organising disclosure of all pertinent financial information concerning quoted firms, such as annual balance sheets, trading, and profit and loss accounts, along with information concerning the structure of capital. Most stock exchanges are also subject to rules prohibiting insider trading, meaning trading by persons such as managers and directors of a firm having private information, not known to the general public, that might lead to unfair trading profits. Many of these rules do not apply, or cannot apply, to organised commodity markets.

A first issue when discussing the concept of informational efficiency is that many of these commodities are characterised by the importance of inventories, which play a key role in price dynamics. The stock of capital in the case of financial assets such as shares, which is usually referred to as the capital or value of shares outstanding, is usually known very precisely at least in global terms for

---

[3] As is well known, the Standard Oil Company, founded in 1871 by John D. Rockefeller, had attained a dominating position on the American market by the 1890s. It was prosecuted under the US antitrust law (the Sherman Act of 1890) and was sentenced in 1911 to be broken up into 31 independent companies in the 31 US states in which Standard Oil was operating.

listed securities. The equivalent concept in the case of physical commodities is not precisely known in the same way. The equivalent of market capitalisation in the case of physical commodities is the amount of private or public inventories, or stocks, of the commodity, which are usually not precisely known and are not subject to any disclosure rules as is the case for listed securities. In fact, the amount of these stocks is usually considered as a strategic secret by firms that are in the commodity business, although in many cases analysts may have some idea of the stocks owned by various market operators. Finally, some particular commodities that now tend to be traded on global or international markets, such as freight and electricity, are not storable commodities so that for them, the equivalent of market capitalisation is completely meaningless.

The cost of storing a commodity is, first, an opportunity cost of capital because the inventory represents a part of invested capital, which yields no income. The opportunity cost is the lost interest on an equivalent amount of capital invested on the money market. There are also direct physical costs of storage, which have to be added to the opportunity cost of capital. In the case of financial assets such as bonds and stocks, costs of storage (custody costs) are usually negligible with respect to the opportunity cost of capital. In the case of commodities, as we have seen, some are not storable. Among other commodities, which are storable, the cost of storage is an important consideration. This might be very low, as is the case for so-called precious metals, which are therefore akin to financial commodities in this sense. Gold, in particular, is a metal that has traditionally been, and still is, considered a financial asset. The role of gold as an industrial commodity is increasing. Silver is now very important in terms of industrial uses, especially in the photographic industry. Platinum and palladium[4] have become key commodities in the automobile industry because of their uses as catalysts and because of the concerns about environmental protection.

In the case of common non-ferrous metals, such as the metals quoted on the LME (aluminium, copper, lead, nickel, tin, and zinc), storage costs are much higher than for the precious metals. Storage is, finally, an important cost in the case of agricultural commodities such as wheat, corn, and soya beans, among others. In Chapter 2 we discuss the theoretical importance of the cost of storage, which is an issue in modelling futures markets. Thus, as we will see below in the section concerning the economics of commodity markets, the existence and the importance of commodity inventories is a key variable in the explanation of price movements on commodity markets. For some commodities that may be considered as financial assets, such as precious metals, stocks are very large and may represent many years of production. For other commodities, stocks are quite limited and depend upon the situation of the industrial markets for the commodity.

---

[4] Palladium is a close substitute for platinum.

A second element of informational efficiency is related to information concerning the fundamentals of commodity prices. In the case of financial assets, a number of accounting data are public and may be used to compute fundamental values of stocks on the basis of their assets and of their expected profits. But similar calculations are not easily done in the case of most, if not all, physical commodities. This does not mean that the concept of a fundamental value is not pertinent in the case of commodities. Clearly, the fundamental value of a commodity may be defined and is really meaningful, although it is usually very different from what is meant by fundamental value in the case of a stock, a bond, or more complex financial instruments such as options. The utility of financial assets is, essentially, to generate some revenues or profits, in either the form of dividends or interest or in the form of capital gains. Physical commodities, besides being capital, or even objects of speculation, will usually have an economic value, which may be defined as their fundamental value, for very different reasons. Commodities are physical objects that are objects of demand and hence are priced because of their industrial uses and, on the supply side, because of their cost of production. Their fundamental value will therefore stem from both their supply value (meaning their competitive cost of production) and their demand value (meaning their input value). Both of these values should be closely related at market equilibrium. However, the economic analysis of commodity prices is even more complex because they may be considered as capital in the form of corporate and other private and public stocks. These are often *speculative* stocks in the sense that they are kept by industrial agents or other agents expecting a speculative profit because of an expected increase in price.

1.2.3 Market Organisation

There are various types of market organisation that apply to any market, including commodity markets. More precisely, one may distinguish between two main market organisations: centralised and decentralised markets.

Centralised markets are markets in which market intermediaries such as brokers and auctioneers, centralise supplies and demands from various sellers and buyers. They include:

1. *Auction markets*, in which the quotations (buyers go up in price, or sellers go down in price, until a suitable price is found) are centralised by an auctioneer;
2. *Centralised exchanges*, in which all orders for buying (with maximum prices) and selling (with maximum prices) are taken by *brokers*, which after processing them, find a suitable market price which clears the markets (meaning that supply and demand are equal), while satisfying all orders.

There are also *decentralised* markets, including:

1. OTC markets, or markets with bilateral contracts, in which all transactions result in a contract negotiated between a buyer and a seller, often through a market intermediary such as a lawyer or an estate agent.
2. Markets with *posted prices*, in which prices are posted or given, usually in some written document such as a catalogue, which is known, or may be known by the buyers.

Physical commodity markets, which are of interest to us here, are mostly OTC markets, with contracts that are freely negotiated between one buyer and one seller, or, so to speak, tailored to suit the needs of a particular transaction between them.

1.2.4   Spot and Forward Markets

In terms of delivery date and of conditions for settlement in general, one may distinguish between several types of markets and the resulting contracts:

1. *Spot markets*, on which the good is paid and physically delivered immediately or on the spot; these are of course a particular case of physical markets.
2. *Physical markets* may also be *forward markets*, on which the good is to be paid and delivered physically at some future date.

1.2.5   The Characteristics of Physical Markets, and Reference Pricing

Physical commodity markets are usually OTC markets on which exchanges are based on bilateral contracts between one particular buyer and one particular producer. Natural gas and coal markets, for example, fall into this category. Physical commodity markets with posted prices also exist. These are generally markets on which there is a dominant producer, or a dominant group of producers, who may impose a posted price or whose price becomes a reference price in national or international contracts, known as a producers' price. A *reference price* is defined as a price that is recognised as a fair price by both parties negotiating a contract. In a forward commercial contract, the price is often stipulated as being the spot price on a reference spot market, which is recognised as such by both parties. Owing to globalisation, markets, including commodity markets, are evolving towards more competition and posted or producers' prices tend to be less important than they were in the past. An example of a market with a posted price, which was also a reference price, was until very recently (2000), the international diamond market. On this market, reference prices tended to be the prices of the Central Selling Organisation controlled by De Beers, the dominant producer. In the past, markets for many commodities operated with posted prices that were imposed by some kind of monopolistic or dominant producer. There are still markets on which there are posted prices in the sense that the price of some dominant producer, or group of producers, is used on these markets as a reference price in the negotiation of OTC contracts. Nowadays, most physical commodity markets are OTC markets, on which commercial contracts are freely negotiated, even if the reference prices that prevail on these markets are producers' or posted prices. Chapter 7 will develop the features of these commercial contracts and of the role of reference prices on them. There are, however, other types of markets (informal auction markets, such as, until recently, the international tea market in London, or the Australian auction market for wool in Sydney, among others). These markets are important in a few cases but, again, they do not usually constitute all of the market. But they are important in providing reference prices for OTC contracts.

Finally, there are organised markets which technically are financial (usually futures) markets. As will be discussed at the end of this chapter and in Chapter 2, a fundamental feature of these markets is that they are closely related to spot and physical markets because of the possibility of physical *arbitrage* between the two markets. In particular, on most futures markets, physical delivery of the commodity at the future delivery date is always possible, thus providing the possibility of profitable arbitrage between the spot and the futures markets and making prices converge at delivery dates. Organised futures markets are thus important for the pricing of physical commodities in that they supply reference prices. They are also used for hedging, that is, for protecting actors on the physical markets against adverse price variations, as will be discussed in Chapter 2.

1.3   FROM PHYSICAL MARKETS TO DERIVATIVE MARKETS

1.3.1   Derivative Markets: Financial vs Physical Trading

A broad definition of *derivative markets* is the following. A derivative market is a financial market on which purely financial instruments representing some underlying physical commodities available for delivery at some future date are traded under various conditions. This future date may be remote in time (from several months to several years), but may also be a nearby date (the commodity will be available in a few days), or even, as a limiting case, the present date. There are several sorts of derivative markets, which correspond to several categories of so-called financial instruments, which are traded on these markets. In particular, one may distinguish between futures and options, which are traded on organised markets, and similar instruments (swaps, caps and floors in particular) that are traded on OTC markets.

Futures markets are financial markets on which a financial instrument representing some underlying asset is to be paid for at some future date, but on which physical delivery is not usually contemplated, although it is, in most cases, possible. To settle the contract, the operator will either offset his/her position by taking an equal and opposite position, perhaps at a different price. After the balance between these two equal and opposite positions has been paid in cash, the operator's contract is terminated. If the contract has not been settled at the date of expiration of the contract, the operator will be ascribed a balance in the commodity, against settlement of an equal and opposite cash balance at the full price.

This type of settlement might be called a financial settlement of the futures contract and is by far the most frequently used. Futures markets, although they are connected to physical markets, are essentially financial markets. However, in most futures markets, the initial position of a trader may also be settled by delivering or receiving the physical commodity. As an order of magnitude, on organised futures exchanges such as the Chicago Board of Trade, no more than 1% of positions are settled in this way. While the operator's commodity balance becomes zero, in general, his/her cash balance will be equal to the usually non-zero difference between initial and final cash balance, because of the difference between initial and final futures prices. To this balance, the brokerage fees must be added or deducted, depending on whether the balance is a debit or a credit.

If *physical speculation* is defined as buying a physical asset in the hope of reselling it at a higher price, it should be remembered that physical speculation on commodities is costly in that it implies paying in cash the initial price of the commodity and then storing the commodity at a cost until its price increases. Storing the commodity implies a capital investment in the facilities for storage as well as other additional storage costs. Physical speculation is thus subject to technical constraints and significant fixed and variable costs. In comparison, the use of futures implies no technical constraints, no fixed or variable costs and little or no initial investment. It therefore makes speculation very easy, whether speculating on a price increase or a price decline. Futures markets also are good vehicles for *hedging*, or protecting oneself against adverse price variations. This having been said, it should be noted that a futures contract traded on an organised exchange generally implies a deposit of cash or marketable securities of about 10% of the initial value of the position. This rule is imposed to avoid any default by an operator as well as to finance the marking-to-market operations at the end of each day. The deposit can, however, be made in certain interest-bearing marketable securities so that the opportunity cost on the deposit is zero.

All these features lead us to a formal definition of futures contracts traded on the organised exchanges. One of the most complete and recent definitions, which has been given by Wilmott (1998), states that:

A forward contract is an agreement whereby one party promises to buy an asset from another party, at some specified time in the future and at some specified price. No money changes hands until the delivery date (or maturity) of the contract. The terms of the contract make it an obligation to buy the asset at the delivery date, no choice in the matter. The asset could be a stock, a commodity or a currency. A futures contract is very similar to a forward contract. Futures contracts are usually traded through an exchange, which standardises the terms of the contracts. The profits of the position are calculated every day and the change of its value is transferred from one party to another.

Similar and equivalent definitions have been formulated by Duffie (1989) and by Kolb (1997). It is possible, however, to give a slightly different definition, emphasising the fact that positions on futures markets are purely financial positions, although physical delivery of the underlying asset is possible at maturity.[5] One can define such a futures contract as follows:

A futures contract is a contract concluded on standardised terms on a centralised market. Under this contract, a financial asset representing a given quantity of some underlying asset, which is either a standardised physical commodity available at a given future date and given location, or some financial asset available at some given future date, is either bought or sold between a given date and the date of availability of the underlying asset (called the maturity of the contract). This implies that any quantity of the financial asset available on the futures market, once it has initially been either bought or sold, may be, respectively, sold back or bought back at any subsequent time before maturity of the contract, thus ending any commitment with respect to that quantity of asset. At maturity, the contract may be fulfilled by the seller through actual delivery of the asset under some standardised conditions and by the buyer through paying the initial futures price. To avoid any default or liability, an initial deposit which is a significant fraction of the value of the contract has to be paid in cash or in marketable securities at the beginning of any contract, with daily settlements of any liability or claim resulting from any daily difference in the value of the contract due to daily market variations. If necessary, other liability settlements (margin calls) are required to maintain a minimum deposit.

A *commodity option* traded on an organised exchange is a different matter. The object of this market is the right but not the obligation either to buy or sell a financial instrument at a given price called the strike or exercise price. This financial instrument may be a share quoted on a stock market. In the case of commodity options, it is usually a position on an underlying commodity futures market before the expiration of the contract or, at the expiration date, another instrument (such as a warehouse receipt) representing the ownership of a given quantity of the commodity underlying the futures contract.[6] Options traded on organised exchanges are generally *American options*, for which the right to buy or to sell a position on a futures market may be effective at any time before the expiration of the contract. Options traded on an organised market may be bought

---

[5] There are also index futures, with no delivery at maturity, but a final settlement in cash.

[6] There are also options on index futures. In that case, if the option is exercised at maturity, there is no physical delivery but a final cash settlement.

and sold at any time before expiration. Options also permit easy speculation and hedging. In Chapter 3 we discuss options contracts in detail. It is nevertheless useful to give here a definition of American options on futures with delivery possible at maturity, which corresponds to the case of usual traded commodity options:

> An option is bought at a price called the premium on a centralised market, with a contract concluded on standardised terms between buyer and seller. The American option on futures gives its owner (the buyer) the right, but not the obligation, to buy (in this case, it is a call option), or to sell (in this case, it is a put option) before or at the date of expiration of the contract, an asset called the underlying asset at a price (the exercise price or the strike price). In the case of commodity options, the underlying asset is a position on an organised commodity futures market with the same maturity as the date of expiration (or at expiration, the physical asset underlying the futures contract) the underlying asset. The seller of an option, who is said to write the option, is accepting to either sell (if the option is a call) or buy (if the option is a put) the underlying asset at the strike price if the option owner requests it, at any time before or at expiration of the contract. An option may be either sold or bought on the market at any time before maturity. At maturity, the owner may choose not to exercise or abandon the option. The option owner who abandons the option loses the premium with no liability. In the case of an option seller, to avoid any default or liability, an initial deposit which is a significant fraction of the value of the underlying contract has to be paid in cash at the beginning of any contract, with daily settlements of any liability resulting from any detrimental daily difference in value of the contract due to daily market variations. If necessary, other liability settlements (margin calls) are required of an option seller to maintain a minimum deposit.

In summary, then, both futures and options are derivative instruments in that they may lead to the ownership of an underlying asset in the form of an account balance or warehouse receipt. Even if the warehouse receipt or balance may be exchanged for the physical commodity, this is by far not the main purpose of the market. Table 1.1 gives a review of the basic features of forward, futures and options markets.

1.3.2 How are Physical and Derivative Markets Prices Related Together?

In most cases due to delays in shipping, physical contracts are forward contracts rather than spot contracts. Spot markets are nonetheless important because, they supply *reference prices* that are used in commercial contracts. However, supplying reference prices is also an important role of futures markets, as will be discussed in Chapter 6. This role of futures markets is logical because futures prices are closely connected to spot prices. In fact, at the maturity of a contract the prices of the two converge. Otherwise, as we will demonstrate in detail in Chapter 2, they are linked through a complicated series of relationships involving opportunity cost, storage cost and convenience yields. Thus, before maturity futures and spot

Table 1.1 A comparison of the characteristics of forward markets, and of organised futures and options markets

Markets	Forward	Futures	Options
Initial cash payment	None or little	Cash deposit (5–10%)	Price of option (premium)
Daily settlements	None	Yes	Yes, in case of option writing (selling)
Physical or financial settlement?	Purely physical	Financial, but physical delivery usually possible	Financial, but physical delivery usually possible
Standardised or not?	Tailor-made	Standardised	Standardised
Final settlement	Mandatory	Mandatory	Optional

prices can and usually do diverge. The difference between the two is called the *basis*.

According to a straightforward definition, the basis may be expressed as

$$\text{basis} = \text{current futures price} - \text{current spot price}$$

Although the Chicago Board of Trade's manual, and some authors, such as Kolb (1997) define the basis with an opposite sign, i.e. as current spot price − current futures price, the definition given here and used in the theoretical developments of Chapter 2 seems more logical, and it follows a tradition that goes back to Keynes and Working, and others. It also has the advantage of giving a positive basis in a quite important case from the theoretical point of view. When the futures price is above the corresponding spot price, the difference reflects an opportunity cost called the cost of carry. Our definition is valid at a given time for the cash price at a given location and for the futures price concerning delivery at a given maturity time t. Some necessary properties of the basis are imposed by the rule of non profitable and riskless arbitrage opportunities (AAO). This rule, which we develop in Chapter 2, states that in an efficient market it should not be possible to observe different prices for the same good at the same time that would make it possible to buy at the low and sell at the high to achieve a certain, riskless profit.

A consequence of the AAO rule is *basis convergence* or *price convergence*, meaning that

$$\lim_{\text{time} \to t} \text{basis} = 0$$

This implies that, at the time of maturity t, the futures price becomes equal to the spot price. In practice, this means that the futures price of a good approaches its spot price when one approaches maturity time t. If this were not true, one could buy on the spot market and resell immediately on the futures market with

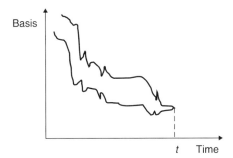

Figure 1.2   Convergence of spot and futures prices (futures price > spot price, case of a contango)

effective physical delivery, or the other way round, thereby achieving an infinite rate of profit. Empirically, convergence is almost always observed (Figure 1.2).

Thus, futures prices are closely connected to spot prices. Inasmuch as they are quoted on large competitive markets with well-defined and standardised rules of conduct, they are usually recognised on physical markets as acceptable reference prices. The same is true of a number of spot and producers' prices, which are also being used as the basis of commercial contracts.

The options price is also closely connected to the spot price of the underlying commodity at the maturity of the contract. In Chapter 3 we develop this relationship in detail. For the moment, suffice it to say that given the AAO rule, the price of an option contract will converge to either zero or the positive difference between the price of the underlying security and the exercise price.

There are also OTC derivatives, including the equivalent of futures and options, which have many of the characteristics of derivatives traded on organised markets, except of course that they are concluded under freely negotiated terms. These OTC derivatives will be discussed in Chapter 4.

The theory of derivatives pricing and their uses for the purpose of hedging and speculation will be discussed in Chapters 2–4. We end this chapter by giving a panorama of international physical and derivatives markets for commodities.

1.4   A PANORAMA OF WORLD PHYSICAL AND DERIVATIVES MARKETS FOR COMMODITIES

1.4.1   Markets for Energy Commodities

The Rotterdam spot market is an informal physical market on which various grades of crude oil (including North Sea 'Brent' oil), and various refined products (gas oil, gasoline, heavy fuel oil, kerosene and heating oil) are traded, together with petrochemical products such as naphtha.

The London International Petroleum Exchange (IPE) is a futures, and possibly a forward, market. The IPE trades futures contracts on North Sea 'Brent' oil (the contract being of 1,000 barrels of 158.987 litres, priced in US$/barrel), and on gas oil (heating oil No. 2 or light fuel oil, the contract being of 1,000 metric tonnes, priced in US$/metric tonne). Options corresponding to the above contracts are also traded on the IPE.

On the New York Mercantile Exchange (NYMEX/COMEX), futures and options for various American crude oils, oil products, and natural gas are traded. These include:

1. 'Light Sweet' crude oil (futures and options contracts for 1,000 barrels, priced in US$/barrel).
2. Heating oil No. 2 (light fuel oil, futures and options contracts for 42,000 US gallons, with 1 US gallon = 3.78541 litres, priced in US$/gallon).
3. Unleaded gasoline (futures and options contracts for 42,000 US gallons, priced in US$/gallon).
4. Natural gas (futures and options contracts for 1,000,000 MBTU, with 1 MBTU = 252 thermic, priced in US$/MBTU).

Other crude oil spot markets include New York (for West Texas Intermediate or WTI, West Texas Sour, Light Sweet, North Slope, and several refined products, with delivery either in Cushing, Oklahoma, or in the Gulf), and Singapore (for Dubai oil).

Besides oil and oil products, and natural gas, other major energy commodities are coal, which used to be traded on one of the major international commodity markets of the nineteenth century. A strong revival of that market was observed after the oil shocks of 1973 and 1979, as analysed by Labys and Lesourd (1988), the main exporters being Australia, Canada, South Africa, and the USA, with spot markets located in these producer countries. Until recently, there was no futures market for coal due to the heterogeneity of its qualities but, since 1999, futures and options on American coal have been traded on the NYMEX/COMEX in New York.

As mentioned above, electricity is an energy source that was not thought of as a commodity until very recently. However, due to the deregulation of electricity utilities in various regions of the world, including North America and Europe, efficient spot markets have appeared since the beginning of the 1990s. The first spot markets that appeared in Europe are in the UK and in the Nordic countries (Denmark, Finland, Norway, and Sweden). In the USA, various states such as California can be mentioned as pioneers in establishing spot markets for electricity. Electricity derivatives soon followed, with futures and options contracts corresponding to American-produced electricity traded on the NYMEX/COMEX in New York, and corresponding to electricity produced in the Nordic countries on the Nord Pool in Oslo. The commoditisation of electricity is, however, expanding very fast and other spot, and perhaps futures markets are

Table 1.2   The most important markets for energy commodities

Commodities	Spot markets	Derivative markets
Oil products		
Crude oil and refined oil products (residual oil, heating oil, diesel fuel, gasoline)	Amsterdam–Antwerp–Rotterdam, New York, Singapore	International Petroleum Exchange (London); NYMEX/COMEX (New York)
Jet fuel (kerosene); petrochemicals (naphtha etc.)	Amsterdam–Antwerp–Rotterdam, New York, Singapore	No organised derivative markets (OTC derivatives)
Liquefied petroleum gas (LPG, propane)	Amsterdam–Antwerp–Rotterdam, New York, Singapore	NYMEX/COMEX (New York)
Other fuels		
Natural gas	OTC contracts with European and North American consumers	NYMEX/COMEX (New York)
Coal	Various spot markets (Australia, USA, South Africa)	NYMEX/COMEX (New York)
Electricity		
Electricity	UK, Nordic countries (Nord Pool, Oslo); California/Oregon; Palo Verde	Nord Pool (Oslo); NYMEX/COMEX (New York)

soon expected to develop in other countries and regions of the world, such as Australia. Table 1.2 summarises the most important of these markets for energy commodities.

1.4.2   Markets for Metal and Non-energy Mineral Commodities

The LME, which is a centralised exchange rather than an OTC market, is the benchmark world reference market for the six most important non-ferrous metals. The originality of the LME is that, contrary to the practice of other recognised futures exchanges, spot prices as well as futures prices are quoted on it with possible delivery in LME warehouses throughout the world. The LME may thus also be used for reference pricing for using both forward and spot prices and physical delivery on LME is at least theoretically possible in many places in Europe, in the USA, and in Asia. However, for some of these basic non-ferrous metals quoted on the LME, physical spot markets that are located in production areas do exist. For instance an important spot market for tin is located at Kuala Lumpur (Malaysia), Malaysia being a major producer. Furthermore, futures and options on both aluminium and copper are traded in the USA on the NYMEX/COMEX.

Spot markets for metal and metal products on which reference pricing uses prices on various spot markets, producers' prices or posted prices, include the markets for steel and steel products, as well as the markets for several rare non-ferrous metals that might be used as alloys in the steel industry. Examples of these metals are:

- cobalt (Gecamines, Zaire, producers' prices)
- iron and steel (various producers' prices)
- magnesium (Dow Pedlock producers' prices)
- vanadium (Highveld producers' prices)
- zirconium (several producers' prices, including those of subsidiaries of Péchiney and Westinghouse)

In addition, antimony, bismuth, cadmium, chromium, cobalt, titanium sponge, ferro-manganese, ferro-molybdenum, mercury, selenium, and tungsten are quoted on an active spot market in London.

Gold and silver are traded on spot, forward and futures markets in many places throughout the world (spot markets exist in London (London Bullion Exchange), New York, Paris, Zurich, Singapore and in many other financial centres). Gold futures and options are traded on both COMEX in New York and CBOT in Chicago (100 oz contracts, priced in US$), while silver futures and options are traded on both COMEX and CBOT (5,000 oz contracts, priced in US$). CBOT offers further 1,000 oz futures contract on silver and a 1 kg gold futures contract. Other precious metals futures and options, such as the platinum group metals (PGM), the most important of which are platinum and palladium, are traded on NYMEX/COMEX (50 and 100 oz contracts, respectively, priced in US$), and on the Tokyo Commodity Exchange (TOCOM) for platinum. Among the other PGM metals, rhodium should be mentioned as a rare and very speculative metal with an active spot market.

Another important market for a mineral commodity other than a metal is the international diamond market, on which reference prices were until very recently prices quoted by De Beers' Central Selling Organisation, which was actually a cartel but was recently (2000) dismantled by De Beers. Therefore, since the end of the 1990s, this market was heading towards more competition. Table 1.3 summarises the most important of these markets for metal and mineral commodities.

1.4.3 Markets for Agricultural Commodities

Markets for agricultural commodities are evolving from markets with controlled or guaranteed price schemes towards more competitive and more liquid markets with more volatile prices, so that, as we will see, a number of new derivative markets concerning agricultural commodities have recently appeared. The Chicago Board of Trade is the largest futures and option market for many American-produced agricultural commodities, including wheat (Hard Red Winter,

Table 1.3 The most important markets for metals and mineral commodities

Commodities	Spot markets	Derivative markets
Metals and other mineral commodities		
Iron and steel products, including scrap	Various spot markets in producing areas (Japan, United States...)	No organised derivative markets
Common non-ferrous metals (aluminium, copper, lead, nickel, tin and zinc)	LME; Kuala Lumpur for tin	LME; NYMEX/COMEX (New York)
Other non-ferrous metals, excluding precious metals	Various spot markets with producers' prices; London for some of these metals	No organised derivative markets
Precious metals		
Gold, silver	Bullion markets throughout the world (London, Zurich, New York, and Tokyo)	LME (silver); NYMEX/COMEX (New York) (silver and gold)
Platinum, palladium	Various spot markets (London, New York, Tokyo)	Tokyo Commodity Exchange (platinum); NYMEX/COMEX (New York) (platinum, palladium)
Other platinum group metals	Various spot markets (London, New York, Tokyo)	No organised derivative markets
Other mineral commodities		
Diamond	Various spot markets, including Antwerp in Belgium. One dominant producer: De Beers	No organised derivative markets

contracts of 5,000 bushels, priced in US$/Bu), corn (No. 2 Yellow, contracts of 5,000 bushels, priced in US$/Bu), soya beans (No. 2 Yellow, contracts of 5,000 bushels, priced in US$/Bu), soya bean meal (contracts of 100 short tons, priced in US$/ton), soya bean oil (contracts of 60,000 lb, priced in US$/lb).[7]

The Chicago Mercantile Exchange (CME), also located in Chicago, has traditionally been another market for agricultural commodities and its derivative products are complementary to those offered by the CBOT. It is quite active in live cattle futures and options (contracts of 40,000 lb, priced in US$/lb) and in boneless beef meat futures and options (contracts of 20,000 lb, priced in US$/lb).

---

[7] 1 bushel (Bu) = 35.239 litres (27.216 kg of wheat, 25.4 kg of corn, 27.216 kg of soybeans); 1 lb = 0.453 kg; 1 short ton = 2000 lb = 906 kg.

It is also active in dairy products, such as milk futures and options (contract of 200,000 lb, priced in US$/lb), runs a butter and cheese spot market and trades contracts on forestry products, including lumber (in particular, Western, North Central, South Western and South Eastern lumber with a 100,000-board square feet contract, priced in US$/1,000-board square feet; this contract concerns standardised board panels of lumber wood that are 4 feet wide, 8 feet long, and 7/16 inch thick).

The New York Board of Trade (NYBOT) that resulted from the recent merger in 1998 of the New York Coffee, Sugar and Cocoa Exchange (CSCE) and of the New York Cotton Exchange, deals with futures and options in coffee (Arabica, contracts of 37,500 lb, priced in US$/lb), cocoa (any origin, contracts of 10 tonnes, priced in US$/tonne), and both international (No. 14) and US origin (No. 11) raw cane sugar futures (any origin, contracts of 112,000 lb or 50 long tons, priced in US$/long ton). The NYBOT also offers futures on cotton (contracts of 50,000 lb, priced in cents of US$), and on orange juice (contracts of 15,000 lb, priced in cents of US$). These contracts were previously traded on the New York Cotton Exchange. Finally, the NYBOT recently developed a contract on milk index futures (contract of 15,000 lb, priced in US$/lb).

The London International Financial Futures Exchange (LIFFE) in London has recently developed its futures and option products on agricultural commodities. It deals with futures in tropical products: coffee (Robusta, contracts of 5 tonnes, priced in US$) and cocoa (contracts of 10 tonnes, priced in US$). It also has a very active futures and option contract in white sugar (any origin, cane or beet sugar, grade No. 5 for contracts of 50 tonnes, priced in US$). More recently, it developed contracts in European Union wheat (contract of 100 tonnes, priced in £/tonne), in European Union barley (contract of 100 tonnes, priced in £/tonne), and in British potatoes (contract of 100 tonnes, priced in £/tonne).

The Paris Marché A Terme International de France (MATIF) deals with futures in milling wheat corn, rapeseed, rapeseed meal, and rapeseed oil (all are contracts of 50 tonnes, priced in Euro/tonne). It is also launching a futures contract on fine wines of the Bordeaux area of the oncoming crop (contracts will be 12 bottles of selected wines at purchaser's choice).

There are a number of other organised markets for agricultural commodities, among which one may mention the Kansas City market, which competes with CBOT for several futures contracts (wheat, etc.), the Winnipeg Commodity Exchange, which offers contracts on cereals such as rye, and the Sydney auction market for wool, which gives a reference quotation on wool. Table 1.4 summarises the most important of these markets for agricultural commodities.

1.4.4 Markets for Other Miscellaneous Commodities and Services

The number of other miscellaneous commodities and services that may be treated as commodities is expanding every day, as mentioned in the first section of

Table 1.4   The most important markets for agricultural commodities

Commodities	Spot markets	Derivative markets
Grains, edible oils, and sugars		
Wheat	Various spot markets in production areas (US Middle West, Western Europe, Australia, Argentina)	CBOT, Kansas City Commodity Exchange, LIFFE, MATIF
Corn	Various spot markets in production areas (US Middle West, Western Europe, Australia, Argentina)	CBOT, MATIF
Soybeans, soybean meal, and soybean oil	Various spot markets in production areas (US Middle West, Brazil)	CBOT
Canola (Canada), rapeseed and rapeseed meal (Europe)	Various spot markets in production areas (Canadian West, Germany etc.)	Winnipeg Commodity Exchange, MATIF
Olive oil	Various spot markets in the areas of production (Seville in Spain, Bari in Italy, and Thessaloniki in Greece)	No organised derivative markets
Raw sugar (usually cane sugar)	Various spot markets in production areas (USA, Latin America, Australia); reference quotations by the International Sugar Organisation	NYBOT (New York); Tokyo Grain Exchange
White or refined sugar	Various spot markets in production areas (Europe, USA, Latin America, Australia); reference quotations by the International Sugar Organisation	LIFFE (London)
Fibres		
Cotton	Various spot markets in production areas (US Southern States)	NYBOT (New York)
Wool	Sydney auction market	Sydney auction market
Silk	Chinese and Japanese spot markets	No organised derivative markets
Tropical commodities		
Coffee	Various spot markets (Brazil, other Latin American, and African producers)	NYBOT (New York)
Cocoa	Various spot markets (various African producers)	NYBOT (New York)
Tea	Various spot markets, including London and areas of production	No organised derivative markets
Natural rubber	Kuala Lumpur, Singapore	No organised derivative markets
Other agricultural commodities		
Cattle, meats	Various spot markets, including Chicago in the USA	CME (live cattle, boneless beef, among other contracts)
Milk and dairy products	Various spot markets, including CME (Chicago) spot market for butter and cheese	CME and NYBOT (milk)
Products of forestry	Various spot markets, including Sweden, the USA and Japan	CME futures on lumber
Pulp and paper	Various spot markets, including London, Scandinavia, Finland, and the USA	Pulpex market in London

this chapter. Among these commodities that can neither be classified as energy or mineral commodities nor as agricultural commodities, are seafood and fish, for which there are spot markets in the various areas of production. There are, for instance, markets for various seawater species of fish in the form of fresh, canned, smoked or frozen fish, and salmon, in the most important ports and areas concerned by fishing and also fish-farming, which is a growing industry. Shrimps and crabmeat are also products for which there is an international market.

There are also a few immaterial services that may be considered as commodities. These include shipping freight, for which there is a large international market, especially in the large seaports, such as London, Rotterdam, and others in Europe, New York in the USA, and Yokohama in Japan, among others. Shipping services include in particular tanker rates, for which there are OTC markets in the Gulf of Mexico and in Rotterdam, and dry cargo rates. There exists a new futures market for one of the representative indexes, which is quoted on the LIFFE in London. This market concerns a shipping freight index, which is the BIFFEX Baltic Panamax Index, a representative index for dry cargo freight.

Another recent innovation is futures and options on weather indexes, recently launched (2000) by the CME in Chicago. It concerns daily heating degree-day indexes (daily HDD indexes) in cities scattered in many American regions under almost all climatic conditions that prevail in the USA. These cities are Atlanta, Chicago, Cincinnati, Dallas, Des Moines, Las Vegas, New York, Philadelphia, Portland, and Tucson. The daily HDD index is defined as

$$\text{daily HDD} = \max \ (0, 65\,^\circ \ \text{Fahrenheit} - \text{daily average temperature})$$

where $65\,^\circ$F is considered as a standard ambient temperature for the utility industry. The HDD value of 100 corresponds to $-35\,^\circ$F, about $-14\,^\circ$C, which is well below freezing point, a temperature at which a significant need for heating is felt. Thus, this index is an index of the need for heating, and, as such, it is closely correlated to the demand for electricity and heating oil. It is therefore useful for the hedging needs of the utility industry. It is also useful for agricultural activities and offers a partial and indirect hedge against the negative effects of some climatic conditions. However, in agricultural activities, the relationship is not a straightforward one, but a sound use of weather derivatives might complete existing insurance systems. It is an important innovation that enables investors to speculate on the economic effects of climatic conditions. As shown in general in Chapter 6 hereafter, this new financial instrument might prove very useful for portfolio investments of banks, insurance and reinsurance companies and other institutional investors. Its usefulness stems from the fact that it provides assets with returns that are either uncorrelated and even negatively correlated with the returns of some traditional assets, such as bonds and shares. This is indeed a very important property for portfolio management which weather derivatives share with traditional commodities and commodity indexes, as shown in Chapter 6. The same is true of new financial instruments that are related to climatic disaster or catastrophes, such as so-called bonds with coupons that are conditioned by the occurrence of catastrophes or *cat bonds* (see e.g. Lesourd and Schilizzi, 2001).

Other important services, which may evolve into marketable commodities, are insurance and reinsurance, in which recently new market instruments, such as catastrophe futures and OTC derivatives have been developed. Other services that may also develop into commodities with global markets are, as mentioned previously, telecommunication services. Finally, there are a number of commodity indexes available. These are useful in allowing for an assessment of the overall international price behaviour of commodities as a whole. While there are a number of futures and option contracts on financial indexes, only two futures and option contracts are traded on commodity indexes, both in the USA, including one futures contract on the Goldman Sachs Commodity Index (GSCI) quoted on the CME in Chicago, and another futures contract on the Bridge–Commodity Research Bureau (Bridge/CRB) index, which is quoted on the NYBOT in New York. Some details on the interest of these contracts for investors will be given in Chapter 6.

Competition between organised futures exchanges, their structure, and the relative importance of the commodity contracts traded on them deserve a few words. Futures exchanges increasingly tend to become suppliers of services that are under competition on global markets, rather than the mutual institutions they used to be. This has reflected in the recent evolution of their legal status. Most futures exchanges (as well as stock exchanges) are changing their status from their previous historical status of mutual institutions to public quoted companies. In particular and among others, the CBOT, the LIFFE, and the LME have thus changed their status and shifted to public company status. There is currently a trend towards stronger competition between exchanges. Exchanges compete more and more on specific commodity futures and option contracts. The size of contracts, in terms of open position (the outstanding position at a given date in terms of number of contracts), and/or rather in terms of volume traded (the number of contracts exchanged during a given period of time), are indicators of the market success of a given commodity contract. It should be stressed that volumes and open interests are expressed in physical units and do not allow comparison between different commodities. Overall comparison between exchanges is meaningless in terms of number of contracts and, in monetary terms, is an aggregate over all sorts of contracts, including commodity and financial futures. However, it seems interesting to give here examples of the importance of several commodity futures exchanges. This is what is done in Table 1.5, which gives data that are comparable for some selected commodity futures contracts.

Table 1.5 merely gives examples of commodity contracts that give information on the importance of respective exchanges. What is observed here may change in time and is therefore only an indication. The table shows that three

Table 1.5 Examples of commodity futures contracts with their sizes

Commodities	Exchange	Open interest[a]	Size of contract	Price[b]	Open interest (10^6 US$)
Energy commodities					
Crude oil	NYMEX/COMEX	123,600	1000 barrels	30.83	3810.59
Crude oil	IPE	60,091	1000 barrels	29.72	1785.90
Metal commodities					
Gold	NYMEX/COMEX	78,636	100 oz	276.9	2177.43
Platinum	NYMEX/COMEX	7,927	50 oz	566.8	224.65
Silver	NYMEX/COMEX	59,069	5000 oz	4.948	1461.37
Agricultural commodities					
Wheat	CBOT	102,270	5000 bushels	2.65	1355.08
Wheat	LIFFE	2,606	100 metric tonnes	£62.50	24.08
Corn	CBOT	204,216	5000 bushels	1.9775	2019.19
Soya beans	CBOT	93,132	5000 bushels	4.905	2284.06
White sugar	LIFFE	14,209	50 metric tonnes	250	177.61
Sugar	NYBOT	87,275	112,000 lb	0.0945	923.72
Cocoa	NYBOT	48,264	10 metric tonnes	797	384.66
Cocoa	LIFFE	55,605	10 metric tonnes	£611	502.32
Coffee	NYBOT	29,043	37,500 lb	0.83	903.96
Coffee	LIFFE	29,900	5 metric tonnes	786	117.50
Financial futures					
US treasury bonds	CBOT	382,058	100,000 US$	98.08%	37472.25

[a] End of September 2000; number of physical contracts for most important nearby contract.
[b] Last settlement price for most important nearby contract in US$ per physical unit, unless otherwise stated.

important agricultural commodities futures, all traded on CBOT, have dollar open interests above US$ 1 billion: these are wheat, corn and soya beans, which total US$ 5.663 billion altogether. This is in line with the fact that the CBOT has consistently been considered as the largest futures market for agricultural commodities such as grains. But this figure is much lower than a typical figure (still concerning CBOT) for a financial commodity (US treasury bonds) with a dollar open interest of more than US$ 37 billion. Clearly, commodity futures are consistently less important in terms of open interest and volumes than financial commodities. The comparison of other commodity futures gives more importance to American exchanges than to European exchanges such as LIFFE. For instance, the dollar open positions of crude oil contracts show that both contracts given as examples (which are comparable nearby contracts) have open positions above US$ 1 billion. However, the open position on the New York NYMEX/COMEX (US$ 3.810 billion) is more than twice the open position on the London IPE

(US$ 1.785 billion). However, for cocoa and coffee, positions on the NYBOT and on the LIFFE are of comparable importance, with the LIFFE being ahead of NYBOT for cocoa. Finally, for futures concerning precious metals, American futures exchanges are dominant, with gold and silver nearby contracts having open positions above US$ 1 billion.

1.5 CONCLUSION

The overview of physical markets for basic commodities that we carried out in this chapter reveals both their diversity and their common features. Indeed, these markets involve a number of very different commodities, including energy commodities, non-energy mineral commodities such as metals, agricultural commodities, and immaterial services such as freight. However, despite the large differences in these commodities, international commodity markets discussed here share a number of characteristics. It should be emphasised that, whenever these markets are truly international and fully competitive, one of these characteristics is the importance of physical trading activities, which are carried out by trading companies. Trading companies, or merchants, are commercial intermediaries that render the indispensable service of making supply and demand meet. But, owing to temporary imbalances between physical supply and demand, trading companies are strongly exposed to price risks because at any time it is likely that they are exposed to this risk, which may be either a risk that prices will increase, or a risk of price decreases according to their order book and their stocks. This means that tools for hedging against price risks and suitable derivative markets play a very important role for those involved in the commodity markets. These instruments and markets therefore require an in-depth analysis, which is carried out in Chapters 2–4 that follow.

BIBLIOGRAPHY

CBOT (1990) *Introduction to Agricultural Hedging*, CBOT, Chicago.
D. Duffie (1989) *Futures Markets*. Prentice-Hall, Englewood Cliffs, New York.
E. Fama (1970) Efficient capital markets: A review of theory and empirical work, *Journal of Finance*, **25**, 383–417.
E. Fama (1991) Efficient capital markets, II, *Journal of Finance*, **46**, 1575–1617.
O. Güvenen, W. C. Labys and J. B. Lesourd (eds), (1991) *International Commodity Market Modelling. Advances in Methodology and Applications*. Chapman and Hall, London, 330 pp.
R. Kolb (1997) *Understanding futures markets*. Blackwell, Oxford.
W. C. Labys and J. B. Lesourd (1988) The New Energy Markets, Chapter 2 in J. K. Jacques, J. B. Lesourd, and J. M. Ruiz (eds), *Modern Applied Energy Conservation. New Directions in Energy Conservation Management*. Ellis Horwood/Halsted Press, Wiley, Chichester / New York, pp. 37–83.

J. B. Lesourd and S. Schilizzi (2001) *The Environment in Corporate Management*. Edward Elgar, Cheltenham, UK.

UNCTAD (General ed. Ph. Chalmin; ed. Ch. Prager, UNCTAD Secretariat; Co-ordinators: O. Matringe and L. Rutten) (2000) *World Commodity Survey 1999–2000. Markets, Trends and the World Economic Environment*. United Nations, Geneva.

P. Wilmott (1998) *Derivatives*. Wiley, New York.

2
Commodity futures

Organised futures markets originated in the middle of the nineteenth century in the celebrated cowtown and windy city of Chicago, Illinois. The Chicago Board of Trade was created in 1848, and around 1865 the first 'modern' futures contracts were developed. Although forward contracts had existed for hundreds of years — Japan and Holland were trading 'forward' type contracts two centuries earlier — the first formalised 'futures' contract originated in Chicago. Since then it has spread all over the world: to New York, Kansas City, Minneapolis and Philadelphia, Montreal, Winnipeg, London, Amsterdam, Paris, Tokyo, Hong Kong, Kuala Lumpur, and Sydney, to mention only a few. Nevertheless, Chicago is still the world's leading 'futures' centre.

The development and growth of futures markets did not come about by chance. Chicago in the nineteenth century, for example, was already at the heart of a fertile agricultural region. Transportation, however, was somewhat hazardous, especially in winter when the rivers would freeze over. This entailed serious risks for the farmers. If the farmers sold at harvest time when supply was abundant, prices were often low. If they waited for winter, prices were often higher, but the ability to deliver was chancy due to the effects of the weather on the transportation system. If they waited till spring, prices would be high or low depending on the size of the harvest and how much was held back. In these conditions, farmers never knew how much they would receive for their produce until it was too late. Futures markets made it possible to overcome this problem.

The same type of phenomenon was present for the development of futures markets in Great Britain at the end of the nineteenth century. London and Liverpool, where the first futures markets sprang up in copper and wool among others, were not production centres for these products. They were, however, the gateways for imports and centres of production and consumption of products that used them as inputs. The international *trade cycle* of economic expansion and contraction combined with the nature of producing many raw materials gave rise to a situation where prices could fluctuate violently from one period to another.[1,2] British industrialists were therefore exposed to considerable uncertainty concerning the price they would pay for their imported inputs. Futures markets for these products enabled them to eliminate or at least control this uncertainty.

From these two historical examples we can see that commodity futures markets developed for basic products subject to wide price fluctuations. They sprang up where there was large-scale trade in the basic products themselves due either to the fact that the region was a production centre for the products or that it was a centre where the basic products were transformed into more elaborate consumer goods. It is interesting to note that if one of these two conditions disappears, the futures market will die. This was the case, for example, with the European raw wool futures markets when the European wool industries disappeared.

Another condition for the creation of a commodity futures market is that the underlying commodity be homogeneous enough to permit contract standardisation. Product differentiability makes delivery too complicated and kills the market. For example, no futures markets have ever developed for sophisticated manufactured products with varied technical characteristics.

For a commodity futures market to function correctly, a competitive spot market in the underlying commodity is indispensable. By competitive we mean that there exists an indeterminate number of traders, all dealing in the same product, and where no one trader can offer or demand a quantity sufficiently large to materially affect the market price. In other words, *monopolistic* and *monopsonistic* markets do not lend themselves to futures trading.[3] For example, as long as OPEC (Organization of Petroleum Exporting Countries) dominated the oil market, no market in petroleum futures ever emerged.

From this little background sketch we can see why futures markets developed and why they have stayed within the realm of certain raw materials like agricultural products, industrial metals, precious metals, and petroleum, and not been generalised to cover all products. The keys to an effectively functioning futures market are a competitive spot market, product homogeneity and price volatility.

---

[1] The trade cycle refers to regular oscillations in the level of business activity over a number of years. Most explanations of the existence and nature of the trade cycle are based on ex ante disequilibrium between savings and investment that can be caused or aggravated by monetary phenomena and the interaction of the multiplier process and the acceleration principle of derived demand. See: Hayek (1933, 1941, 1975); Hicks (1950, 1987).

[2] Wide price fluctuations are often associated with the production of perishable raw materials in what is known as the *cobweb effect*. The cobweb effect refers to the graphic representation of the conditions that may exist in a competitive market when the sale of a perishable good, requiring a period of time to produce, is confined to a short seasonal demand but enjoys a fairly constant demand from year to year during that season. The seasonal sales period is too short and the time required for production too long to permit changes in the supply by any producer after sales have begun. Each year, therefore, the supply depends on the market price of the previous year. This tends to cause price oscillations from year to year, a relatively high price and short supply alternating with a relatively low price and plentiful supply.

[3] A monopoly is where one supplier dominates the market and a monopsony is where one buyer dominates it.

2.1 FORWARDS AND FUTURES

As discussed in Chapter 1, a forward contract is an agreement to buy or sell an asset at a certain future time for a certain future price, whereas a spot contract is an agreement to buy or sell an asset today. Forward contracts are traded in the OTC market and usually involve a financial institution on one side of the deal and either a client or another financial institution on the other side of the deal. One party to the deal takes a long position and agrees to purchase the asset. The other party takes the short position and agrees to sell the asset. The agreed price in the forward contract is called the delivery price, which is chosen so that the value of the contract to both sides is equal to zero. Consequently, it costs nothing to enter into a forward agreement.

A futures contract is very similar to a forward contract. It is an agreement between two parties to buy or sell an asset at a certain time for a certain price. Futures contracts are traded on organised exchanges. To facilitate trading the exchange specifies certain standardised features of the contract and trading takes place in such a way that the exchange is the ultimate counterparty to each transaction. Futures contracts differ from forward contracts in two other ways. First of all, payments are made over the life of the contract in what is called marking to market.[4] Secondly, most futures contracts are closed out before maturity.

2.1.1 Hedging against Price Declines

Futures markets make it possible for producers of raw materials to respect the delivery requirements of their clients while eliminating the price risk associated with sales that will take place in the future. Let us take the example of an American producer of soya bean meal in the month of January. He is used to spreading his sales out over the year depending on prices and the habits of his clients. He has equipped himself with an efficient storage facility that protects his raw materials and output adequately from damage caused by sunlight and cold. He has 500 tons of meal that he expects to sell in March. The current price is $147.40 per ton and the March contract on the CBOT is $147.40. Thus, the spot (cash) price and the March futures price are the same. This, of course, is a happy coincidence that makes the example easier to understand without changing anything important to the exercise. If the American producer wants to eliminate the risk of a fall in the price of soya bean meal, he can cover himself by selling five March contracts. Each contract is for 100 tons on the CBOT.

Suppose that he sells the five contracts and that the price falls to $120 per ton. He will be able to sell his 500 tons of meal to his regular clients only at this price and receive $500 \times \$120 = \$60,000$. He then instructs his broker to close out his

---

[4] Marking to market and its effects are discussed below.

futures position right before the expiry limit. Since the futures price converges to the spot price at expiry, he buys back his five contracts at $120 and receives the difference between $147.40 and $120, multiplied by the five contracts multiplied by 100 tons per contract:

$$(\$147.40 - \$120) \times 5 \times 100 = \$13,700$$

His total income from the spot sale and the futures transaction is

$$\$60,000 + \$13,700 = \$73,700$$

an average price of $147.40 per ton. Because he hedged his position with the five futures contracts, he supplied his regular March customers and lost nothing by waiting even though the price fell from $147.40 to $120 per ton in the interim.

Guaranteeing against an unfavourable price movement by means of a futures contract has a cost. The cost is what is lost if there is a favourable price move. Suppose, for example, that instead of falling to $120, the price of meal rises to $170 per ton. In this case the producer sells his meal to his regular March customer at $170 per ton and receives $85,000. When he instructs his broker to close out his position by buying five futures contracts, he finds that the futures price has converged to the spot price and that he must pay $170. He loses the difference between the sales price and the purchase price ($170 − 147.40) multiplied by the five contracts multiplied by 100 tons per contract

$$(\$170 - \$147.40) \times 5 \times 100 = \$11,300$$

His total income from the two transactions is

$$\$85,000 - \$11,300 = \$73,700$$

an average price of $147.40 per ton. This is the same outcome as in the case of a price fall. The cost of hedging against a potential price fall is the loss of the potential gain in the case of a price rise.

2.1.2   Hedging against a Price Rise

Primary producers are not the only ones to benefit from commodity futures markets. Raw materials traders and industrial firms that use raw materials as direct inputs can also benefit. Consider the case of a raw materials trader. In January a Japanese importer contacts the trader about a March delivery of 2,000 tons of soya bean meal and asks him to make an offer. The trader checks the current price and finds it is $147.40 per ton. The trader could, of course, offer this price plus a commission, but he/she is only an intermediary. He/she has no meal and no means of stocking it, so he cannot buy it now. If he offers $147.40 as the basis of his offer, he is running a big risk. Between January and March when the trader will purchase the meal to be shipped to his Japanese customer, the price could rise, thereby costing him dearly. He/she can make a firm offer and still cover his risk by using the futures market.

Remember that the March futures price is $147.40, the same as the spot price. The trader offers his Algerian customer this price plus a commission and proceeds to buy 20 contracts worth $294,800. If the price rises above $147.40 to $160, for example, the trader will have to pay $320,000 when the meal is purchased on the spot market. However, when he/she closes out his futures position by selling 20 contracts at the $160 price of the futures contract at maturity, he/she will earn the difference between $160 and 147.40 multiplied by the 20 contracts multiplied by 100 tons per contract:

$$(\$160 - \$147.40) \times 20 \times 100 = \$25,200$$

His total cost will be

$$\$320,000 - \$25,200 = \$294,800$$

$147.40 per ton. If prices fall, he will be able to purchase the potatoes more cheaply on the spot market, but he will lose the difference on his futures position so that his cost will always be $147.40 per ton.

The two foregoing examples serve to point out the principles of commodities hedging with futures contracts. Long positions in the commodity (the producer, for example) take short positions in futures while short positions in the commodity (the trader, for example) take long positions in futures contracts. At maturity, the position can be closed out by making an offsetting buy or sell. It is interesting to notice that in neither case was the futures market used as a source of supply. The desired goal was a price differential that would offset unfavourable moves in the spot price. Furthermore, it is clear that both buyers and sellers have an interest in the market and are likely to be present on a continuous basis. This is important for liquidity where the presence of both is indispensable.

2.2   ORGANISATION OF THE FUTURES EXCHANGES

Commodities futures markets are organised like the financial futures markets. Trading takes place in public in a designated area (the pit or the ring) among brokers accredited by the exchange. The clearing house is the ultimate counter-party to all transactions.

2.2.1   Public and Competitive Trading Procedures

Only commission houses registered as member firms are allowed to trade on the exchange. Anyone else who seeks access to the market must do so through a commission house by opening an account. All orders are then executed through the commission house. In the USA, for example, opening an account is subject to strict rules. Before opening an account, the client must read a number of documents and declare that he has understood them. This is to ensure that the client understands the risks associated with the futures markets. Furthermore, opening an account is also subject to certain financial guarantees such as a deposit of cash or marketable securities.

When a client wants to trade, the order is transmitted to the 'registered representative' that manages the account for the clearing house. Different types of conditions can be attached to the order. The order can be limited to a certain period of time or to a certain price range or both. When the registered representative receives the order, it is transmitted directly to the offices of the clearing house in the city where the futures market is located. From there it is sent to the commission house's order desk or the trading floor. A messenger takes it to the commission house's trader in the pit. At each stage of the operation the order is time stamped so as to control the speed of execution and serve as proof in the case of a complaint.

Transactions take place either around a ring or inside a pit. The traders, either from the different commission houses or independent speculators, take their places around the ring or on different steps of the pit based on the maturity date of the commodity being traded. The messengers bring them the orders for execution and large electronic panels flash information that keeps them constantly informed of what is happening in the market. Trading is done by an auction system of open outcry where any trader can take the opposite side of a trade if he wants to. In this system, the voice is combined with a particular sign language to communicate prices, quantities and buys or sells. If, for example, a trader wants to buy 10 February contracts at 1.05 FF per kilo, he signals this to the other traders. Any trader can answer and if several do, the fastest to respond is the one who gets the deal. If no one responds, the trader knows that his price is off. He either has to wait to execute his order or he has to offer a better price. This system guarantees that at any particular moment there is only one price on the market.

Exchange employees permanently monitor what is going on in each pit or ring. After each order is executed they enter the price in the computer system. In this way all exchange members are kept informed of the market's evolution. Some exchanges link their computer systems to the outside for public distribution of the information.

Once an order has been executed, the floor broker uses a messenger to transmit the information to his desk. The desk then informs the client and transmits the information to the commission house's accounting services where the appropriate entries are recorded. Recording requirements do not end here, however. The clearing house, which is the ultimate counterparty to each trade, must also be informed. For this purpose, floor brokers are obliged to fill in a *trading card* for each transaction indicating the type of contract, its maturity, the number of contracts, the price, the commission houses code numbers, and the initials of the floor broker.

2.2.2   The Role of the Clearing House

The role of the clearing house is threefold. It records the existence of the contract, it manages settlement of day-to-day operations, and it guarantees delivery at the contract's maturity. Thus, there is no individual counterparty risk because all clients have the clearing house as the ultimate counterparty.

The modern system of clearing used today by almost all futures markets was developed in the USA about 1920. Most clearing houses are specific to each exchange, although some clearing corporations such as ICCH in London act on behalf of several markets. Their role is always the same. They act as third-party guarantors to all futures contracts and they manage the financial implications associated with their guarantee.

Once a trade has been completed, the commission houses on either side of the trade do not have an obligation to each other. They each have an obligation to the clearing house. Thus, the commission house on the buy side of the trade has an obligation to the clearing house to buy. The commission house on the sell side of the trade has an obligation to the clearing house to sell and the clearing house has an obligation to sell to the buyer and an obligation to buy from the seller.

The role of the clearing house is essential for a smooth functioning futures market. Clients do not have to worry about the solvability of the commission house nor do commission houses have to worry about the solvability of other exchange members. The only risk is the solvability of the clearing house itself. This risk is minimal since the clearing house is required to maintain an impregnable financial position. All contracts are with the financially impregnable clearing house and, thus, for a given type are strictly equivalent. This facilitates trading and fosters liquidity. When a client wants to close out a position on a purchased futures contract, for example, he simply sells a contract to someone else. No one cares who makes the transaction because the ultimate counterparty is the clearing house. The clearing house keeps its accounts with each member and knows at all times the net position of each one.

Because of its role as ultimate counterparty, the clearing house is at risk from all the members with whom it does business. Consequently, it requires certain guarantees from each one. One of the most important guarantees of an exchange's financial system is the strict *clearing margin* imposed on members. A clearing margin is a deposit in the form of cash, government-issued securities, stock in the clearing corporation, or letters of credit issued by an approved bank that clearing members leave with the clearing house. The size of the deposit is fixed by the clearing house based on the member's net position or on its long and short positions and it can be revised upward or downward at any time depending on how the clearing house feels the market is going. Clearing margins are calculated every day in an exercise similar to the way that clients are marked to market. They must be large enough to cover maximum fluctuations in futures prices. Since prices vary from day to day, initial margins may become inadequate if prices move strongly against one or more members. In this case, the clearing house can make a margin call against the deficient members. They then have one hour to effect a 'wire transfer of funds'. These funds will be included in the end of day settlement procedures when all accounts are marked to market. It is clear that much care is taken to ensure the exchange's solvability and that the clearing house wields extensive power over its members.

2.2.3   Margin Calls and Marking to Market

As would be expected, member commission houses require the same type of guarantees from their clients that the clearing house requires of them. In fact, the margins that commission houses require of their clients are often higher than the margins required by the clearing house, although the deposits represent only a small proportion of the total contract and are virtually costless since interest-bearing treasury bonds can be used. Clients' accounts are marked to market at the end of each day and clients are subject to margin calls if their position deteriorates. Margins and daily marking to market make client defaults a rare occasion and reinforce the overall financial soundness of the exchange.

Marking to market means that profits and losses are paid every day at the end of trading and is equivalent to closing out a contract each day, paying off losses or receiving gains, and writing a new contract. The procedure can best be illustrated by an example.

On Monday morning an investor takes a long position in a hog futures contract of 30,000 pounds at a price of $0.70 per pound. At the end of the day the price has risen to $0.72. Since the amount of the contract is 30,000 lb, the investor's gain is

$$(\$0.72 - \$0.700) \times 30,000 = \$600$$

He receives his $600 and is the owner of a contract whose price is now $0.72. On Tuesday evening the price has fallen to $0.68. Therefore, he has to pay:

$$(\$0.72 - \$0.68) \times 30,000 = \$1,200$$

and he owns a contract whose price is $0.68.

In this context, the margin procedure is straightforward. An *initial margin* is deposited when a position is taken on a futures contract. This initial margin is usually set high enough so that the cost and inconvenience of frequent small payments can be avoided as the futures price is marked to market each day. Small losses are simply deducted from the initial margin until a predetermined lower bound, called the *maintenance margin*, is reached. At this point, the commission house issues a *margin call* requesting the client to deposit the funds necessary to bring the margin back to the initial level.

2.2.4 Delivery Procedures

Except for isolated rare exceptions, futures positions that remain open at maturity are closed out by physical delivery of the commodity in question. Most futures positions, however, are closed out before maturity. When physical delivery is required, the clearing house manages the transaction. It assigns buyers to sellers and fixes exactly how the exchange is to take place. Exchange rules specify the quality of the merchandise to be delivered, where it is to be delivered, storage and other costs, compensation differentials for discrepancies in quality, appraisal procedures, and conditions for refusal by the buyer. It is indispensable for the exchange that physical delivery be effected smoothly and with the least conflict possible. The exchange knows, however, that the seller maintains an advantage in being able to choose the merchandise that will be delivered and oftentimes where it will be delivered. The buyer has little latitude and must pay the price determined by the last known settlement price.

Although physical delivery concerns only 1–3% of all contracts, it is nevertheless a fundamental element of the arbitrage operations that ensure an efficiently functioning futures market. If, for example, futures prices are much higher than spot prices as the maturity date approaches, traders will be able to earn a riskless profit by buying the commodity on the spot market, stocking it, selling a futures contract, and making physical delivery at maturity. The difference in price, of course, has to be large enough to cover the storage costs and the financial opportunity cost of buying spot. On the other side of the coin, if futures prices are too low, traders can sell the commodity short, make a futures purchase and take delivery at maturity. The commodity can then be resold at a profit or consumed directly. Thus, the possibility of physical delivery ensures that the spot and futures prices will converge as maturity approaches and the futures market is linked directly to the reality of the spot market in the underlying commodity.

2.3 BASIS AND EFFECTIVE HEDGING

Although spot and futures prices converge at maturity, they can and do differ significantly before maturity. The difference between the futures price and the spot price is called the *basis*. The basis and how it varies through time are important elements in hedging strategies that use the organised futures exchanges.

The flexibility afforded by the possibility of closing out a futures position at any time before the contract's maturity is an important element for hedging strategies on the organised futures exchanges. Suppose, for example, that in May a Swiss chocolate manufacturer forecasts a need for 400 tons of sugar to be purchased at the end of June. He feels that sugar prices are likely to rise in the interim and wants to cover himself. Although he is used to undertaking hedging transactions on the Paris exchange, he has some doubt as to the most effective instrument to use in this particular case. A hedge can be constructed with a futures contract having a different maturity than the asset being hedged. This brings up the question of basis risk. In this section we will first look at the conditions for choosing the maturity of the futures contract. We will then look at what determines the basis on the commodities markets.

2.3.1   Choosing the Maturity of the Futures Contract

Futures delivery dates, being relatively infrequent, will often not correspond perfectly with the maturity of the risk to be hedged. Consequently, the hedge might not eliminate all risk. This is because although the futures price and spot (cash) price will converge at maturity, before maturity they can and do differ significantly.[5] Thus, the choice of a maturity date will affect the effectiveness of the hedge. This can be seen with an example.

Suppose that on 16 May the spot price for sugar is $286.50 per ton. At the same time, an August futures contract on the Paris exchange is selling at $279.50 per ton. To cover himself, the Swiss manufacturer decides to purchase eight August contracts (each contract is for 50 tons). On 20 June he purchases 400 tons of sugar from his regular suppliers at a price of $327.50 per ton. He simultaneously closes out his futures position at $325 per ton for a gain of

$$(\$325 - \$279.50) \times 8 \times 50 = \$18,200$$

The cost of purchasing the 400 tons of sugar was

$$\$327.50 \times 400 = \$131,000.$$

Including the gain on the futures contract the net cost was

$$\$127,000 - \$18,200 = \$108,800$$

or a price of $282 per ton.

His hedging operation turned out to be pretty effective in so far as the spot price of the sugar on the day that he purchased it was $327.50 and he only paid

---

[5] Samuelson (1965) showed that futures prices will become more volatile as they approach maturity. Rutledge (1985) found empirical support for this law. Other studies supporting Samuelson's law are R. Anderson, some determinants of the volatility of Futures prices, *Journal of Futures Markets*, Fall (1985) 331–348 and Milonas (1986). This means that the volatility of the basis for a particular contract may tend to increase as the contract approaches maturity.

$282. This outcome is due to the fact that the futures price followed an evolution parallel to the spot price. The spot price went from $286.50 to $327.50, a gain of $41, while the futures price went from $279.50 to $325, a gain of $45.50. As long as the two prices evolve in a parallel fashion, it does not matter too much if the maturity dates differ.

We can also see that the hedge made it possible to get a better price than what was available on 16 May, $282 instead of $286.50. The reason for this is that the forward price went up by more ($45.50) than the spot price ($41). The $4.50 difference explains the difference between the $282 and $286.50. This brings up the question of the basis. Remember that the basis is the difference between the futures price and the spot price. On 16 May the basis was

$$\$279.50 - \$286.50 = -\$7$$

On 20 June the basis was

$$\$325 - \$327.50 = -\$2.50$$

The basis increased by $4.50 from −$7 to − $2.50 and this is what explains the difference between the spot price of $286.50 on 16 May and the $282 effective cost of the sugar on 20 June.

Unfortunately, there is no reason why the basis should always increase. It could also decrease. Suppose that instead of $325 the futures price had been $317.50 on 20 June. The basis would have been

$$\$317.50 - \$327.50 = -\$10$$

a fall of $3. The gain on the futures contracts would have been

$$\$317.50 - \$279.50 = \$38 \text{ per ton}$$

The net cost of the sugar would have been

$$\$327.50 - \$38 = \$289.50 \text{ per ton}$$

$3 higher than the spot price on 16 May. The $3 fall in the basis is responsible. A hedger purchasing futures benefits from a rise in the basis and suffers from a fall. An imperfect hedge using futures contracts like the one above where the maturities do not match is called a delta hedge. In practice, a delta hedge will never eliminate all the risk. Basis risk will always exist in so far as the futures price is not perfectly correlated with the spot price. Choosing the maturity of the futures contract, then, is important for the effectiveness of the hedge and depends on how the price of the futures contract is expected to evolve relative to the spot price. The expected evolution of the basis, then, is the key to choosing the maturity of the hedging instrument.

Before getting into the factors that determine the basis we should remember that all hedgers, both buyers and sellers are subject to basis risk. Whereas buyers benefit when the basis increases and lose when the basis decreases, sellers benefit when the basis decreases and lose when the basis increases. This is only logical since they are on opposite sides of the fence with buyers hedging against a rise in the spot price and sellers hedging against a fall.

2.3.2   Determining the Basis

Cost of carry   The evolution of the basis is crucial for the effectiveness of the hedge. Consequently, it is important to understand what determines the basis. The basis in financial futures is straightforward and depends on the difference between the short and long-term interest rates. The underlying instruments on the financial futures markets, however, have no supply problems associated with production costs, weather, and the like, nor do they have inventory problems related to storage facilities, damage, and obsolescence. The underlying instruments on the commodity futures markets do have these problems, which makes the determination of the basis more complicated.

First of all, we have seen that when the maturity of the futures contract and the commodity transaction are the same, arbitrage ensures that the basis will tend to zero as the maturity date approaches. Convergence is never perfect, however, because arbitrage transactions are costly. Transport costs, insurance against litigation, and eventual differences in the quality of the merchandise, among others, can be the source of differences between the futures price and the spot price at maturity. Nevertheless, on the whole, convergence is satisfactory for most commodities. If it were not, commodities futures would lose their attraction for professional traders and eventually die out.

When the maturity date is somewhere in the future, there is no reason for the basis to be equal to zero. On the contrary. In practice it can be either positive or negative. When it is positive, it is referred to as *contango*. When it is negative, it is called *backwardation*. There are two major elements that explain the existence of a positive or negative basis. The first is the cost of setting up an arbitrage operation, called the *carrying cost*, and the second is the expected evolution of the spot market.

When the commodity in question is stockable (grain, gold, oil, etc.), it is easy to show that the futures price 'F' with maturity 't' should verify the following inequality:

$$F_t \leq (S + K)(1 + r)^t \qquad (2.1)$$

where S = the spot price of the commodity, r = the riskless rate of interest per period, and K = the present value of storage costs. It is easy to see that if the futures price, F, is larger than the right-hand side of the equation, a trader could make a riskless profit by borrowing $S + K$ at the rate, r, using the proceeds of the loan to purchase the commodity on the spot market, sell a futures contract for F, and then sit back and wait. On the maturity date, physical delivery would be made, storage costs and the loan would be paid off out of F with the difference remaining as the arbitrager's profit. Consequently, the upper limit of the futures price is determined by the carrying cost of the arbitrage transaction. In certain commodity markets, relation (2.1) is particularly binding. On the gold market, for example, where storage costs are low and stable, it is almost an equality.

While this arbitrage relation is important, it has some practical shortcomings. First of all, it defines only the upper limit of the futures price. It tells us nothing about how low the price can go. Secondly, it supposes that storage costs are easily observable. Thirdly, it is entirely inapplicable to commodities such as cattle on the hoof that are not stockable.

Convenience yield   Working was the first to make a partial answer to the first two shortcomings.[6] He demonstrated in a formalized argument that storage costs cannot be considered as fixed. They depend on the level of stocks as depicted in Figure 2.1. The explanation is straightforward. In the weeks following a harvest, the silos are full and storage space is rare and costly. As time goes on, stocks are run down, storage space becomes available and its cost falls.

Working's analysis of storage costs explains why the basis is higher or lower, depending on the maturity in question. It also explains how the basis can be negative. In practice, the basis is often negative for certain commodities. During the Iraq–Kuwait crisis of 1990, for example, the spot price of crude oil rose to over $40 a barrel while the futures price hovered at about $24 per barrel. With such a large negative basis it is hard to understand why traders would continue to hold stocks. It seems like it would be better to sell spot and assure future supplies at a lower price by buying a futures contract. The fact that this does not always happen proves that there must be certain advantages in holding stocks. The advantages come in the form of the planning benefits of having a secure supply and the elimination of costs associated with stock outs or avoiding stock

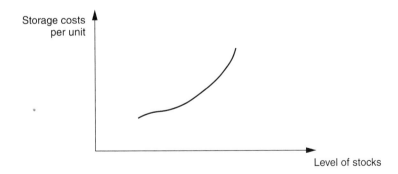

Figure 2.1   Storage costs and level of stocks

---

[6] Working (1934) and Hoss and Working (1938).

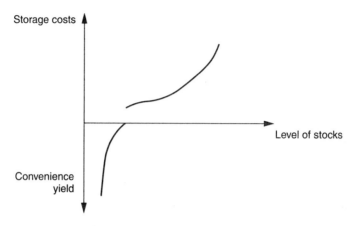

Figure 2.2 Storage costs, convenience yield and level of stocks

outs when it seems they might occur. Benefits of this type are referred to as *convenience returns* or *yields*. Lower stocks make a stock out more likely and raise the convenience yield. Figure 2.2 completes Figure 2.1 with the notion of convenience yields. At high levels of stocks, convenience yields are negligible or non-existent. At low stock levels, convenience yields rise rapidly and push down the price of the futures contract.

We can summarise the determination of the basis as follows. When stocks are high and expected to remain adequate, convenience yields are non-existent and the carrying cost of arbitrage determines the futures price at a level above the spot price. On the other hand, when stocks are very low or expected to get very low, convenience yields rise and storage costs fall. The futures price is determined by the difference between convenience yields and carrying costs. Convenience yields higher than carrying costs can push the futures price below the spot price and make the basis negative.

Normal backwardation   Another theory of the determination of the basis borrows from expectations theory and the role of the speculator. Do not forget that spot and futures prices should converge at maturity. Furthermore, it is reasonable to assume that today's futures price represents the market's expectation of what the spot price will be on the maturity date of the futures contract. This assumption is called the forward rate parity hypothesis. It can be written

$$F_t = E(S_t) \qquad (2.2)$$

where E is the expectations operator. Equation (2.2) represents forward rate parity and says that today's future rate for maturity 't' is the best estimate of what the spot rate will be on that date. If it is true, this is a valuable statistic. Unfortunately, it is not compatible with the presence of speculators in the market, at least according to Keynes.[7] In fact, if a speculator holds his position until maturity, his/her expected gain will be zero: $F_t - E(S_t) = 0$. Since there are many speculators on the market and since they have to make a profit on the average in order to stay in business, something else must be at work. Keynes's solution to the problem is the hypothesis of *normal backwardation*, whereby the rate of profit for a speculator with a long position in futures should be positive. The hypothesis can be written as follows:

$$E(S_t) - F_t = \lambda \qquad (2.3)$$

where λ represents the level of remuneration necessary for the speculator to finance the margin requirements, transactions costs, and profits necessary to keep him in business. A negative basis reflects all these elements when the expected spot price at time 't' is just equal to the current spot price. This proposition is important because it fixes a lower limit to the futures price. The futures price cannot fall below the expected spot price at time 't' less the premium λ. Otherwise, speculators will all take up long positions. The same type of argument can be made for speculators with short positions. The futures price cannot exceed the sum of the expected spot price at maturity plus the speculator's premium. Otherwise, all speculators would sell futures in order to benefit from the excessively high expected profits, thereby lowering the futures price.

Systematic risk and return   Modern portfolio theory leads to the conclusion that there are two types of risk in the economy — risk that can be eliminated through diversification, called unsystematic risk, and risk that cannot be eliminated through diversification, called systematic risk.[8] Since unsystematic risk can be eliminated, investors should not worry about it. Systematic risk arises from correlations of returns across all assets or, as in the capital asset pricing model (CAPM), from the correlation between returns on the investment and the market as a whole. Since this risk cannot be diversified away, investors should require a return above the riskless rate of interest for taking on positive amounts of systematic risk. They should also be prepared to accept a return below the riskless rate if their systematic risk is negative. Equations (2.2) and (2.3) can be interpreted in this context.

Consider an investor that purchases a futures contract for F_t at time 0 for delivery at t and invests the amount $F_t/(1 + r)^t$ in the riskless asset. On the delivery date, the proceeds from the loan are used to pay off the futures contract and take delivery of the underlying asset, which is then sold for its market price. The cash flows to this investment are $S_t - F_t$, the price received for the underlying asset less the futures price. If the capital markets are in equilibrium,

---

[7] Keynes (1930).

[8] For an excellent, in depth presentation of modern portfolio theory see, for example, Elton and Gruber (1990).

the present value of this investment at time 0 is

$$\frac{E(S_t)}{(1+R)^t} - \frac{F_t}{(1+r)^t} = 0$$

where R is the required rate of return on the underlying asset necessary to compensate investors for its systematic risk. This can be written as

$$F_t = E(S_t)\frac{(1+r)^t}{(1+R)^t} \tag{2.4}$$

Thus, R depends on the systematic risk of the underlying asset. If it has positive correlation with the market, $R > r$, which suggests that $F_t < E(S_t)$; if it has negative correlation $R < r$ and $F_t > E(S_t)$; if it is uncorrelated with the market $R = r$ and $F_t = E(S_t)$.

It is clear that there are two types of actors on the futures markets. There are those who trade for the purpose of hedging and those who trade for the purpose of speculating. Some are short; others are long. Taken together, their actions determine the basis. The elements that motivate their actions can be summarised as follows:

- the expected evolution of the spot price
- carrying costs
- convenience returns
- the speculators' premium
- the systematic risk premium

All these elements are not necessarliy present simultaneously at all times. There are times when simple arbitrage will determine the basis. There are other times when convenience costs and the speculators' premium will come into play. The fact is that although the basis converges to zero at maturity, in practice, its evolution can be erratic. Basis risk is real. For this reason hedging operations require technical expertise and should be undertaken carefully.

2.4 THE RELATIONSHIP BETWEEN SPOT AND COMMODITY FUTURES PRICES

In this section we need to formalise the relationship between the spot and futures prices. The notation is as follows:

T = delivery date of the futures contract (years)
t = current date (years)
τ = T-t
$F_{t,T}$ = price of a futures contract at time t for delivery at time T
S_t = spot (cash) price at time t

K = present value of storage costs or other known intermediate
    payouts
r = riskless rate of interest
k = proportional cost of storage
c = convenience yield
δ = dividend yield
r_D = the riskless rate on domestic currency
r_F = the riskless rate on foreign currency.

2.4.1 No Intermediate Payouts, No Storage Costs and No Convenience Yield

First we consider an underlying asset with no intermediate cash payments and no storage costs such as a pure discount bond or a stock that pays no dividends. The no-arbitrage relationship between the futures price and the cash (spot) price is

$$F_{t,T} = S_t\, e^{r\tau} \qquad (2.5)$$

If this were not true and $F_{t,T} > S_t\, e^{r\tau}$, it would be possible to make an arbitrage profit by selling F, borrowing S at the riskless rate and using the proceeds to purchase the underlying at the cost of S. At maturity we would take delivery and use F to pay off the loan. The profit would be $F_{t,T} - S_t\, e^{r\tau}$. If $F_{t,T} < S_t\, e^{r\tau}$, an arbitrage profit could be made by purchasing F, selling S short, and using the proceeds to invest in the riskless asset. At maturity we would use the proceeds from the investment in the riskless asset to take delivery. The profit would be $S_t\, e^{r\tau} - F_{t,T}$.

2.4.2 Non-proportional Storage Costs

Suppose that the present value of storage costs are equal to K. The no-arbitrage relationship between F and S must be

$$F_{t,T} \leq (S_t + K)\, e^{r\tau} \qquad (2.6)$$

If this were not true and $F_{t,T} > (S_t + K)\, e^{r\tau}$, it would be possible to make an arbitrage profit by selling F, borrowing $S + K$ at the riskless rate, using the proceeds to: (1) purchase the underlying at the cost of S, and (2) invest in the riskless asset for maturities corresponding to payments for storage costs. Over the life of the contract we use the proceeds of the investments in the riskless asset to pay off the storage costs as they come due. At maturity we would take delivery and use F to pay off the loan. The profit would be $F_{t,T} - (S_t + K)\, e^{r\tau}$. If $F_{t,T} < (S_t + K)\, e^{r\tau}$, the problem is more complicated because it is usually not possible to short the commodity in such a way that the storage costs are paid to the short position. Thus, the strategy of buying the futures contract and shorting the commodity will not work. However, for precious metals like gold and silver that are held as investments as well as for consumption, an arbitrage profit could be made by those holding the commodity as an investment. This could be done by purchasing F, selling S out of stocks (thereby saving K in storage costs, which for expository purposes we can assume are invested in the riskless asset) and using the proceeds to invest in the riskless asset. At maturity we would use the proceeds from the investment in the riskless asset to take delivery. The profit with respect to their original position would be $(S_t + K) e^{r\tau} - F_{t,T}$.

2.4.3 Non-proportional Convenience Yield

Suppose that the present value of the convenience yields is equal to K. The no-arbitrage relationship between F and S must be

$$F_{t,T} = (S_t - K) e^{r\tau} \tag{2.7}$$

If this were not true and $F_{t,T} > (S_t - K) e^{r\tau}$, it would be possible to make an arbitrage profit by selling F, borrowing S at the riskless rate, and using the proceeds to purchase the underlying at the cost of S. The convenience yields received over the life of the contract are invested in the riskless asset. At maturity we would take delivery and use F plus the proceeds from the income invested in the riskless asset to pay off the loan. The profit would be $F_{t,T} - (S_t - K) e^{r\tau}$. If $F_{t,T} < (S_t - K) e^{r\tau}$, the arbitrager can purchase F, sell S short, and use the proceeds to invest in the riskless asset for maturities corresponding to the intermediate convenience yield payouts. At maturity we would use the proceeds from the investment in the riskless asset to take delivery. The profit would be $(S_t - K) e^{r\tau} - F_{t,T}$.

2.4.4 Commodities with a Proportional Convenience Yield

Consider a commodity that pays a known, constant convenience yield equal to c expressed as a percentage of the commodity price. The relationship between F and S is

$$F_{t,T} = S_t e^{(r-c)\tau} \tag{2.8}$$

To see this, set up a portfolio by selling a futures contract (cash flow $= 0$), borrowing $F e^{-r\tau}$ (cash flow $= +Fe^{-r\tau}$) and buying $S e^{-c\tau}$ of the commodity (cash flow $= -Se^{-c\tau}$). If the convenience yields are reinvested in the commodity, at maturity we will have $+S_T$ from the commodity purchase, $-F$ from paying off the loan, and $+F - S_T$ from the futures contract. This is equal to zero. The value of a portfolio with a certain zero outcome is equal to zero. Thus, $F_{t,T} e^{-r\tau} - S_t e^{-c\tau} = 0$. Rearranging gives equation (2.8).

2.4.5 Commodities with Proportional Storage Costs and a Proportional Convenience Yield

If the futures contract refers to a commodity with proportional storage costs and a proportional convenience yield, equation (2.8) becomes

$$F_{t,T} = S_t \, e^{(r+k-c)\tau} \tag{2.9}$$

where k represents storage costs as a proportion of the price of the commodity.

2.5 HEDGING STRATEGIES

The futures markets are easy to use. To cover a short position in a commodity, a futures contract can be bought. To cover a long position in the commodity, a futures contract can be sold. Because the contracts are standardised and guaranteed by the clearing house, they are liquid and represent no counterparty risk. Hence, futures are generally cheaper than forwards and positions can be closed out or rolled over more easily and cheaply than they can with forwards. A short position in futures can be closed out by a purchase of the same contract. It can be rolled over by a simultaneous purchase of the same contract and the sale of a similar contract with a later maturity date. A long position in futures can be closed out by a sale of the same contract. It can be rolled over by a simultaneous sale of the same contract and purchase of a similar contract with a later maturity date.

The facility of opening and closing out positions makes it possible to manage relatively small levels of exposure on a continuous basis. Furthermore, arbitrage ensures that pricing advantages between futures and forward markets should also be negligible. It is true, though, that because of marking to market, forward and futures prices can theoretically differ, with the difference between the futures price minus the forward price depending on the correlation of the riskless interest rate with the futures price.[9] If the futures price falls when the riskless interest rate rises and vice versa, the correlation is negative and the futures price will be below the forward price. If the futures price rises when the riskless interest rate rises and vice versa, the correlation is positive and the futures price will be higher than the forward price. The reason is straightforward. Marking to market generates interim cash flows. A negative correlation between the futures price and the riskless rate means that for the buyer of a futures contract, on the average, financing costs of interim outflows when interest rates rise and futures prices fall will be higher than interest gains on interim inflows when interest rates fall and futures prices rise. For example, financing a $1,000 loss on a futures contract when the interest rate goes from 8% to 10% costs the annual equivalent of $100. A $1,000 gain

---

[9] See Cox *et al.* (1981).

on a futures contract when the interest rate goes from 8% to 6% only brings in an annual equivalent of $60. The expected return on the interim cash flows is negative. Consequently, to compensate for the expected losses on the interim cash flows, the buyer's price is lower than it would be for a forward contract that has no interim cash flows. For the seller of the futures contract, losses and gains are reversed and the seller is willing to accept a lower price than for a forward contract. If the correlation between the futures price and the riskless interest rate is positive, financing costs and gains are reversed and marking to market is an advantage for the buyer and a disadvantage to the seller, thereby causing the price of the futures contract to rise above that of the forward contract. In the case where the correlation is zero, futures and forward prices are the same. All this having been said, differences seem to be negligible. Comparisons of futures and forward prices in the foreign exchange market, for example, have consistently revealed the absence of a significant difference between the two.[10] Consequently, for all practical purposes, the prices of futures contracts can be determined as if they were forward contracts.

Although futures contracts exhibit definite advantages with respect to forwards in transaction costs and ease of use because of standardisation and liquidity, they also have some definite disadvantages:

1. Futures contracts are only available for short maturities. The maximum maturity is one year and markets are usually thin for maturities exceeding six months. Hence, for long-term hedging the futures markets are not a viable alternative to the forward and swap markets.
2. The fixed contract size makes it difficult to make an exact match with the position to be hedged. As mentioned, however, the size of the contracts is sufficiently small that most users' needs can be approximated quite well.
3. The infrequent maturity dates make it unlikely that the futures contract will correspond perfectly with the maturity of the cash flow to be hedged. In this case, hedging with futures requires setting up what is called a *delta hedge*.
4. There are many commodities for which no corresponding futures market exists. In this case, hedging with futures requires setting up what is called a *cross hedge*.

2.5.1 The Delta Hedge

Because the infrequent maturity dates on futures contracts make it unlikely that the maturity of the futures contract will correspond perfectly with the maturity of the cash flow to be hedged, basis risk must be taken into consideration when setting up a hedging strategy. To see how this can be done, consider the situation of a grain producer holding C bushels of corn that will be sold at time 1. His

---

[10] See, for example, Cornell and Reinganum (1981); Park and Chen (1985); Chang and Chang (1990).

hedge involves selling N futures contracts of size Q bushels that mature at time 2. Ignoring the interest rate risk associated with marking to market, at time 1 when the C bushels of corn are sold, the agent will receive the dollar value of C bushels of corn times the spot price less N times the difference between the futures price at time 1 and the futures price contracted at time 0 multiplied by Q bushels, the size of the contract. The problem is to determine the optimum number of futures contracts to be sold. To answer this question let S_1 be the spot (cash) price at time 1 (the number of dollars per bushel), $F_{0,2}$ the futures price of 1 bushel at time 0 for delivery at time 2, and $F_{1,2}$ the futures price of 1 bushel at time 1 for delivery at time 2. Selling the corn at the time 1 spot price gives $S_1 \times C$ dollars. The difference between the futures prices gives $-N(F_{1,2} - F_{0,2}) \times Q$ dollars. Thus the dollar value of the portfolio will be

$$S_1 C - N(F_{1,2} - F_{0,2})Q \tag{2.10}$$

Divide by C and define the hedge ratio as $\beta = NQ/C$ and equation (2.10) can be written as

$$S_1 - \beta(F_{1,2} - F_{0,2}) \tag{2.11}$$

The idea is to choose β so that the variance of equation (2.11) is minimized. Let *Var* represent variance and *Cov* represent covariance. Since $F_{0,2}$ is known, the variance of equation (2.11) is

$$Var(S_1) - 2\beta \, Cov(S_1, F_{1,2}) + \beta^2 \, Var(F_{1,2}) \tag{2.12}$$

Taking the derivative of (2.12) with respect to β and setting it equal to zero gives

$$-2 \, Cov(S_1, F_{1,2}) + 2\beta \, Var(F_{1,2}) = 0$$

which implies that[11]

$$\beta = \frac{Cov(S_1, F_{1,2})}{Var(F_{1,2})} \tag{2.13}$$

Thus, the optimal number of contracts is equal to

$$N = \beta \frac{C}{Q} \tag{2.14}$$

The delta hedge: an example Starting with the following information: $C =$ 100,000 bushels to be sold in one month, $Q = 5,000$ bushels, maturity date of the futures contract is two months, we want to find N, the optimal number of

---

[11] Since futures prices are the markets' estimate of cash prices expected to be prevailing at the time of contract maturity, one might expect the cash/futures price correlation to increase as the amount of time between futures maturity and cash market delivery is decreased. However, based on Samuelson's law (see footnote 4), this intuition is probably false.

futures contracts to be sold. The first step is to estimate β. Going back to equation (2.13), we can see that β is equal to the slope coefficient in the equation

$$S_1 = \alpha + \beta F_{1,2} + \varepsilon \tag{2.15}$$

In theory, equation (2.15) should be estimated as a forecast. In practice, because the data necessary for making a reliable forecast is generally unavailable, equation (2.15) is usually estimated in a time series regression using historical data. Using monthly historical data over a five-year period we find $\beta = 0.95$. Hence, the number of contracts to be sold is

$$N = 0.95 \frac{100,000}{5,000} = 19$$

2.5.2   The Cross Hedge

There are many commodities for which no corresponding futures market exists, for example, lettuce, peanuts, tomatoes, sunflowers, and wine. These non-futures commodities can be hedged in a related market where prices are highly correlated with the non-futures' cash commodity price. The problem is similar to that of a maturity mismatch except here the disparity arises because the spot (cash) price of the hedged currency and the futures price of the proxy commodity are likely to differ at maturity. The problem is to minimise the difference between the two. The first and most obvious step is to choose a proxy commodity with a close relationship to the commodity to be hedged. The second step is to adjust the hedge for likely divergencies.

To see how this can be done, consider the situation of a refinery with a capacity of C gallons of kerosene per month. There is no futures market for the kerosene, but there is a close relationship between the price of kerosene and the price of heating oil, which is traded on the NYMEX. In the absence of a futures contract on kerosene, the refiner decides to use the heating oil futures contract to hedge against a fall in the cash price of his kerosene output. His hedge involves selling N futures contracts of size Q gallons that mature at time 1, the same time as the projected sale of the month's kerosene output. Ignoring the interest rate risk associated with marking to market, at time 1 when the C gallons are sold, the agent will receive C times the cash price for his kerosene less N times the difference between the futures price of 1 gallon of heating oil on a contract maturing at time 1 and the futures price contracted at time 0 multiplied by Q gallons, the size of the contract. The problem is to determine the optimum number of heating oil futures contracts to be sold. To answer this question let $S_1(x)$ be the cash (spot) price of kerosene or heating oil at time 1, $F_{0,1}$ the futures price of heating oil at time 0 for delivery at time 1, and $F_{1,1}$ the futures price of heating oil at time 1 for delivery at time 1.

Selling the C gallons of kerosene on the cash (spot) market gives $S_1 \times C$ dollars. The difference between the futures prices gives

$$-N[F_{1,1} - F_{0,1}] \times Q \text{ dollars} \tag{2.16}$$

At maturity, the futures price converges to the spot price so that equation (2.16) becomes

$$-N[S_1(\text{heating oil}) - F_{0,1}] \times Q \text{ dollars} \tag{2.17}$$

Thus, the value of the portfolio will be

$$S_1(\text{kerosene})C - N[S_1(\text{heating oil}) - F_{0,1}]Q \tag{2.18}$$

Divide by C and define the hedge ratio as $\beta = NQ/C$ and equation (2.13) can be written as

$$S_1(\text{kerosene}) - \beta[S_1(\text{heating oil}) - F_{0,1}] \tag{2.19}$$

As with the delta hedge, the idea is to choose β so that the variance of equation (2.19) is minimised. Since $F_{0,1}$ is known, the variance of equation (2.19) is

$$Var(S_1(\text{kerosene})) - 2\beta \, Cov(S_1(\text{kerosene}), S_1(\text{heating oil}))$$

$$+ \beta^2 \, Var(S_1(\text{heating oil}))$$

Taking the derivative with respect to β and setting it equal to zero gives

$$\beta = \frac{Cov[S_1(\text{kerosene}), S_1(\text{heating oil})]}{Var(S_1(\text{heating oil}))} \tag{2.20}$$

Thus, the optimal number of contracts is equal to

$$N = \beta \frac{C}{Q} \tag{2.21}$$

The cross hedge: an example   Starting with the following information: $C = 4{,}200{,}000$ gallons of kerosene to be sold in one month. $Q = 42{,}000$ gallons, we want to find N, the optimal number of futures contracts to be sold. The first step is to estimate β. Going back to equation (2.20), we can see that β is equal to the slope coefficient in the equation

$$S_1(\text{kerosene}) = \alpha + \beta S_1(\text{heating oil}) + \varepsilon \tag{2.22}$$

Suppose that a time series regression using monthly historical data over a five-year period yields $\beta = 0.875$. The number of contracts to be sold is

$$N = 0.875 \frac{4{,}200{,}000}{42{,}000} = 87.5$$

Rounded to the closest full contract $N = 88$.

2.5.3   The Delta Cross Hedge

Having solved the problems of the maturity and currency mismatches, it is easy
to solve the problem when both mismatches occur simultaneously. To see how
this can be done, consider a sweet corn producer that wants to hedge against a
fall in price one month forward. Since there is no sweetcorn futures market, the
producer decides to use the feedcorn futures contract on the CBOT, the nearest of
which matures two months forward. Thus, his hedge involves selling N futures
contracts of size Q that mature at time 2, the closest maturity date to the projected
sale. This information can be resumed as follows:

S_1 (sweet) = the cash (spot) price of sweet corn at time 1
   $F_{0,2}$ = the futures price of one bushel of feed corn at time 0 for
           delivery at time 2
   $F_{1,2}$ = the futures price of one bushel of feed corn at time 1 for
           delivery at time 2

Proceeding as in the previous examples, we seek to determine the optimum
number of feedcorn futures contracts to be sold. The value of the cash flow at
time 1 is equal to

$$S_1(\text{sweet}) - \beta[F_{1,2} - F_{0,2}] \tag{2.23}$$

and the minimum variance hedge ratio is found by estimating the equation

$$S_1(\text{sweet}) = \alpha + \beta F_{1,2} + \varepsilon \tag{2.24}$$

Using $C = 100,000$ bushels to be sold in one month, $Q = 5,000$, and estimating

$$\beta = \frac{Cov[S_1(\text{sweet}), F_{1,2}]}{Var(F_{1,2})} = 0.85$$

the optimal number of contracts is equal to

$$N = 0.85\frac{100,000}{5,000} = 17 \text{ contracts}$$

2.6   INVENTORY MANAGEMENT[12]

Futures transactions can and should play an integral role in managing supplies
of raw materials and inventory levels. Two examples will be used to illustrate
the techniques and issues involved.

---

[12] In this section we follow Clark *et al.* (1993).

2.6.1 Managing Inventories of Raw Materials: The Case of an Expected Price Rise

Consider the case of a manufacturer at the beginning of September who is expecting a large jump in the price of copper for the end of the year. The current price of copper is $1.025 per pound. He feels that this relatively low price is due to a momentary excess supply that will disappear in short order. He realises that if he is wrong, however, the price is likely to drop lower than it is now. A December futures contract is selling at $1.0825 per pound and it is a contango market with a positive basis of 5.75 cents per pound.

The manufacturer could buy a December futures contract to protect himself against the expected price rise, but if he does and the price falls, he will be a big loser. In order to take advantage of his analysis of the current and expected market situation, the manufacturer decides to increase his inventory at the current spot price of $1.025 beyond what his normal needs would be. But, just in case he is wrong and the price falls rather than rising, he decides to hedge the excess stock he is going to carry by selling a December futures contract at $1.0825 per pound.

At the end of December the price of copper has risen to $1.22 per pound and his futures contract is settled at this price. Thus, the manufacturer has lost 13.75 cents per pound ($1.0825 − $1.22) on his futures contract. However, the cost of his excess stock is only $1.1625, the $1.025 spot price he paid plus the 13.75 cent loss on the futures contract. This is 5.75 cents lower than the spot price of $1.22. On the other hand, it is 8 cents higher than he would have paid if he had made a straightforward purchase of a futures contract at $1.0825 per pound. The disadvantage of the straightforward futures purchase is that if the spot price had fallen — to $1.00, for example — he would still have paid $1.0825 for his copper supply. With the solution that he actually chose, a fall in the spot price to $1.00 would give him a gain of 8.25 cents on the futures and his net cost would be $0.9425 per pound, 5.75 cents lower than the spot price of $1.00. Thus, by adjusting his inventory and using the futures market, he was able to secure his supply of raw materials at a price more favourable than the going market price. Of course, he would have to compare his 5.75 cent gain with his carrying costs and convenience returns to determine his net benefit on the operation.

2.6.2 Inventory Management: The Case of an Expected Price Decline

Suppose that at the beginning of March the spot price of copper is $1.1725 per pound. The market is expecting the price to fall and the June futures contract is selling for $0.9925 per pound. The market is in a situation of backwardation and the basis is negative by 18 cents.

The manufacturer decides to avoid paying the high spot price by running down his inventory. Nevertheless, he wants to cover himself in case prices do not fall and proceeds to buy a June contract at $0.9925 per pound. By the end of April the bottom has fallen out of the market and the spot quote is $0.885 while the June futures contract is selling at $0.95. It is now a contango market and the basis is positive by 6.5 cents.

Having run down his inventory, the manufacturer must now make a purchase at $0.885 per pound. He closes out his futures position and loses 4.25 cents per pound ($0.95 − $0.9925). His total cost is $0.9275 per pound ($0.885 + $0.0425). This is 24.5 cents better than the $1.1725 he would have paid in March. Of course, he would have to compare this gain with his convenience losses due to lower inventory levels and the savings on foregone carrying costs to determine his net benefit on the operation.

In any case, this example as well as the preceding one give an idea of how futures markets can be combined with the timing of inventory supplies to contribute to more cost-efficient inventory management.

2.7   SPECULATION AND SPREADING

The economic rationale for the existence of futures markets is based on the principle of hedging, which makes it possible for producers of goods and services to operate more efficiently by reducing uncertainty and risk. In order for futures markets to function effectively, however, arbitragers and speculators are indispensable. Arbitragers are necessary to maintain the links between the underlying cash market and the different maturities of the futures market. Speculators are also necessary because it is they who ultimately assume the risk laid off by the hedgers.

2.7.1   Speculation and Portfolio Management

The prospect of extraordinarily high returns will undoubtedly attract a large number of speculators. Participation in the futures market does not require access to large sums of money or quantities of raw materials. The only requirement is sufficient funds to put up the initial margin and enough back-up funds to make good on any margin calls that might be forthcoming. The initial margin represents only a small percentage of the total value of a contract, in practice between 5% and 10%. For a contract worth $20,000, an agent might only have to put up $1,000. If the agent's position gains 5% — not a rare event — he makes $1,000, a yield of 100%. Futures contracts, then, are highly levered. The leverage can be measured by taking the reciprocal of the initial margin, which in this case is $1/0.05 = 20$.

It should not be forgotten that the leverage effect works both ways. If, for example, the futures price had moved against the speculator by 5%, his yield would have been a negative 100% (-100%). Thus, speculation is very risky. A typical speculation on a price rise involves an uncovered purchase of a futures contract while speculation on a fall involves an uncovered sale.

It is easy to see that individual speculative transactions are too risky to be of interest to most investors. However, in the context of a portfolio, a speculative position in futures might offer some opportunity for diversification benefits. This, of course, depends on the correlation of the returns of the futures position with the returns of the other assets in the portfolio (see Chapter 8). In practice, the financial futures markets are becoming popular with professional portfolio managers and there has been considerable growth in commodities futures funds.[13]

2.7.2 Professional Speculation

A private speculator can often hold a position for several days or even several weeks. Professional speculators, on the other hand, are position traders and more often than not day traders. They hold an open position for no longer than one trading session, closing out all open positions before the end of the session. Furthermore, they are usually members of the exchange and execute their transactions themselves.

The *scalper* is a particular type of speculator that trades directly for his own account in the pit. His technique is to take advantage of small price variations during one trading session. His profit on each transaction is very small but so are his losses. His overall profit comes from the large volume of trades that he makes. He is important for market liquidity in so far as he stands ready to buy at the ask price and sell at the bid price.

2.7.3 Spreading

The idea behind spreading is simple. It is a variation of the old 'buy cheap, sell dear' adage where a futures contract that seems abnormally cheap is purchased while another contract on the same underlying commodity that seems abnormally expensive is simultaneously sold. If the expected price corrections are realised, a tidy little profit can be made with limited risk.

---

[13] A recent study finds that publicly offered commodity funds, of which there were over 130 in 1988, do not offer high enough returns to make them attractive investments. Not only does the time pattern of their returns show an extremely high variance but the probability of a fund dissolving within five years is just under 25%, while the probability of its dissolving within 10 years is almost 50%. Furthermore, the expected returns on the commodity funds and the correlation between commodity funds returns and returns on other assets does not justify the inclusion of commodity funds in a portfolio of stocks and bonds. See Elton *et al.* (1990).

There are four basic types of spreads:

1. *Interdelivery spreads*   The purchase of a futures with one maturity and the simultaneous sale of another contract on the same commodity with a different maturity. For example, the purchase of a December contract and the sale of a March contract on crude oil.
2. *Intermarket spreads*   The simultaneous purchase and sale of the same contract with the same maturity but on different exchanges. For example, purchase an April contract on potatoes in Lille and sell an April contract on potatoes in Amsterdam. In this operation there is an exchange risk.
3. *Intercommodity spreads*   The simultaneous purchase and sale of contracts with the same maturity on different commodities, but where the two commodities are related. For example, buy a December contract on primary aluminum in London and sell a December contract on secondary aluminum.
4. *Commodity-product spreads*   The simultaneous purchase of a contract on one commodity and the sale of a contract with the same maturity on another commodity that is produced from the first commodity. For example, the purchase of a March contract on soya beans and the sale of a March contract on soya bean oil.

BIBLIOGRAPHY

C. W. Chang and J. S. K. Chang (1990) Forward and futures prices: evidence from the foreign exchange markets, *Journal of Finance*, **45**, 1333–1336.
E. Clark, M. Levasseur and P. Rousseau (1993) *International Finance*. Chapman & Hall, London.
B. Cornell and M. Reinganum (1981) Forward and futures prices: evidence from the foreign exchange markets, *Journal of Finance*, **36**, 1035–1045.
J. Cox, J. Ingersoll, Jr and S. Ross (1981) The relation between forward prices and futures prices, *Journal of Financial Economics*, **9**, 321–346.
E. J. Elton, M. J. Gruber and J. Rentzler (1990) The performance of publicly offered commodity funds, *Financial Analysts Journal*, July–August, 23–30.
E. J. Elton and M. J. Gruber (1995) *Modern Portfolio Theory and Investment Analysis*, 5th edn. Wiley, New York.
F. Hayek (1941) *The Pure Theory of Capital*. (Routledge and Kegan Paul, London; F. Hayek, *Monetary Theory and the Trade Cycle*, trans. N. Kaldor and H. M. Croome London: Jonathan Cape, 1933.).
F. Hayek (1975) *Prix et Production*, trans. Tradecom. Calmann-Levy, Vienna.
J. Hicks (1950) *A Contribution to the Theory of the Trade Cycle*. Clarendon Press, Oxford.
J. Hicks (1987) *Capital and Time: A Neo-Austrian Theory*. Clarendon Press, Oxford.
S. Hoss and H. Working (1938) Wheat futures prices and trading at Liverpool since 1886, *Wheat Studies of the Food Research Institute*, November.
J. C. Hull (2000) *Options, Futures and Other Derivatives*. Prentice-Hall International, London.
J. M. Keynes (1930) *A Treatise on Money*. Macmillan, London, tome 2, pp. 142–144.

N. Milonas (1986) Price variability and the maturity effect in futures markets, *Journal of Futures Markets* Spring. This means that the volatility of the basis for a particular contract may tend to increase as the contract approaches maturity.

H. Y. Park and A. H. Chen (1985) Difference between futures and forward prices: a further investigation of marking to market effects, *Journal of Futures Markets*, **5**, 77–88.

D. Rutledge (1985) A note on the variability of futures prices, *Review of Economics and Statistics*, **58**, 118–120; R. Anderson, Some determinants of the volatility of futures prices, *Journal of Futures Markets*, Fall, 331–348.

P. A. Samuelson (1965) Proof that properly anticipated prices fluctuate randomly, *Industrial Management Review*, **6**, 41–49.

P. Wilmott (1998) *Derivatives*. Wiley, New York.

H. Working (1934) Price of cash wheat and futures at Chicago since 1883, *Wheat Studies of the Food Research Institute*, November.

APPENDIX 2A

Other relationships between futures and spot prices

The notation is as follows:

T = delivery date of the futures contract (years)
t = current date (years)
τ = T-t
$F_{t,T}$ = Price of a futures contract at time t for delivery at time T
S_t = spot (cash) price at time t
K = present value of storage costs or other known intermediate payouts
r = riskless rate of interest
k = proportional cost of storage
c = convenience yield
δ = dividend yield
r_D = the riskless rate on domestic currency
r_F = the riskless rate on foreign currency.

2A.1 Intermediate Cash Payments

Consider a security such as a coupon paying bond or a stock with a known dividend. Suppose that the present value of these payments is equal to K. The no-arbitrage relationship between F and S must be

$$F_{t,T} = (S_t - K)\,e^{r\tau} \qquad (A2.1)$$

If this were not true and $F_{t,T} > (S_t - K)\,e^{r\tau}$, it would be possible to make an arbitrage profit by selling F, borrowing S at the riskless rate, and using the proceeds to purchase the underlying at the cost of S. The income that is received from the security over the life of the contract is invested in the riskless asset. At maturity we would take delivery and use F plus the proceeds from the income invested in the riskless asset to pay off the loan. The profit would be $F_{t,T} - (S_t - K)\,e^{r\tau}$. If $F_{t,T} < (S_t - K)\,e^{r\tau}$, the arbitrager can purchase F, sell S short, and use the proceeds to invest in the riskless asset for maturities corresponding to the intermediate cash payouts. At maturity we would use the proceeds from the investment in the riskless asset to take delivery. The profit would be $(S_t - K)\,e^{r\tau} - F_{t,T}$.

2A.2   Known Dividend Yields

Consider a security such as a currency or a stock that pays a known, constant yield equal to δ expressed as a percentage of the security price. The relationship between F and S is

$$F_{t,T} = S_t \, e^{(r-\delta)\tau} \qquad (A2.2)$$

To prove this, set up a portfolio by selling a futures contract (cash flow $= 0$), borrowing $F_{t,T} \, e^{-r\tau}$ (cash flow $= +F_{t,T} \, e^{-r\tau}$), and buying $S_t \, e^{-\delta\tau}$ (cash flow $= -S_t \, e^{-\delta\tau}$).

If dividends are reinvested in the stock, at maturity we will have $+S_T$ from the stock purchase, $-F_{t,T}$ from paying off the loan, and $+F_{t,T} - S_T$ from the futures contract. This is equal to zero. The value of a portfolio with a certain zero outcome is equal to zero. Thus, $F \, e^{-r\tau} - S \, e^{-\delta\tau} = 0$. Rearranging gives equation (A2.2).

2A.3   Currency Futures

If the security in question is a foreign currency, using the same arguments, equation (A2.2) becomes:

$$F_{t,T} = S_t \, e^{(r_D - r_F)\tau} \qquad (A2.3)$$

where r_D is the riskless rate on domestic currency and r_F is the riskless rate on foreign currency.

3
Options

The forward and futures markets make it possible to set up a fixed hedge. A fixed hedge enables the investor to avoid a loss when the spot price moves against him, but it also eliminates the possibility of making a gain if it moves in his favour. A fixed hedge strategy is appropriate when the investor assigns a strong probability to a move against him and a weak probability for a move in his favour. A fixed hedge is less appropriate, however, in the case where the investor feels that there is an equally strong chance for favourable and unfavourable moves. This is because the advantage of avoiding the loss is offset by the disadvantage of missing out on the gain. The fixed hedge is still useful, but its usefulness is considerably diminished. Another type of coverage in the form of an option might therefore be preferable. Options make it possible to take advantage of potential gains while limiting downside risk. Proper use of options requires a clear understanding of what an option is and the elements that determine its price. This is the object of this chapter.

3.1 OPTIONS: CHARACTERISTICS AND MARKETS

3.1.1 An Introduction to Options

An option is a contract that gives its owner the right for a given period of time to buy or sell a given amount of an underlying asset at a fixed price, called the *exercise price* or the *strike price*. The underlying asset can be a financial security such as a stock or a bond, a financial commodity such as an interest rate or a currency, or a physical commodity such as oil, gas, coffee, and potatoes. If the right can be exercised at any time during the life of the option it is called an *American option*. If the right can be exercised only at the option's expiration date, it is called a *European option*. The right to buy is called a *call*. The right to sell is called a *put*. The buyer of the option pays the seller, or the *writer*, a certain sum, called the *premium*, for the right to buy or sell at the prescribed price. The characteristic elements of an option contract can be summed up as follows:

- the nature of the transaction: call or put
- the underlying asset
- the amount of the underlying asset
- the strike or exercise price
- the expiration date
- the premium.

Consider a European call option on 100 shares of ATT with a maturity of 15 March and a strike price of $55. It gives the buyer the right to buy 100 shares of ATT at the rate of $55 per share on 15 March. The underlying asset is the share of ATT, the amount is 100 shares, the strike price is $55, and the expiration date is 15 March. If the premium is $1.50, this means that the buyer has to pay the writer 100 shares × $1.50 = $150 at the outset.

A European put option on GBP 500,000, a strike price of 1.60, and a maturity of six months gives the buyer the right to sell GBP 500,000 at the rate of US$1.60 per pound in six months. If the premium is 2.58%, the buyer has to pay the writer GBP 12,900 (£500,000 × 2.58%) at the outset. The premium can also be expressed in dollars by using the spot exchange rate. If, for example, the spot bid rate is 1.65, the premium will be US$21,285 (£12,900 × 1.65).

Option contracts are listed according to the underlying asset, the expiration date, and the strike price. The two *types* of options are calls and puts. All options of the same type in the same underlying asset constitute an option *class*. All options in the same class with the same expiration date and the same strike price constitute an option *series*.

3.1.2 Over-the-counter Markets

In the over-the-counter (OTC) market, options are written by financial institutions. This market is similar to the forward market described in Chapters 1 and 2. Like forward contracts, OTC options can be made to order with the expiration date, contract size, and strike price determined at the buyer's discretion. OTC options, however, can be more liquid than forward contracts since the institutions that write these contracts often quote regular bid–ask prices and stand ready to buy them back at any moment. This is the case in the foreign currency market, for example, but the increased liquidity has a cost in that the bid–ask spreads are relatively high.

In the absence of buyer preference, it is customary in the OTC market to write options with the strike price equal to the spot price of the moment and to quote the premium to clients as a percentage of the underlying value. The norm for quoting strike prices is two decimal places. Among themselves, traders do not usually quote a price. Instead they quote volatility from which the price can be inferred. Later in this chapter we will see why this is so.

3.1.3   Organized Options Markets

Organised options markets have many features of the futures markets described in the preceding chapter. First of all, contracts are standardised. On the Philadelphia Stock Exchange, for example, all currency options are American style and expire on the third Wednesday of March, June, September, or December. Early exercise is possible until the last Saturday of the option's life. Each currency has a standard contract size: e.g. JPY 6,250,000, with strike prices conforming to prearranged formulas depending on the currency: e.g. multiples of 5 US cents for the GBP. Premiums are quoted in US cents per unit of foreign currency.

Organised options exchanges also utilize a *clearing house* that records the transactions concluded by each one of its members. Each member also has the obligation to keep records of its clients' accounts. Just as in the futures markets, the role of the clearing house is essential. It guarantees the execution of all contracts negotiated on the exchange and effectively becomes the counterparty to both sides of the transaction. The role of the clearing house and contract standardisation facilitate trading and make the market more liquid as the exchanges continually write new options as well as closing out ongoing positions. An investor who has written an option can close out his position by buying an equivalent option, while an investor who has bought an option can close out his position by selling an equivalent option. Since the contracts are standardised and the clearing house is the counterparty to both sides of the contract, all options in the same series are equivalent no matter who are the end buyers and sellers.

The scope for commodity options extends into the futures markets. In this case, the buyer of a call has the right to buy a given futures contract on the exchange at a price equal to the option's strike price. The buyer of the put has the right to sell a given futures contract at a price equal to the option's strike price. If a call futures option is exercised, the buyer acquires a long position in the underlying futures contract plus a cash amount equal to the difference between the most recent futures settlement price and the strike price. If a put futures option is exercised, the buyer acquires a short position in the underlying futures contract plus a cash amount equal to the difference between the strike price and the most recent futures settlement price. Options on futures contracts are more attractive to investors than options on the underlying asset when it is cheaper or more convenient to deliver a futures contract on the underlying asset than the underlying asset itself. This is true of many physical commodities and, in fact, most options on physical commodities are options on futures contracts. For example, it is cheaper, easier, and more convenient to make or take delivery of a hogs futures contract than it is to make or take delivery of the hogs themselves.

Table 3.1 Information on soya bean meal futures options

Soya bean meal (CBT)— 100 tons; $ per ton

	Calls— settle			Puts— settle		
Strike price	Sept	Oct	Dec	Sept	Oct	Dec
130	—	—	—	—	—	1.45
135	—	—	—	1.00	2.75	2.25
140	3.25	4.30	7.00	2.50	4.75	4.45
145	1.75	2.80	4.75	6.00	8.15	7.20
150	0.85	1.60	3.25	10.00	11.60	10.50
155	0.65	1.30	2.25	14.75	16.30	14.45

Est. vol. 2,000 Mon 1,479 calls 2,672 puts.
Open int Mon 43,757 calls 30,794 puts.

Thus, exercise of a futures option does not normally lead to delivery of the underlying asset because, as we mentioned in Chapter 2, most futures contracts are closed out before delivery.

Information on traded options is published daily in the financial press. Table 3.1 is an example of the information on futures options on soya bean meal on 4 August 1998.

The first line of Table 3.1 tells us that the options are on a futures contract of 100 tons of soya bean meal. Line 2 shows that the table is divided into information on calls and puts. Column 1 gives the strike price. Columns 2–4 give the prices for calls expiring in September, October, and December and columns 5–7 give the prices for puts expiring in September, October, and December. For example, the last traded price of a put with a strike price of US$145 expiring in December was US$7.20. The last two lines give the trading volume and the number of options outstanding.

3.2 VALUING OPTIONS

Option pricing theory is one of the most important contributions to the theory and practice of finance over the last 50 years. Much of the credit goes to F. Black, M. Scholes, and R. Merton for the development of a workable option pricing formula for European calls and puts on non-dividend paying stocks.[1] Since then option pricing has been extended to a myriad of instruments including, among many others, dividend paying stocks, indexes, interest rates, currencies, commodities, and futures. It has even been extended into the realm of what are called 'real options' as a tool for strategic management and capital budgeting.[2] In this chapter

[1] For the original option pricing formula, see: F. Black and M. Scholes, The pricing of options and corporate liabilities, *Journal of Political Economy* (June, 1973) 637–659.
[2] See, for example, Dixit and Pindyck (1994) and Trigeorgis (1996).

we will develop the option pricing methodology in a general framework that includes intermediate pay-outs such as dividends on stocks, interest on currencies, and convenience yields on commodities. This will enable us to understand the OTC products that are discussed in the next chapter. Once the general framework has been presented, we go on to develop the pricing model for futures options.

3.2.1   The Elements of Option Value

The value of an option depends, first of all, on the value of the underlying asset and its volatility. Secondly, it depends on the specific characteristics of the contract itself concerning the strike price and the expiration date. Finally, it depends on the level of the risk-free interest rate.

The premium and the spot price: European options   The premium on a call option is higher when the price of the underlying asset is higher. This is easy to understand. If the spot price of a stock is $12, an investor will be willing to pay more for the right to purchase the stock at $10 than if the spot price were $8. On the other hand, the premium on a put will be higher when the spot price of the underlying asset is lower. An investor will be willing to pay more for the right to sell a stock for $10 if the spot price is $8 than if it is $12.

No matter what the value of the underlying asset is, the premium on a call or a put will always be positive, although sometimes it might be very small. This is because there is always at least a remote possibility that something will happen to make the option profitable. Even if the spot price is $15.00 and the strike price on a call with a week to expiration is $30, some exceptional event like a new discovery, a huge contract, a take-over bid, etc. could possibly take place before the option expires that would push the value of the stock above $30. If it does not take place, the option expires worthless, but still only costs the investor the premium that he paid for it. The right to a possible gain with no chance of a loss is clearly worth something.

When the spot price is very high compared to the strike price, the probability that the call option will be exercised is also very high. Since exercise uncertainty decreases with the rise in the spot price, the value of a European call will tend to approach the value of the spot price minus the strike price (multiplied by the nominal amount of the contract). In this situation the option starts to resemble a fixed forward contract where the strike price is the forward price. Similarly, when the spot price is very low compared to the strike price, the probability that a European put option will be exercised becomes very high. Its value approaches the difference between the strike price and the spot price. Again, because of the high probability of exercise, the option begins to resemble a fixed forward contract.

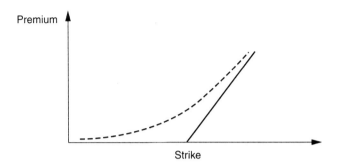

Figure 3.1   The relationship between the value of a European call and the spot price

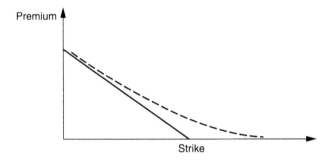

Figure 3.2   The relationship between the value of a European put and the spot price

Figures 3.1 and 3.2 summarise the relationship between the value of European calls and puts respectively and the spot price of the underlying security. The solid line in Figure 3.1 represents the difference between the spot price and the strike price. The broken line represents the value of the call. At very high levels of the spot price, the value of the call comes close to this line. At very low levels of the spot price, the value of the option approaches zero.

In Figure 3.2 the solid line represents the difference between the strike price and the spot price. At very low levels of the spot price, the value of the option comes very close to this line. At very high levels of the spot price, it approaches zero.

The premium and the strike price   The higher the strike price, the lower the value of a call and the higher the value of a put. On the other hand, the lower the strike price, the higher the value of a call and the lower the value of a put. The reason is straightforward. A call is the right to buy at a given price. The lower the strike price, the more chance there is that the market price of the underlying asset will surpass it for a profit. A put is the right to sell at a given price. The higher the strike price, the more chance there is that the market price of the underlying asset will fall below it for a profit. At a lower strike price, the results are reversed.

When the strike price is higher than the spot price, the value of a call is due entirely to the possibility that the spot price will rise above the strike price before the option expires. The call is then said to be *out-of-the-money* and its value is called *time value*. On the other hand, if the strike price is lower than the spot price, there is an immediate gain equal to the difference between the spot price and the strike price. The option is said to be *in-the-money*. Since the option buyer acquires the right to this gain, called the *intrinsic value*, he must pay for it. Besides the in-the-money value, though, the possibility that the rate could go higher before the option expires still exists. Hence, the value of an in-the-money option is equal to its intrinsic value plus its time value. When the spot rate and the strike price are equal, the option is said to be *at-the-money*.

The same expressions are used to qualify puts. If the strike price is higher than the spot rate, there is an immediate gain for the buyer in so far as the writer contracts to pay a higher price than the current market price. The put is in-the-money. Conversely, if the strike price is lower than the spot rate, the put has only time value and is said to be out-of-the-money. When the spot rate and the strike price are equal, the put is at-the-money.

The premium and volatility   The volatility of the underlying asset is an important factor in determining the time value of an option. The higher the volatility of the price of the underlying asset, the higher is the probability that a strong rise or fall will occur. As we have seen, this is exactly what the buyer of the option is hoping for. A sharp rise in the spot price will be extremely profitable for the owner of a call. On the other hand, if a sharp fall occurs, he loses nothing but the premium he paid for the option.

The outcome is similar for a put. In this case the put owner is hoping for a fall in the spot price. The larger the fall, the greater is his gain. On the other hand, if there is no fall or even a sharp rise, the option expires worthless and the owner only loses the premium he paid to buy it. The value of a put increases with the volatility of the spot price.

The premium and the expiration date   The expiration date plays an important role in determining the value of an option. When the time to expiration is longer, the chances for fluctuations in the spot price of the underlying asset are increased. In other words, volatility is increased. An option that expires in six months is worth more than an option that expires in three months.

It is interesting to note that an option's time value is not proportional to its time to expiration. In fact, as far back as 1900, Bachelier showed that it is the square root of the time to expiration that influences an option's time value. Exactly why this is so is the object of the next section.

3.3   BINOMIAL APPROACH TO OPTION PRICING

Option prices (premiums or values) reflect all the complex interrelationships among the foregoing variables as well as all the factors that could possibly affect the judgement of the participants in a free market. Using the analysis based on arbitrage opportunities, professional traders and arbitragers, who have very low transaction costs, have developed pricing rules that they use in their day-to-day operations. Theorists have summarised their experiences in a number of pricing models that are useful tools for effective risk management. The binomial model is the simplest and easiest to understand.

3.3.1   The One-period Model for European Style Options

The binomial option pricing model is a simple approach to option pricing that makes it possible to understand what is going on in the more complicated models of the Black–Scholes type. The binomial model assumes that, given the current value of the underlying asset, there are only two values for next period's price — an upward move or a downward move. Hedging is then combined with borrowing and lending to determine the option's value. The following numerical examples will show how the binomial model works for an underlying asset with a proportional payout such as a currency option or a commodity option with a proportional convenience yield.

We start with the following notation:

C_t = the value of the call on one unit of the underlying asset
        after t moves
u = an upward move equal to 1 plus a percentage gain
d = a downward move equal to 1 minus a percentage loss
δ = the proportional payout on the underlying asset
r_d = the risk-less interest rate in domestic currency
R_d = $1 + r_d$
X = exercise price
Δ = delta: the number of units of the underlying asset to be
        held per option shorted to create a riskless hedge.

For simplicity, we assume that u, d, δ, and the domestic interest rate are constant over time. In order to rule out risk-free arbitrage profits, we also have the constraint that

$$d < \frac{1 + r_d}{1 + \delta} < u$$

Valuing a one-period call   Now consider the following information:

S = 100
u = 1.10

$$d = 0.90$$
$$\delta = 0.05$$
$$r_d = 0.08$$
$$1 + \delta = 1.05$$
$$R_d = 1 + r_d = 1.08$$
$$X = 100$$

Figure 3.3a shows the stock price movements with probability q of an up move and probability $1 - q$ of a down move. Figure 3.3b shows the value of the option if the price of the underlying asset moves up or down. Notice that the probabilities q and $1 - q$ are absent from Figure 3.3b. This is because the procedure for option valuation eliminates the need to make assumptions about the probability distribution of the price of the underlying asset.

We want to determine the value of a call option with one period until expiration during which the asset price can either move up to uS or down to dS. The evaluation process includes four steps.

1. First, we build a portfolio by selling a call on one unit of the asset and simultaneously purchasing Δ units of the same asset. Table 3.2 shows the cash flows associated with this portfolio. When we sell the call, we receive C_0 and we pay ΔS when we purchase the asset. If the asset price moves up

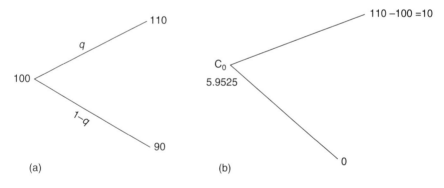

Figure 3.3 (a) Stock price in a one-step binomial tree; (b) Call price in a one-step binomial tree

Table 3.2 One-period cash flows

	Flows at period 0	Flows at period 1	
		$uS = 110$	$dS = 90$
Write a call	$+C_0$	$-C_u = -10$	0
Purchase Δ units of the asset	$-\Delta S$	$+\Delta uS(1 + \delta) =$ $\Delta 115.5$	$+\Delta dS(1 + \delta) =$ $\Delta 94.5$
Total	$+C_0 - \Delta S$	$\Delta 115.5 - 10$	$\Delta 94.5$

to uS, the call will be worth 10, the difference between the asset price and the exercise price. Since we sold the call, we have to pay this amount. We receive ΔuS, the value of our investment in the asset, plus $\delta \Delta uS$, the pay-out which is proportional to the asset price. This is equal to $\Delta 115.5$ for a net inflow of $\Delta 115.5 - 10$. If the asset price moves to dS, the call expires worthless and we receive $\Delta 94.5$, the value of the asset plus the proportional payout, from the investment in the asset.

2. The second step is to make the portfolio risk free. To do this, we choose Δ so that the outcome will be the same whether the price moves up or down. Setting the two possible outcomes in period 1 equal gives $\Delta 115.5 - 10 = \Delta 94.5$ and $\Delta = 0.4762$. Thus, if we purchase 47.62% of one unit of the underlying asset, the outcome of the portfolio will be the same whether the price moves up or down.

3. In step three, we expand the portfolio by borrowing an amount that will yield a net cash flow of zero in period 1. This amount is equal to the present value of the portfolio's cash flows in period 1: $\Delta 94.5/1.08$ (or $(\Delta 115.5 - 10)/1.08$ since they are equal). Table 3.3 shows the flows associated with this portfolio.

4. In step four, we find the value of the call by applying the well known fact that the value of an investment with zero net cash flows is equal to zero. Thus:

$$+C_0 - \Delta S + \frac{\Delta 94.5}{1.08} = 0$$

Substituting the values for S and Δ gives the price of the call: $C_0 = 5.9525$.

The one-period binomial formula   Using the same methodology as above we can derive a simple formula for one-period binomial option pricing. Table 3.4 shows the cash flows. To find the value of Δ that makes both outcomes independent of the move in the underlying security, set the two possible period 1 outcomes equal and solve. This gives:

Table 3.3   One-period cash flows with borrowing

	Flows at period 0	Flows at period 1	
		$uS = 110$	$dS = 90$
Write a call	$+C_0$	$-C_u = -10$	0
Purchase Δ units of asset	$-\Delta S$	$+\Delta uS(1 + \delta) = \Delta 115.5$	$+\Delta dS(1 + \delta) = \Delta 94.5$
Borrow	$+\dfrac{\Delta 94.5}{1.08}$	$-(\Delta 115.5 - 10)$	$-\Delta 94.5$
Total	$+C_0 - \Delta S + \dfrac{\Delta 94.5}{1.08}$	0	0

Table 3.4 Cash flows

	Flows at period 0	Flows at period 1	
		uS	dS
Write a call	$+C_0$	$-C_u$	$-C_d$
Purchase Δ units of the asset	$-\Delta S$	$+\Delta uS(1+\delta)$	$+\Delta dS(1+\delta)$
Borrow	$\dfrac{(-C_d + \Delta dS(1+\delta))}{R_d}$	$C_u - \Delta uS(1+\delta)$	$C_d - \Delta dS(1+\delta)$
Total	$\begin{array}{l} +C_0 - \Delta S \\ +\dfrac{-C_d + \Delta dS(1+\delta)}{R_d} \end{array}$	0	0

$$-C_u + \Delta uS(1+\delta) = -C_d + \Delta dS(1+\delta)$$

$$\Delta = \frac{C_u - C_d}{S(u-d)(1+\delta)} \tag{3.1}$$

We then borrow $-C_d + \Delta dS(1+\delta)/R_d$ so that the net outcomes in period 1 are zero. Since the investment generates zero net cash flows, its value is also zero. Thus

$$C_0 - \Delta S + \frac{-C_d + \Delta dS(1+\delta)}{R_d} = 0 \tag{3.2}$$

Substituting the value of Δ from equation (3.1) and rearranging gives:

$$C_0 = \frac{C_u\left[\dfrac{(R_d/(1+\delta)) - d}{u-d}\right] + C_d\left[1 - \dfrac{(R_d/(1+\delta)) - d}{u-d}\right]}{R_d} \tag{3.3}$$

This can be simplified even further by defining

$$P = \frac{(R_d/(1+\delta)) - d}{u - d}$$

Substituting this definition into equation (3.3), we have

$$C_0 = \frac{C_u P + C_d[1 - P]}{R_d} \tag{3.4}$$

Delta and risk neutral valuation   We defined delta as the number of units of the underlying asset to be held (shorted) per option shorted (held) to create a riskless hedge. The creation of the riskless hedge then made it possible to derive equation (3.4). It is important to notice that the original probabilities given in Figure 3.3a are absent from this equation. In fact, we were able to price the option without making any assumptions at all about the probabilities of up and down moves in the asset price. However, we can interpret P as the probability of an up move in a world without risk and $1 - P$ as the probability of a down move.[3] The absence of risk makes it possible to discount and compound the expected cash flows at the riskless rate.

This result is an example of what is called *risk-neutral valuation*. It means that we can correctly value an option by using the risk-neutral probabilities and pretending that investors are neutral to risk. This is an application of what is known as the *Girsanov theorem*. The new probabilities change the mean but leave the volatility structure intact. The answers obtained in this way are valid in all worlds, not only in the risk-neutral world.

In practice, the construction of a binomial tree involves defining the volatility of the price of the underlying security σ so that $\sigma\sqrt{dt}$ is the standard deviation of the return on the security over a short period of time. We then choose the parameters u and d to match the volatility of the asset price. The values for u and d suggested by Cox *et al.* (1979) are: $u = e^{\sigma\sqrt{dt}}$ and $d = e^{-\sigma\sqrt{dt}}$.

3.3.2 The Multi-period Model

Valuing a two-period call   Valuing a call with more than one period to expiration involves the same procedure as before, although the calculations are more complicated. We start at the option's value on the expiration date and work backward to the present. Figure 3.4a shows the different possible values of the asset

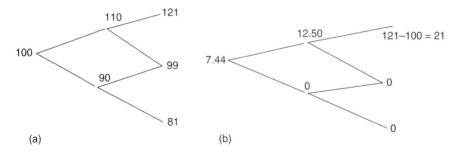

Figure 3.4   (a) Stock price in a two-step binomial tree; (b) Call price in a two-step binomial tree

---

[3] We can verify that $E(S_1)$ is equal to

$$S_0 \frac{R_d}{1+\delta} = PuS_0 + [1 - P]dS_0$$

by substituting the value of P.

price in a two-period binomial tree, and Figure 3.4b shows the corresponding value of the option at each period. There are three steps to the valuation procedure.

Step 1 Use C_{u^2} and C_{ud} to calculate C_u, the value of the option if the asset price makes one upward move. C_{u^2} is the terminal value of the option if the asset price makes two upward moves, and C_{ud} is the terminal value of the option if it makes one upward and one downward move.

Step 2 Use C_{ud} and C_{d^2} to calculate C_d, the value of the option if the asset price makes one downward move. C_{d^2} is the terminal value of the option if the asset price makes two downward moves.

Step 3 Use the calculated values of C_u and C_d to calculate the value of C_0.

In step 1 we proceed as we did for a one-period option. Table 3.5 consolidates the information from Figures 3.4a and 3.4b necessary to calculate the value of C_u. First we find Δ by equating the cash flows for the two possible outcomes and solving:

$$-21 + \Delta 127.05 = \Delta 103.95 \qquad \Delta = 0.9091$$

Next, we borrow

$$\frac{0.9091 \times 103.95}{1.08} = 87.50$$

so that net cash flows are equal to zero. Since the net cash flows are zero the value of the investment is also zero. Thus

$$C_u = 0.9091 \times 110 - 87.50 \qquad C_u = 12.50$$

In step 2, $C_d = 0$ because both C_{ud} and C_{d^2} are equal to zero. Since we know C_u and C_d, step 3 boils down to calculating the value of a one-period option.

Table 3.5 Two-period cash flows

	Flows at period 1	Flows at period 2	
		$u^2 S = 121$	$u\,dS = 99$
Write a call	$+C_u$	$-C_{u^2} = -21$	$-C_{ud} = 0$
Purchase Δ units of asset	$-\Delta uS$	$+\Delta u^2 S(1+\delta) = \Delta 127.05$	$+\Delta u\,dS(1+\delta) = \Delta 103.95$
Borrow	$\dfrac{(-C_{ud} + \Delta u\,dS(1+\delta))}{R_d}$	$C_{u^2} - \Delta u^2 S(1+\delta) = C_{ud} - \Delta u\,dS(1+\delta) =$	
		$21 - \Delta 127.05$	$0 - \Delta 103.95$
Total	$+C_u - \Delta uS$ $+\dfrac{-C_{ud} + \Delta u\,dS(1+\delta)}{R_d}$	0	0

First we find Δ using equation (3.1)

$$\Delta = \frac{12.5 - 0}{100 \times (1.05) \times (1.1 - 0.9)} \qquad \Delta = 0.5952$$

Next, we borrow

$$\frac{0.5952 \times 90 \times 1.05}{1.08} = 52.08$$

so that net cash flows will equal zero. Finally, we set the investment in period 0 equal to zero and find that

$$C_0 = 0.5952 \times 100 - 52.08 \qquad C_0 = 7.44$$

The general n-period binomial pricing formula for European calls   Finally, we can use the foregoing discussion to develop the general binomial option pricing formula. Rather than go through the steps of hedging and borrowing, we could apply the formula expressed in equation (3.4). If we apply equation (3.4) to value C_u, we will have

$$C_u = \frac{C_{u^2}P + C_{ud}[1 - P]}{R_d} \tag{3.5}$$

For C_d, we have

$$C_d = \frac{C_{ud}P + C_{d^2}[1 - P]}{R_d} \tag{3.6}$$

Substituting equations (3.5) and (3.6) into equation (3.4) gives

$$C_0 = \frac{P\left[\dfrac{C_{u^2}P + C_{ud}(1 - P)}{R_d}\right] + (1 - P)\left[\dfrac{C_{ud}P + C_{d^2}(1 - P)}{R_d}\right]}{R_d}$$

Simplifying

$$C_0 = \frac{P^2 C_{u^2} + 2P(1 - P)C_{ud} + (1 - P)^2 C_{d^2}}{R_d^2} \tag{3.7}$$

where $C_{u^i d^j}$ is the value of the call at expiration if there are i up movements and j down movements. We can use this formula to verify that the value of the call in the preceding example is indeed 7.44.

Figure 3.5a shows a three-period binomial tree for the asset evolution and Figure 3.5b shows the corresponding value of the call at expiration. By adjusting the subscripts, we can use equation (3.7) to calculate the values of C_u and C_d:

$$C_u = \frac{P^2 C_{u^3} + 2P(1 - P)C_{u^2 d} + (1 - P)^2 C_{ud^2}}{R_d^2}$$

$$C_d = \frac{P^2 C_{u^2 d} + 2P(1 - P)C_{ud^2} + (1 - P)^2 C_{d^3}}{R_d^2}$$

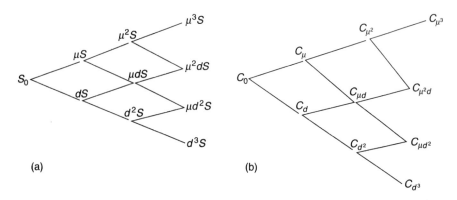

Figure 3.5 (a) Stock price in a three-step binomial tree; (b) Call price in a three-step binomial tree

Applying these values in equation (3.4) gives

$$C_0 = \left\{ P \left[\frac{P^2 C_{u^3} + 2P(1-P)C_{u^2 d} + (1-P)^2 C_{ud^2}}{R_d^2} \right] + (1-P) \left[\frac{P^2 C_{u^2 d} + 2P(1-P)C_{ud^2} + (1-P)^2 C_{d^3}}{R_d^2} \right] \right\} R_d^{-1}$$

Simplifying

$$C_0 = \frac{P^3 C_{u^3} + 3P^2(1-P)C_{u^2 d} + 3P(1-P)^2 C_{ud^2} + (1-P)^3 C_{d^3}}{R_d^3} \qquad (3.8)$$

In Appendix 3A we show that starting from the option's value after n moves and working backwards in the foregoing manner gives

$$C_0 = S(1+\delta)^{-n} \Phi(a, n, P') - X R_d^{-n} \Phi(a, n, P) \qquad (3.9)$$

where $\Phi(a, n, P)$ is the probability of realizing at least a upward moves when the probability at each trial is P and $\Phi(a, n, P')$ is the cumulative probability, given that at least a upward moves have been attained where the probability at each trial is P' with $P' = Pu(1+\delta)/R_d$

Valuing European puts   The same recursive methodology used to value European calls can be used to value European puts. We build a risk-less portfolio composed of the put and Δ units of the underlying asset, borrow the appropriate amount and end up with the equivalent of equation (3.4) where p represents the value of the put:

$$p_0 = \frac{p_u P + p_d[1-P]}{R_d} \qquad (3.10)$$

Continuing with the information in the previous examples, consider a one-period European put with a strike price of 100. If the spot price moves up to 110, the put expires worthless. If the spot price falls to 90, the put will be worth 10. Thus $p_u = 0$, $p_d = 10$ and

$$P = \frac{1.08/1.05 - 0.9}{1.10 - 0.9} = 0.6429$$

$$p_0 = \frac{(0 \times 0.6429) + (10 \times 0.3571)}{1.08}$$

$$p_0 = 3.31$$

Valuing American style options   The main difference between European and American style options is that American style options can be exercised at any time over the option's life, whereas European style options can only be exercised at maturity. This added flexibility makes the American style option more valuable than the European style option, but it also makes it more complicated to compute the price. In fact, two extra steps must be added in the computation of the price of an American style option:

Step 1   Start from the right-hand side as before and compute the expiration values of the option.

Step 2   Work towards the left using the expiration values and the risk neutral probabilities to compute the option value if it is not exercised.

Step 3   *Compute the option's value if it is exercised.*

Step 4   *Compare the two values and choose the higher of the two.*

Step 5   Return to step 2 and repeat this process until the initial period is reached.

Consider the following information which is the same as before except that $\delta = 15\%$ instead of 5%: $S = 100$, $u = 1.10$, $d = 0.90$, $\delta = 0.15$, $r_d = 0.08$, $X = 100$.

Figure 3.6a shows the evolution of the asset price. Figure 3.6b shows the value of the European style call option in parentheses and the value of the American style call option in bold. In the upper middle node we can see that the option is worth 3.80 alive. If it is exercised it is worth 10. Thus, to compute the value of the American style option at the initial period, we use 10. The value of the American style option is considerably higher than the equivalent European style option (1.8116 versus 0.6884).

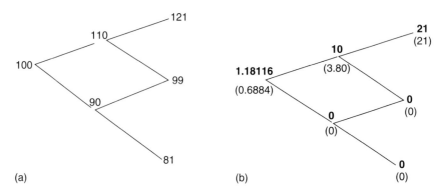

Figure 3.6   (a) Stock price; (b) American and European call prices

3.3.3   Binomial Valuation of European Options on Futures Contracts

The foregoing binomial model can be used to value options on assets with different types of yields. All we need to know are the yields to calculate the probabilities P and P'. As mentioned above, because of the convenience and low cost of delivery of a futures contract relative to the underlying asset, options on most physical commodities are options on futures contracts relating to the underlying asset rather than on the underlying asset itself. Most futures contracts are closed out prior to delivery and settled in cash. With this important practical consideration in mind, we will spend time developing the relationship between the cash and futures markets in the following sections and derive Black's continuous time option pricing model on futures contracts.

For the binomial form of a futures option remember that

$$P = \frac{(R_d/(1+\delta)) - d}{u - d}$$

When a futures position is taken, there is no cash outlay and therefore its value is zero. An asset with a value of zero has an expected return equal to zero. If this were not true there would be arbitrage possibilities. Since there is no yield and no return on a *futures contract* in a risk-neutral world, the risk neutral probability of an up move is

$$P = \frac{(1+0)/(1+0) - d}{u - d} = \frac{1 - d}{u - d} \quad \text{and} \quad P' = Pu$$

and the value of the option is

$$C_0 = SR_d^{-n}\Phi(a, n, P') - XR_d^{-n}\Phi(a, n, P) \tag{3.14}$$

3.4   THE CONTINUOUS TIME FUTURES OPTION MODEL

The Black–Scholes option pricing model is a general form of the preceding multi-period binomial model. The difference between the two is that the binomial model refers to a limited number of discrete time periods, whereas the Black–Scholes model was developed in the context of a multitude of infinitely small periods, known as continuous time. In this section we develop the model developed by Black (1976) for an option on a futures contract.

3.4.1   A Weiner Process

Let F represent the futures price. Suppose that the change of the futures price in the time interval dt follows a continuous stochastic process of the type

$$dF(t) = \mu F(t)\,dt + \sigma F(t)\,dz(t) \qquad (3.15)$$

where μ is the expected percentage change in the asset price, called the drift, σ the volatility, and $dz(t)$ a standard Weiner process sometimes referred to as Brownian motion (from here on we drop the time argument for notational simplicity). A Weiner process is a particular type of stochastic process, called a Markov process, where only the present value of the variable is relevant for predicting its future evolution. The major properties of a standard Weiner process are as follows:

1. $dz = \varepsilon\sqrt{dt}$, where ε is a standardised random variable following the normal law with a mean of 0 and variance of $1 : N(0, 1)$.
2. The values of dz for any two different short time intervals are independent. From property 1 it follows that
3. $E(dz) = 0$.
4. $E(dz^2) = dt =$ the variance of dz.

   If we heuristically define dt as the smallest positive real number such that $dt^x = 0$ whenever $x > 1$, it follows that
5. $E(dz\,dt) = 0$
6. The variance of $dz^2 = 0$
7. $E[(dz\,dt)^2] = 0$
8. The variance of $dz\,dt = 0$

3.4.2   Ito's Lemma

Equation (3.15) is a generalised Weiner process known as geometric Brownian motion with drift equal to μ and volatility equal to σ. It is also called an Ito process after the mathematician who discovered an important result on stochastic processes. The result is called *Ito's lemma*. Ito's lemma shows that a function of an Ito process is itself an Ito process.

Let $C(F, t) = C$ represent the value of a call on one unit of the futures contract. To apply Ito's lemma expand C in a Taylor series

$$dC = \frac{\partial C}{\partial F} dF + \frac{\partial C}{\partial t} dt + \frac{1}{2} \frac{\partial^2 C}{\partial F^2} dF^2 \qquad (3.16)$$

In stochastic calculus, the term dF^2 does not disappear as it would in ordinary calculus even though higher-order terms do vanish. This is because dF is a normally distributed random variable whose variance is proportional to dt. To see this compute

$$dF^2 = \mu^2 F^2 dt^2 + 2\mu\sigma F^2 dz\, dt + \sigma^2 F^2 dz^2 \qquad (3.17)$$

The first term on the right-hand side vanishes because terms of order $dt^x; x > 1$ are neglected. From 5 and 8, $dz\, dt = 0$ and the second term also vanishes.[4] From properties 4 and 6, $dz^2 = dt$ so that equation (3.17) reduces to:[5]

$$dF^2 = \sigma^2 F^2 dt \qquad (3.18)$$

We now proceed as in the binomial case by creating a portfolio of one call and Δ units of the futures contract:

$$V = C + \Delta F \qquad (3.19)$$

Choose Δ so that the change in the value of the portfolio over a short period of time will be equal to zero. To do this, we take the derivative of V with respect to F and set it equal to zero:

$$\frac{\partial V}{\partial F} = \frac{\partial C}{\partial F} + \Delta = 0 \longrightarrow \Delta = -\frac{\partial C}{\partial F}$$

The portfolio will be riskless when $\Delta = -\partial C / \partial F$.[6] Since we are now in a risk-neutral world, equation (3.15) becomes:[7]

$$dF = \sigma F\, dz \qquad (3.15)$$

Now differentiate equation (3.19)

$$dV = dC - \frac{\partial C}{\partial F} dF \qquad (3.20)$$

---

[4] Since the variance of property 5 is zero because of property 8, the expectations operator is redundant.

[5] Since the variance of property 4 is zero because of property 6, the expectations operator is redundant.

[6] This is the continuous time equivalent to the binomial

$$\Delta = \frac{C_u - C_d}{S(u - d)}$$

[7] To see this start from the continuous time version of equation (2.4): $F_{0,T} = E(S_T) e^{rT} / e^{RT}$. In a risk-neutral world all assets yield the riskless rate so that $R = r$ and $F_{0,T} = E(S_T)$. At maturity, the futures price and the spot price will converge so that $F_{T,T} = S_T$. Applying the expectations operator gives $E(F_{T,T}) = E(S_T)$. Thus, $E(dF) = 0$.

Substitute equations (3.16) and (3.18) into equation (3.20)

$$dV = \frac{\partial C}{\partial t} dt + \frac{1}{2}\frac{\partial^2 C}{\partial F^2}\sigma^2 F^2 dt \qquad (3.21)$$

The only element of uncertainty was contained in dF and all terms containing dF have been eliminated. Thus, V is riskless. Since V is riskless, it should earn the riskless rate through time, but it is important to remember that because the futures contract has a value of zero (there is no cash outlay at the outset), the equity in the portfolio is equal to C. Thus, $dV = rC\,dt$ and

$$rC\,dt = \frac{\partial C}{\partial t} dt + \frac{1}{2}\frac{\partial^2 C}{\partial F^2}\sigma^2 F^2 dt \qquad (3.22)$$

Rearranging and simplifying gives the Black differential equation:

$$\frac{1}{2}\frac{\partial^2 C}{\partial F^2}\sigma^2 F^2 - rC + \frac{\partial C}{\partial t} = 0 \qquad (3.23)$$

The solution to this equation depends on the boundary conditions. For a European call option we know

$$C(F, T) = \max(F_{T,T} - X, 0) \qquad (3.24a)$$

and

$$C(0, t) = 0 \qquad (3.24b)$$

Solving the differential equation and using the value for C at the expiration date yields an exact analytical solution:

$$C_t = e^{-r(T-t)}[F_{t,T}N(d_1) - XN(d_2)] \qquad (3.25)$$

where $N(d)$ is the value of the cumulative normal distribution evaluated at d.

$$d_1 = \frac{\ln(F_{t,T}/X) + \sigma^2/2(T-t)}{\sigma\sqrt{T-t}}$$

$$d_2 = \frac{\ln(F_{t,T}/X) - \sigma^2/2(T-t)}{\sigma\sqrt{T-t}} = d_1 - \sigma\sqrt{T-t}$$

In Appendix 3B we show how this result can be obtained by computing the true expectation.

The corresponding formula for the put is

$$p = e^{-r(T-t)}[XN(-d_2) - F_{t,T}N(-d_1)] \qquad (3.26)$$

where d_1 and d_2 are defined above.

3.5 USING THE CONTINUOUS TIME MODEL

3.5.1 Calculating the Premium: An Example of a Futures Call Option

In spite of the apparent complexity of the formula, using the model to derive the theoretical value of an option is quite simple. All that is necessary is an estimate of the volatility of the futures price. The other information is observable. Consider, for example, the following information on a corn futures call option: $r = 5\%$, $T - t = $ three months $= 0.25$ year, $X = 200$ cents per bushel, current futures price $= 200$ cents per bushel. The estimated volatility is $\sigma = 35\%$.

Substituting this information into equation (3.25) gives

$$13.75 = e^{-0.05 \times 0.25}[200N(d_1) - 200N(d_2)]$$

The call premium is $13\frac{3}{4}$ cents per bushel. Since each contract is for 5,000 bushels the cost of the option is $687.50.

3.5.2 Implied Volatility

Although the Black–Scholes model and its extensions are easy to use, it has a number of shortcomings. First of all, it can only be used for European options. Because of the possibility of early exercise, we have seen that American options are worth more than European options. Money managers should be careful about this.

Another practical difficulty resides in the choice of the volatility parameter, σ. One possible solution is to estimate volatility using past values of the underlying security. Unfortunately, experience has shown that volatility is not stable and tends to fluctuate considerably over time. The volatility estimate necessary for the Black–Scholes-type models is not past volatility in any case, but the volatility expected over the life of the option. This variable is not directly observable, of course, because it depends on the anticipations of all the participants in the market. Consequently, investors have developed another use for the model. Rather than using it to determine the theoretical price of an option, they take the price observed on the market and use the model to determine the volatility that the market price implies. In fact, professional options traders do not quote a price for an option. Instead they quote a level of volatility from which the price can be deduced.

Take, for example, an at the money call on wheat futures that expires in six months with a strike price of 250 and quoted at 32.25 cents per bushel. The investor can substitute the value 32.25 into equation (3.25):

$$32.25 = e^{-0.05 \times 0.5}[250N(d_1) - 250N(d_2)]$$

and solve for σ. The only unknown in the equation is σ in the formulas for $N(d_1)$ and $N(d_2)$. There is no explicit solution to the equation, but an iterative trial and error method can get the job done quickly. In fact, 47% is the solution to this problem, which means that 47% is the value of σ that makes it possible to find the market price of 32.25 cents per bushel. This is called *implied volatility*.

Because there are numerous calls with different strike prices and expiration dates quoted on the same currency, implied volatility can be used in several ways. First of all, it can be used as a gauge of the relative expensiveness of the different calls. Those with the highest volatility are the most expensive and to be avoided by buyers. Secondly, if we make the assumption that market anticipations only evolve slowly, the best estimation of anticipated risk is the weighted average of all the different implicit volatilities. In fact, this use seems to give the best results.

3.6 FUTURES OPTION MANAGEMENT TOOLS

The usefulness of the Black–Scholes model goes beyond the limited scope of pricing European call options. The model expresses in a relatively simple manner the relationships between the price of the option and the principal variables: the spot price, volatility, time, and the domestic and foreign interest rates. It allows investors to anticipate the effects of a change in one of these variables on the value of the overall position. There are five basic tools to be derived from the model: the delta (Δ), the gamma (Γ), the theta (Θ), the vega (v), and rho, the sensitivity to the interest rate.

3.6.1 The Delta

We have seen that when the futures price is higher, the option premium is also higher. Mathematically, we can say that the option premium is an increasing function of the futures price. The Black–Scholes model makes it possible to state the relationship precisely. In fact, we can use the first partial derivative of the option premium with respect to the futures price. It is equal to

$$\Delta = \frac{\partial C}{\partial F} = e^{-r(T-t)} N(d_1) \tag{3.27}$$

and is referred to by professionals as the call's *delta*.[8] A call's delta is always positive and measures the sensitivity of the premium to a small change in the

---

[8] When deriving the 'Greeks', keep in mind that $F e^{-r(T-t)} N'(d_1) = X e^{-r(T-t)} N'(d_2)$, where $N'(\cdot)$ is the first derivative of the cumulative normal distribution. To see this, take the logs of both sides:

$$\ln F - r(T-t) + \ln \frac{1}{\sqrt{2\pi}} - \frac{d_1^2}{2} = \ln X - r(T-t) + \ln \frac{1}{\sqrt{2\pi}} - \frac{d_2^2}{2}$$

futures price. For the writer of a call wanting to hedge his exposure, it represents the number of units of the underlying asset to be bought spot. For the owner of a call wanting to hedge his exposure, it represents the number of units of the underlying asset to be sold. When an investor has accumulated a position composed of calls with different strike prices and expiration dates, he would like to know how sensitive his overall position is to changes in the futures price. Individual call deltas can be used for this purpose.

His overall position can be defined as the weighted sum of the value of the premiums of all the calls he has bought or written. Let H be the overall position. Then:

$$H = \sum x_i C_i \qquad (3.28)$$

where x_i is the number of calls in series i that have been bought if $x > 0$ and the number of calls that have been written if $x < 0$. The sensitivity of his overall portfolio to a change in the futures price, Δ_H, will then be the weighted average of the sensitivities of the different calls:

$$\Delta_H = \sum x_i \Delta_i \qquad (3.29)$$

The investor can evaluate how well he is covered by comparing the delta of his overall position in calls with his futures exposure. This technique is frequently used by professional investors.

For a put option

$$\Delta = \frac{\partial p}{\partial F} = e^{-r(T-t)}(N(d_1) - 1) \qquad (3.30)$$

It is negative. Therefore, a long position in a put option should be hedged by a long position in the futures contract and a short position in a put option should be hedged by a short position in the futures contract.

3.6.2 The Gamma

Delta only measures the sensitivity of the premium to changes in the futures price in the vicinity of the actual price. If the price undergoes a large change, the delta will change considerably. Hence, if options are used to hedge risk, the level of exposure would automatically change if there is a large move in the asset price. The rate at which delta changes, then, is an important factor in the riskiness of

---

$$\Leftrightarrow \ln F - \ln X = \frac{1}{2}\left[d_1^2 - (d_1 - \sigma\sqrt{T-t})^2\right]$$

$$\Leftrightarrow \ln(F/X) + \frac{\sigma^2(T-t)}{2} = d_1\sigma\sqrt{T-t}, \text{ which is true by definition}$$

the investor's position. *Gamma*, which is the second partial derivative of C or p (gammas for calls and puts are the same) with respect to F, measures the rate of change in delta:[9]

$$\Gamma = \frac{\partial \Delta}{\partial F} = \frac{\partial^2 C}{\partial F^2} = e^{-r(T-t)} \frac{1}{\sigma F \sqrt{2\pi(T-t)}} e^{-(d_1)^2/2} \tag{3.31}$$

As with delta, the gamma of the overall position can be calculated by taking a weighted average of all the calls:

$$\Gamma_H = \sum x_i \Gamma_i \tag{3.32}$$

Since the x_i can be negative (calls sold), the gamma of a portfolio can be negative as well. Negative gammas can be dangerous in the case of a wide swing in the futures price. A negative gamma will make hedging a short position with sold puts less and less effective in the case of a rise in the asset price because delta will fall as the price rises. Covering a long position in futures with sold calls is also less and less effective when the asset price falls because delta will decrease as the price falls. Furthermore, in the case of opposite moves, the position will immediately show a tendency to be over-hedged, which is costly.

3.6.3 Theta

The value of an option is indisputably a function of the time to expiration. The first partial derivative of the value of an option with respect to time is called *theta*. For a call it is

$$\Theta = \frac{\partial C}{\partial t} = -\frac{FN'(d_1)\sigma e^{-r(T-t)}}{2\sqrt{T-t}} + rF e^{-r(T-t)}N(d_1) - rX\sigma e^{-r(T-t)}N(d_2) \tag{3.33}$$

---

[9] The value of gamma can be worked out as follows:

$$\frac{\partial^2 C}{\partial F^2} = e^{-r(T-t)} \frac{\partial N(d_1)}{\partial d_1} \frac{\partial d_1}{\partial F}$$

Where from the normal distribution

$$\frac{\partial N(d_1)}{\partial d_1} = \frac{1}{\sqrt{2\pi}} e^{-(d_1)^2/2}$$

$$\frac{\partial d_1}{\partial F} = \frac{1}{\sigma F \sqrt{(T-t)}}$$

Putting these together yields the derivative in the text.

For a put it is

$$\Theta = \frac{\partial p}{\partial t} = -\frac{FN'(d_1)\sigma\,e^{-r(T-t)}}{2\sqrt{T-t}} - rF\,e^{-r(T-t)}N(-d_1)$$
$$+ rX\sigma\,e^{-r(T-t)}N(-d_2) \tag{3.34}$$

Normally, the value of an option diminishes as time passes and it usually diminishes faster as the expiration date approaches. Therefore, theta is usually negative. Theta is not the same type of hedge parameter as delta or gamma. Delta and gamma refer to hedging against uncertainty about changes in the futures price. Since there is no uncertainty about the passage of time, it does not make sense to hedge against it. It is useful as a descriptive statistic.

3.6.4 Vega

The value of an option is a direct function of the volatility of the spot price. Higher volatility raises the value of the option. On the organised exchanges, most options positions are closed out before expiration. Consequently, the price of the option comes into play twice, once when it is bought and once when it is sold. It is thus important for an investor to have an idea of what the effect of an anticipated change in the volatility of an option will have on its premium. For example, a fall in volatility will cause a fall in the call's premium.

The relationship between the option's premium and volatility can be expressed as the first partial derivative of C or p (vega is the same for calls and puts) with respect to σ:[10]

$$\frac{\partial C}{\partial \sigma} = F\sqrt{T-t}\,\frac{1}{\sqrt{2\pi}}\,e^{(d_1)^2/2}\,e^{-r(T-t)} \tag{3.35}$$

This derivative is called *vega*. It measures the increase in the premium for a small change in volatility. As with the other parameters, vegas can be added to calculate a global position consisting of different calls.

3.6.5 Interest Rate Sensitivity: rho

To show the sensitivity of the option premium to the small changes in the interest rate, we can do as we have done for the other parameters and take the first partial derivative of C and p with respect to the interest rate.

---

[10] The other member of the derivative disappears because

$$F\,e^{-r(T-t)}N'(d_1) - X\,e^{-r(T-t)}N'(d_2) = 0$$

$$\frac{\partial C}{\partial r} = (T - t)X\,e^{-r(T-t)}N(d_2) \tag{3.36}$$

$$\frac{\partial p}{\partial r} = -(T - t)X\,e^{-r(T-t)}N(-d_2) \tag{3.37}$$

The result shows that for a call a higher interest rate has a positive effect on the premium. A higher interest rate lowers the present value of the strike price $[e^{-r(T-t)}X]$ and increases the difference with the current asset price, thereby increasing the premium. For a put the effect is the opposite.

3.7 HEDGING WITH OPTIONS

3.7.1 Exercising a Futures Option

The maturity date of a futures option is usually on, or just a few days before, the earliest delivery date of the underlying futures contract. Remember that when a call futures option is exercised, the buyer acquires a long position in the under-lying futures contract plus a cash amount equal to the difference between the most recent futures settlement price and the strike price. When a put futures option is exercised, the buyer acquires a short position in the underlying futures contract plus a cash amount equal to the difference between the strike price and the most recent futures settlement price.

Suppose, for example, that on 24 December an investor exercises one February call option on a February gold futures contract with a strike price of $280 per ounce. Each contract is for 100 troy ounces. The settlement price for the February futures contract on 23 December was $288.50. Thus, the investor receives a cash amount equal to

$$100 \times (\$288.50 - \$280) = \$850$$

The investor also acquires one February gold futures contract. Suppose that the futures price for February gold is currently trading at $289. If the position is closed out

$$100 \times (\$289 - \$288.50) = \$50$$

is received. The investor's total gain on 24 December is $900, which is equal to $100 \times (F - X)$, where $F = \$289$ is the futures price at the time of exercise and $X = \$280$ is the exercise or strike price.

Now consider an investor who, on 24 December exercises a put option on the February gold futures contract with an exercise price of $295. A cash amount equal to

$$100 \times (\$295 - \$288.50) = \$650$$

is received. The investor is also short one February gold futures contract. If he closes out his position by purchasing one February gold futures contract he/she pays

$$100 \times (\$289 - \$288.50) = \$50$$

His/her total gain on 24 December is \$600, which is equal to $100 \times (X - F)$, where $F = \$289$ is the futures price at the time of exercise and $X = \$295$ is the exercise or strike price.

3.7.2 Hedging against a Price Rise by Purchasing Calls

Consider a manufacturer on 5 July with a need for 25,000 pounds of copper in September. The current spot price for copper is \$0.75 per pound. It is felt that the price could go as high as \$0.90 per pound by September and the manufacturer does not want to be left holding the bag if it does. He/she also feel that the price could fall as low as \$0.60 per pound. The current price for a September copper futures contract is \$0.80 per pound. If he/she purchases one September contract he/she can lock in his price at \$0.80 per pound, but if the price falls, the manufacturer will reap none of the benefits of a lower price. He/she decides to purchase one September futures call option with a strike price of \$0.76 currently selling for \$0.0375 per pound for a cost of

$$25,000 \times \$0.0375 = \$937.50$$

Outcome if the price rises to \$0.90 on the expiry date   The manufacturer exercises his/her option and closes out the futures contract. Since the futures price converges to the spot price on expiry, he/she receives:

$$25,000 \times (\$0.90 - \$0.76) = \$3,500$$

The total gain is \$2562.50, the difference between the cash payment and the cost of the option. When he/she purchases the 25,000 pounds of copper at the spot price of \$0.90 his all-in cost is

$$25,000 \times \$0.90 - \$2562.50 = \$19,937.50$$

This works out to a cost of \$0.7975 per pound.

Outcome if the price falls to \$0.60 on the expiry date   The manufacturer lets the option expire worthless and buys his copper at \$0.60 per pound. When the cost of the option, is added in the total cost is

$$25,000 \times \$0.60 + \$937.50 = \$15,937.50$$

This works out to \$0.6375 per pound. The price is higher than the spot price, but is much lower than if it had been locked into the futures contract at \$0.80 per pound.

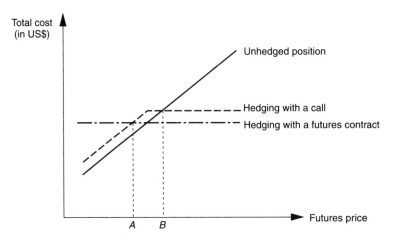

Figure 3.7   Pay-out profile of three strategies

Outcome if the price remains unchanged   The benefits of an option strategy can only be realised if there is a sizeable move in the price. If, for example, the price in September was $0.75, the option would expire worthless, but the cost per pound would be $0.7875 because of the cost of the option. Figure 3.7 shows the payoff profile for a hedge with a call compared with a futures hedge and an unhedged position.

3.7.3   Hedging against a Price Fall by Purchasing Puts

Consider a copper broker on the same day, 5 July, with an excess 25,000 pounds of copper on his hands in September. The situation is the same as above. The current spot price for copper is $0.75 per pound. The copper broker has made the same analysis as the manufacturer. He feels that the price could go as high as $0.90 per pound by September and would like to take advantage of the situation if it does. The broker also feels that the price could fall as low as $0.60 per pound and does not want to get hurt. The current price for a September copper futures contract is $0.80 per pound. If one September contract is sold he can lock in his price at $0.80 per pound, but if the price rises, he/she will reap none of the benefits of a higher price. He/she decides to purchase one September futures put option with a strike price of $0.76, currently selling for $0.0475 per pound for a cost of

$$25,000 \times \$0.0475 = \$1187.50$$

Outcome if the price rises to $0.90 on the expiry date   The option contract expires worthless and the copper is sold for

$$25,000 \times \$0.90 = \$22,500$$

His total income is $22,500 less the cost of the option

$$\$22,500 - \$1187.50 = \$21,312.50$$

for an all-in price of $0.8575 per pound.

Outcome if the price falls to $0.60 on the expiry date   The broker exercises his option and takes delivery. Since the futures price converges to the spot price on expiry, he/she receives a cash amount for the option equal to

$$25,000 \times (\$0.76 - \$0.60) = \$4,000$$

He/she also receives $25,000 \times \$0.60 = \$15,000$. His/her total gain is $15,000 + $4,000 less the cost of the option. This works out to $0.7125 per pound.

Outcome with a small price change   Again, the benefits of an option strategy can only be realised if there is a sizeable move in the price. If, for example, the price in September rose to $0.82, the option would expire worthless, but the price per pound would be only $0.7725 because of the cost of the option.

3.7.4   Hedging by Selling Options

One of the main criticisms of options as hedging instruments is their cost. The premium is relatively high because it reflects the fact that the hedger is protected against adverse price movements, but can take advantage of favourable ones. Consequently, hedging by purchasing options is only appropriate if relatively large swings in the price of the underlying asset are forecast. If the forecast is for relative stability (low volatility), it might be better to sell options.

Hedging against a price rise by selling puts   Consider the manufacturer on 5 July with a need for 25,000 pounds of copper in September who feels that the price will not vary more than plus or minus 5% around the current price of $0.75 per pound. The current price for a September copper futures contract is still $0.80 per pound. If the manufacturer purchases one September contract he can lock in his price at $0.80 per pound, but if the price falls, he will reap none of the benefits of a lower price. If sells a September futures put with a strike price of $0.76, he receives $0.0475 per pound. If the price of the futures contract rises by 5% to $0.7875 at maturity, the put option expires worthless and his all-in, per pound cost is the maturity spot price less the option premium:

$$\$0.7875 - \$0.0475 = \$0.74$$

If the price falls by 5% to $0.7125, the option is exercised and $0.76 - \$0.7125 = $0.0475 is paid out for the option plus the maturity spot price for the copper. His/her total cost per pound will thus be $0.7125.

In fact, this strategy will be the best to follow as long as the futures price stays between $0.7125 and $0.8475 (the current price of the September futures contract plus the put premium). If the price falls to $0.60, for example, the all-in cost will be $0.7125, far higher than the maturity spot price. If the price rises to $0.90 the all-in cost will be $0.90 less the option premium = $0.8525, far higher than the current price of the September futures contract.

Hedging against a price fall by selling calls   Consider the copper broker on 5 July with the excess 25,000 pounds of copper on his hands in September. He still has not hedged his position. The spot price is $0.76 and the current price of a September futures contract is $0.76. He decides to sell a September futures call with a strike price of $0.76 and receives $0.035. If at maturity the price of the September futures contract has fallen to $0.74, the option expires worthless. His total per pound income is equal to the maturity price of $0.74 plus the option premium of $0.035 = $0.775. This is better than the $0.76 he would have received if he had sold a September futures contract.

If the price of the September futures contract has risen to $0.78, the option will be exercised and he will pay the difference between this and $0.76, the exercise price, $0.02. His total income will be $0.78 − $0.02 + $0.035 = $0.795. This is a better price than the $0.76 fixed hedge that could have been obtained by selling the September futures contract.

This strategy will be the best if the price of the September futures contract stays between $0.795 (the exercise price + the option premium) and $0.725 (the price of the futures contract minus the call premium). If it goes above $0.795, no hedging would be the preferable strategy. If it goes below $0.725, the fixed hedge would be the preferable strategy.

3.7.5   Hedging with Sales and Purchases of Options

The tunnel   As we have already mentioned, hedging by purchasing options is costly because of the premium and effective only in times of high volatility. Hedging by selling options can be advantageous in times of low volatility. The two strategies are complementary.

Consider a gold trader in August who will need 100 ounces of gold for delivery in December. The December futures contract is trading at $285. He purchases an out-of-the money call on a December futures contract with a strike price of $300 for $4.90 and sells an out-of-the money put on the contract with a strike price of $280 for $4.90. His outlay on the two transactions is zero. He can never pay more than the strike price of the call and never pay less than the strike price of the put. The two strike prices determine the tunnel's limits. Within the tunnel limits, the outcome varies with the price of the December futures contract. This kind of strategy is popular because risk is limited and the cost is low.

Put–call parity   Put–call parity illustrates the relationships between calls and puts as well as the other positions that incorporate calls and puts. The starting point is the tunnel. The position is not entirely riskless because outcomes can fluctuate within the tunnel. Remember that the tunnel limits are the strike prices for the calls and puts. As they come closer together, the tunnel gets smaller. When the strike prices are equal the tunnel is similar to a forward or a futures contract in that it gives a fixed outcome equal to the strike price. We start where the strike prices and expiry dates are equal. The arbitrage can then be summarised as follows:

Operation	Cash flow at time 0	Outcome if $F_T > X$	Outcome if $F_T < X$	Outcome if $F_T = X = S$
Buy one call	$-C$	$F_T - X$	0	0
Sell one put	$+p$	0	$-(X - F_T)$	0
Sell forward	0	$+F_{t,T} - F_T$	$+F_{t,T} - F_T$	$+F_{t,T} - X$
Result	$p - C$	$F_{t,T} - X$	$F_{t,T} - X$	$F_{t,T} - X$

We can see that the outcomes are all the same no matter what happens to the price of the forward (futures) contract. If we borrow the amount $(F_{t,T} - X)\,e^{-r(T-t)}$, all the outcomes will become equal to zero.[11] A portfolio with a certain zero return has a value of zero.

$$p - C + (F_{t,T} - X)\,e^{-r(T-t)} = 0 \qquad p = C - (F_{t,T} - X)\,e^{-r(T-t)} \qquad (3.38)$$

This relationship is known as put–call parity.

BIBLIOGRAPHY

F. Black and M. Scholes (1973) The pricing of options and corporate liabilities, *Journal of Political Economy*, **81**, 637–659.

F. Black (1976) The pricing of commodity contracts, *Journal of Financial Economics*, **3**, 167–179.

E. Clark, M. Levasseur and P. Rousseau (1993) *International Finance*. Chapman & Hall, London.

J. Cox and M. Rubenstein (1985) *Options Markets*. Prentice-Hall, Englewood Cliffs, NJ.

J. Cox, S. Ross and M. Rubenstein (1979) Option pricing: a simplified approach, *Journal of Financial Economics*, **7**, 229–264.

A. K. Dixit and R. S. Pindyck (1994) *Investment Under Uncertainty*. Princeton University Press, Princeton, NJ.

J. C. Hull (2000) *Options, Futures and Other Derivatives*. Prentice-Hall International, London.

---

[11] Alternatively, we can say that we have invested $C - p$ in the portfolio. Since its outcome is certain it should yield the riskless rate. Thus, $(C - p)\,e^{r(T-t)} = F_t - X$.

S. N. Neftci (1996) *An Introduction to the Mathematics of Financial Derivatives*. Academic Press, San Diego, CA.

M. Garman and S. Kohlhagen (1983) Foreign currency options values, *Journal of International Money and Finance*, 231–237.

R. C. Merton (1990) On the mathematics and economic assumptions of continuous time models, in *Continuous Time Finance*. Basil Blackwell, Cambridge MA, 57–93.

L. Trigeorgis (1996) *Real Options*. The MIT Press, Cambridge, MA.

P. Wilmott (1998) *Derivatives*. Wiley, New York.

APPENDIX 3A

The binomial option pricing model with known, proportional payouts

Remembering that the option's expiration value after j upward moves and $n - j$ downward moves is equal to $\max[0, u^j d^{n-j} S - E]$. Thus, n periods before its expiration date, the value of the call is

$$C_0 = \frac{\displaystyle\sum_{j=0}^{n} \frac{n!}{j!(n-j)!} P^j (1-P)^{n-j} \max\left[0, u^j d^{n-j} S - X\right]}{R_d^n} \tag{A3.1}$$

This expression can be simplified by defining a as the minimum number of upward moves in the asset price for the option to finish in the money. This will be the case when $u^a d^{n-a} S - X > 0$. Taking logs gives

$$a > \ln \frac{X}{Sd^n} \Big/ \ln \frac{u}{d}$$

When there are fewer than a upward movements, the call will not be exercised and it will expire worthless. The maximum can then be written as $u^j d^{n-j} S - X$ over $j = a \ldots n$. With these changes we can write equation (3.9) as

$$C_0 = \frac{\displaystyle\sum_{j=a}^{n} \frac{n!}{j!(n-j)!} P^j (1-P)^{n-j} \left[u^j d^{n-j} S - X\right]}{R_d^n} \tag{A3.2}$$

Rearranging

$$C_0 = S(1+\delta)^{-n} \sum_{j=a}^{n} \frac{n!}{j!(n-j)!} \frac{(1+\delta)^n (Pu)^j ((1-P)d)^{n-j}}{R_d^n}$$

$$- XR_d^{-n} \sum_{j=a}^{n} \frac{n!}{j!(n-j)!} P^j (1-P)^{n-j} \tag{A3.3}$$

The second summation is the binomial formula with P as the probability. The first summation is also the binomial formula with $P' = Pu(1+\delta)/R_d$ as the probability if

$$(1 - P') = (1 - P)d \frac{1+\delta}{R_d}$$

This is indeed the case since

$$(1 - P') = 1 - Pu\frac{1+\delta}{R_d} = 1 - u\frac{1+\delta}{R_d}\left[\frac{\dfrac{R_d}{1+\delta} - d}{u-d}\right]$$

$$= 1 - \frac{u\dfrac{R_d}{1+\delta} - ud}{u\dfrac{R_d}{1+\delta} - d\dfrac{R_d}{1+\delta}} = \frac{u\dfrac{R_d}{1+\delta} - d\dfrac{R_d}{1+\delta} - u\dfrac{R_d}{1+\delta} + ud}{u\dfrac{R_d}{1+\delta} - d\dfrac{R_d}{1+\delta}}$$

$$= \frac{d}{\dfrac{R_d}{1+\delta}}\left[\frac{u - \dfrac{R_d}{1+\delta}}{u-d}\right] = \frac{d}{\dfrac{R_d}{1+\delta}}\left[\frac{u - d - \dfrac{R_d}{1+\delta} + d}{u-d}\right]$$

$$= \frac{d(1+\delta)}{R_d}\left[1 - \frac{\dfrac{R_d}{1+\delta} - d}{u-d}\right]$$

which is what we wanted to show. Thus, we can write the general binomial foreign currency option pricing model as

$$C_0 = S(1+\delta)^{-n}\Phi(a, n, P') - XR_d^{-n}\Phi(a, n, P) \tag{A3.4}$$

where $\Phi(a, n, P)$ is the probability of realising at least a upward moves when the probability at each trial is P and $\Phi(a, n, P')$ is the probability of obtaining at least a upward moves when the probability at each trial is P'.

APPENDIX 3B

Derivation of the expected expiration value of the call option

In this appendix we derive the expected expiration value of the call option on the futures contract. This involves solving the equation

$$C = e^{-r(T-t)}E[\max(F_T - X, 0)] \qquad (B3.1)$$

We know that F is lognormally distributed. Applying the lognormal distribution to equation (B3.1) gives

$$C = e^{-r(T-t)} \int_{\ln X}^{\infty} \frac{1}{\sqrt{2\pi\sigma^2(T-t)}} \frac{1}{F_T} e^{-(\ln F_T - m)^2/2\sigma^2(T-t)}[F_T - X]\, dF_T$$

$$= e^{-r(T-t)} \left[\frac{1}{\sqrt{2\pi\sigma^2(T-t)}} \int_{\ln X}^{\infty} e^{-(\ln F_T - m)^2/2\sigma^2(T-t)}\, dF_T \right.$$

$$\left. -X\frac{1}{\sqrt{2\pi\sigma^2(T-t)}} \int_{\ln X}^{\infty} \frac{1}{F_T} e^{-(\ln F_T - m)^2/2\sigma^2(T-t)}\, dF_T \right] \qquad (B3.2)$$

where m is the mean of $\ln F_T$.

First we evaluate the second interval on the right-hand-side (RHS) of equation (B3.2). Let

$$\varepsilon = \frac{\ln F_T - m}{\sigma\sqrt{T-t}}$$

and make the change of variable, knowing that

$$\frac{d\varepsilon}{dF_T} = \frac{1}{F_T\sigma\sqrt{T-t}}$$

This gives

$$-X\frac{1}{\sqrt{2\pi}} \int_{(\ln X - m)/(\sigma\sqrt{T-t})}^{\infty} e^{-\varepsilon^2/2}\, d\varepsilon \qquad (B3.3)$$

Equation (B3.3) is X multiplied by the probability that $F_T > X$. This probability can be visualised as the area under the standard normal curve to the right of the cut-off point. The convention in option pricing is to use areas to the left of the cut-off point. This translation is easy to achieve, since the standard normal curve is symmetrical around zero. The probability that

$$\varepsilon > \frac{\ln X - m}{\sigma\sqrt{T-t}}$$

is the same as the probability that

$$\varepsilon < -\frac{\ln X - m}{\sigma\sqrt{T - t}}$$

Making this transformation gives

$$-X\frac{1}{\sqrt{2\pi}}\int_{\infty}^{(m-\ln X)/(\sigma\sqrt{T-t})} e^{-\varepsilon^2/2}\,d\varepsilon \tag{B3.4}$$

and, since we are in a risk-neutral world we also know that S follows the process

$$dF = \sigma F\,dz \tag{B3.5}$$

To find the parameters for $\ln F$, let

$$y = \ln F \tag{B3.6}$$

Apply Ito's lemma:

$$dy = \frac{1}{F}\,dF - \frac{1}{2F^2}\,dF^2$$

$$dy = \frac{1}{F}\sigma F\,dz - \frac{1}{2F^2}\sigma^2 F^2\,dt$$

$$dy = \left(-\sigma^2/2\right)dt + \sigma\,dz \tag{B3.7}$$

Integrate equation (B3.7)

$$y_T = y_t + \left(-\sigma^2/2\right)(T - t) + \sigma\varepsilon\sqrt{T - t} \tag{B3.8}$$

The mean of the $\ln F$ is $y_t + (-\sigma^2/2)(T - t)$ and the variance is $\sigma^2(T - t)$. Thus equation (B3.3) is evaluated at

$$d_2 = \frac{\ln(F_t/X) + \left(-\sigma^2/2\right)(T - t)}{\sigma\sqrt{T - t}} \tag{B3.9}$$

To evaluate the first integral on the RHS of equation (B3.2) we proceed as before. Let

$$\varepsilon = \frac{\ln F_T - m}{\sigma\sqrt{T - t}}$$

and make the change of variable, knowing that

$$\frac{d\varepsilon}{dF_T} = \frac{1}{F_T\sigma\sqrt{T - t}}$$

This gives

$$\frac{1}{\sqrt{2\pi}}\int_{(\ln X - m)/(\sigma\sqrt{T-t})}^{\infty} F_T\,e^{-\varepsilon^2/2}\,d\varepsilon \tag{B3.10}$$

Substituting equation (B3.8) into F_T gives

$$\frac{1}{\sqrt{2\pi}} F_t e^{(-\sigma^2/2)(T-t)} \int_{(\ln X - m)/(\sigma\sqrt{T-t})}^{\infty} e^{\sigma\varepsilon\sqrt{T-t}} e^{-\varepsilon^2/2} \, d\varepsilon \qquad \text{(B3.11)}$$

Add

$$\frac{\sigma^2(T-t)}{2} - \frac{\sigma^2(T-t)}{2}$$

to the exponents in the integral to complete the square. This gives

$$\frac{1}{\sqrt{2\pi}} F_t e^{(-\sigma^2/2)(T-t)+(\sigma^2/2)(T-t)} \int_{(\ln X - m)/(\sigma\sqrt{T-t})}^{\infty} e^{-1/2\left(\varepsilon^2 - 2\sigma\varepsilon\sqrt{T-t}+\sigma^2(T-t)\right)^2} \, d\varepsilon$$

$$\text{(B3.12)}$$

Make the change of variables $\omega = \varepsilon - \sigma\sqrt{T-t}$

$$\frac{1}{\sqrt{2\pi}} F_t \int_{(\ln X - m)/(\sigma\sqrt{T-t})-\sigma\sqrt{T-t}}^{\infty} e^{-\omega^2/2} \, d\omega \qquad \text{(B3.13)}$$

Substituting the value for m and translating from the right of the cut-off point to the left gives

$$\frac{1}{\sqrt{2\pi}} F_t \int_{-\infty}^{d_1} e^{-\omega^2/2} \, d\omega \qquad \text{(B3.14)}$$

where

$$d_1 = \frac{\ln\dfrac{F_t}{X} + \dfrac{\sigma^2}{2}(T-t)}{\sigma\sqrt{T-t}} \qquad \text{(B3.15)}$$

Substituting equations (B3.4), (B3.9), (B3.14), and (B3.15) into equation (B3.2) gives the solution in the text:

$$C = e^{-r(T-t)}[F_t N(d_1) - X N(d_2)] \qquad \text{(B3.16)}$$

where

$N(d) = $ the value of the cumulative normal distribution evaluated at d

$$d_1 = \frac{\ln(F_t/X) + \sigma^2/2(T-t)}{\sigma\sqrt{T-t}}$$

$$d_2 = \frac{\ln(F_t/X) - \sigma^2/2(T-t)}{\sigma\sqrt{T-t}} = d_1 - \sigma\sqrt{T-t}$$

4
Exotic options and other over-the-counter products

4.1 FORWARDS AND SWAPS

4.1.1 Forward Contracts

In Chapters 1 and 2 we saw that a forward contract is very similar to a futures contract. It is an agreement to buy or sell an asset at a certain future time for a certain future price. Forward contracts are traded in the OTC market and usually involve a financial institution on one side of the deal and either a client or another financial institution on the other side of the deal. One party to the deal takes a long position and agrees to purchase the asset. The other party takes the short position and agrees to sell the asset. The agreed price in the forward contract is called the delivery price, which is chosen so that the value of the contract to both sides at the outset is equal to zero. Like a futures contract, it costs nothing to enter into a forward agreement. A forward contract differs from a futures contract in that it is made to order. Dates and amounts can be chosen to correspond perfectly to the purchaser's needs. In spite of these minor differences, forward and futures contracts are very similar and generally serve the same purpose.

4.1.2 Commodity Swaps

A swap is an agreement between two institutions to exchange cash flows in the future. The agreement specifies the dates when the cash flows are to be paid and the way that they are to be calculated. A forward contract is a simple example of a swap. Whereas a forward contract leads to the exchange of cash flows on only one future date, swaps typically involve exchanges of cash flows on several future dates.

Commodity swaps are direct descendants of the interest rate swaps that grew up in the early 1980s. In an interest rate swap one party agrees to pay the other a fixed interest rate on a given notional amount at certain specified dates while the other party agrees to pay the first party a floating interest rate, LIBOR, for example, on the same notional amount at the same specified dates. In a commodity swap, one party agrees to pay the other a fixed price for a given quantity of a commodity at certain specified dates in the future while the other party agrees to pay the first party a variable price, the ongoing spot price or the futures price, for example, for the same quantity of the commodity on the same specified dates. An example would be an airline company that consumes 20,000 tons of kerosene per month hedging against a price rise by making a deal with the bank whereby it agrees to pay the bank $200 per ton on the first day of every month for the next 12 months. In return the bank agrees to pay the company the price recorded on the Rotterdam spot market on the last working day of the preceding month. Thus, on the first of every month, the company owes $200 × 20,000 tons = $4,000,000. The bank's liability will depend on the spot price. Suppose that on the last working day of the first month the spot price on the Rotterdam market is $225. The bank will owe $225 × 20,000 tons = $4,500,000. The bank will pay the company the difference between the two liabilities: $4,500,000 − $4,000,000 = $500,000. If on the last working day of the second month, the Rotterdam spot price is $195, the company must pay the bank ($200 − $195) × 20,000 tons = $100,000. No kerosene changes hands. The company obtains its kerosene on the Rotterdam market where its effective price is always $200 no matter what the spot price of the moment happens to be.

A swap can also be used to hedge against a price fall. An example would be a small oil producer with 5,000 barrels of oil per month hedging by making a deal with the bank whereby it agrees to pay the bank on the first working day of every month for the next 24 months the spot price on the last working day of the preceding month reported by Platt's for Brent crude. In return the bank agrees to pay the company $25 per barrel for 5,000 barrels on the first working day of every month. Thus on the first working day of the month the company would receive ($25 − S) × 5,000. If the spot price were $20, it would receive ($25 − $20) × 5,000 = $25,000. Its total income from the oil plus the contract would be $20 × 5,000 + $25,000 = $125,000. If the spot price rises to $30 per barrel in the next month, its total income would still be $125,000. It would receive $150,000 from the sale of the oil on the spot market, but would have to pay the bank $25,000 on the difference between the fixed price and the flexible price.

Commodity swaps started off with petroleum products but have since branched out into most commodities including gas, precious metals, non-ferrous metals, and the soft commodities. They are especially effective for commodities such as kerosene that do not have a functioning futures market. Although cross hedging is possible (see Chapter 2), this type of hedge is risky because the price correlations with the hedging instruments are not necessarily stable. In many cases it might be preferable to enter into a swap agreement to avoid the spread risk in a cross hedge or the volatility of the spot price in spite of the often costly nature of a swap.

Swaps can be arranged for any commodity that has a reliable reference price. These prices can be futures prices or spot prices reported by a reliable specialist organisation such as Platt's. Professionals prefer futures prices on the organised exchanges because they are public and cannot be manipulated. Furthermore, the futures markets offer the hedging instrument that the floating price payer can use to offset his risk.

4.2 CAPS

A cap is an option offered by financial institutions in the OTC market that permits hedging against a rise in the commodity price. It is designed to provide insurance against the price of the underlying commodity rising above a certain level, known as the *cap* price. It is similar to a swap in that it concerns a series of cash flows. In the swap, the floating price was reset periodically according to a predefined formula. The time between resets is called the *tenor*. The tenor could be monthly, quarterly, bi-annually, etc. If, for example, the tenor is monthly as in the swap examples above, the floating price will be reset every month. The cap differs from the swap in that a payment will be made only if the floating price rises above the cap price.

Let us go back to the airline company that consumes 20,000 tons of kerosene per month. Rather than a swap to hedge against the price rise, the company could purchase a cap with the same reset conditions. The cap price would be $200 per ton. The tenor would be one month. On the first day of every month for the next 12 months, the company would compare the floating price, defined as the price recorded on the Rotterdam spot market on the last working day of the preceding month, with the cap price. If it is lower than the cap price, the option would not be exercised and the company would pay the spot rate for its 20,000 tons of kerosene. If, however, the Rotterdam spot price is higher than the cap price, the company will exercise the option and receive the difference between the two prices times the 20,000 ton size of the contract. Suppose, for example, that on the last working day of the first month the spot price on the Rotterdam market is $225. The bank will pay the company ($225 − $200) × 20,000 tons = $500,000. In our example the contract lasts for 12 months. Therefore there are 12 reset dates.

4.2.1 The Cap as a Series of Call Options

It is clear from the foregoing example that the cap is a contract composed of a series of call options, where X is the cap price, S_t the price of the underlying commodity at time t, Q the amount of the contract, and F_{t,T_i} the forward price of S at time t on a contract with maturity T_i. Each individual option is called a *caplet*. On the exercise dates $T_1, T_2 \ldots T_n$ the payoff will be

$$Q \max(S_{T_i} - X, 0); \quad i = 1, 2 \ldots n \tag{4.1}$$

To value each caplet we assume risk neutrality so that $E(S_{T_i}) = F_{t,T_i}$ and that S_{T_i} has a lognormal distribution.

$$C_t^i = Q e^{-r(T_i - t)} E \max(S_{T_i} - X, 0) \tag{4.2}$$

We then compute the true expectation (see appendix B, Chapter 3) and make the substitution $E(S_{T_i}) = F_{t,T_i}$. This gives the Black formula

$$C_t^i = Q e^{-r(T_i - t)} [F_{t,T_i} N(d_1) - X N(d_2)] \tag{4.3}$$

where $N(d)$ is the value of the cumulative normal distribution evaluated at d.

$$d_1 = \frac{\ln(F_{t,T_i}/X) + \sigma^2/2(T_i - t)}{\sigma \sqrt{T_i - t}}$$

$$d_2 = \frac{\ln(F_{t,T_i}/X) - \sigma^2/2(T_i - t)}{\sigma \sqrt{T_i - t}} = d_1 - \sigma \sqrt{T_i - t}$$

The total value of the cap is

$$\text{cap} = \sum_{i=1}^{n} C_t^i \tag{4.4}$$

Consider the aviation company consuming 20,000 tons of kerosene per month that purchases a cap for the next three months with the following characteristics:

X = \$200 per ton
S_0 = the current Rotterdam spot price = \$200.
Q = the amount of the contract = 20,000 tons.
r = 5%
σ = 20%
c = the convenience yield = 3%
k = proportional storage costs = 3%

There will be three resets: at the end of month 1, the end of month 2, the end of month 3. We calculate the futures price as[1]

$$F_{0,1/12} = \$200 \, e^{0.05 \times 1/12} = \$200.835$$

---

[1] The equation is given as $F_t^T = S_t e^{(r+k-c)(T-t)}$. Since the convenience yield is equal to the proportional storage cost, it reduces to $F_t^T = S_t e^{r(T-t)}$.

$$F_{0,1/6} = \$200\,e^{0.05 \times 2/12} = \$201.674$$

$$F_{0,1/4} = \$200\,e^{0.05 \times 3/12} = \$202.516$$

Using this information in equation (4.3) gives

$$C_0^1 = 20{,}000 \times \$4.9925 = \$99{,}850$$

$$C_0^2 = 20{,}000 \times \$7.2756 = \$145{,}512$$

$$C_0^3 = 20{,}000 \times \$9.1761 = \$183{,}522$$

From equation (4.4), the value of the cap is

$$\mathrm{cap} = \sum_{i=1}^{3} C_t^i = \$428{,}884$$

At the current price of kerosene, 60,000 tons is worth $12,000,000. Thus, the premium represents 3.574% of the current value of 60,000 tons of kerosene.

4.3 FLOORS

A floor is similar to a cap except that it is designed to provide insurance against the price of the underlying commodity falling below a certain level, known as the *floor price*.

Let us go back to the small oil producer of 5,000 barrels of oil per month. Instead of the swap he could purchase a comparable floor from his bank. If the spot price on the last working day of the preceding month reported by Platt's for Brent crude is above the floor price of $25 per barrel, the option expires worthless. If it is below the floor price, the company exercises the option and receives the difference between the two prices multiplied by 5,000 barrels.

Thus, the floor is equivalent to a series of put options, called *floorlets*. Using the same assumptions and notation as above, each floorlet can be valued with the following equation:

$$p_t^i = Q\,e^{-r(T_i - t)}[XN(-d_2) - F_{t,T_i}N(-d_1)] \tag{4.5}$$

where d_1 and d_2 are defined above.

The value of the floor is

$$\mathrm{floor} = \sum_{i=1}^{n} p_t^i \tag{4.6}$$

Suppose, for example that the company purchases a floor for the next three months with the following characteristics:

X = \$25 per barrel
S_0 = the current spot price = \$25.
Q = the amount of the contract = 5,000 barrels
r = 5%
σ = 20%
c = the convenience yield = 3%
k = proportional storage costs = 3%

There will be three resets: at the end of month 1, the end of month 2, the end of month 3. From equation (2.9), we calculate the futures price as[2]

$$F_{0,1/12} = \$25\,e^{0.05 \times 1/12} = \$25.104$$

$$F_{0,1/6} = \$25\,e^{0.05 \times 2/12} = \$25.209$$

$$F_{0,1/4} = \$25\,e^{0.05 \times 3/12} = \$25.314$$

Using this information in equation (4.5) gives

$$p_0^1 = 5{,}000 \times \$0.5203 = \$2{,}601$$

$$p_0^2 = 5{,}000 \times \$0.7058 = \$3{,}529$$

$$p_0^3 = 5{,}000 \times \$0.8366 = \$4{,}183$$

From equation (4.6) the value of the floor is

$$\text{floor} = \sum_{i=1}^{3} p_t^i = \$10{,}313$$

This represents about 2.75% of the current value of 15,000 barrels of oil.

4.4 COLLARS

A collar is an instrument designed to guarantee that the price of the underlying commodity always lies between two given levels. It is the multi-period equivalent of the tunnel presented in Chapter 3. A collar consists of a long position in the cap and a short position in the floor when hedging against price rises. It consists of a short position in the cap and a long position in the floor when hedging against price falls. A collar is usually constructed so that the price of the cap is initially equal to the price of the floor. In this case the initial cash outlay of entering into the collar is zero. Although there is no cash outlay, the collar is not free. The cost comes in the potential gains that have been surrendered in the option that was sold.

---

[2] See note 1.

Consider the aviation company with 20,000 tons of kerosene consumption per month. It wants to hedge against a rise in the price of kerosene above $225 per ton in three months. It decides to purchase one three-month caplet. The strike price on the caplet is the cap price of $225. The other information is the same as above. Using equation (4.3), the cost of the caplet is calculated as

$$C_t^3 = 20{,}000 \times e^{-0.05 \times 3/12}[\$202.516 \times N(d_1) - \$225 \times N(d_2)] = \$31{,}047.47$$

In order to offset the initial outlay on the caplet, the company sells the bank a floorlet with the same maturity and a strike price of $183.244. Using equation (4.5), the price of the floorlet is calculated as

$$p_t^i = 20{,}000 \times e^{-0.05 \times 3/12}[183.244 \times N(-d_2) - \$202.516 \times N(-d_1)]$$
$$= \$31{,}045.47$$

a negligible difference of $2. Thus, the most the company can pay is $225. If the price rises above $225 the option will be exercised and the company receives the difference between the two. The least the company can pay is $183.244. If it falls below 183.244, the option will be exercised and the company will pay the difference. Between the two strike prices the company will pay the ongoing market price.

4.5 SWAPTIONS

European options on swaps or *swaptions* are another increasingly popular innovation in the commodities markets borrowed from interest rate derivatives. They give the holder the right to enter into a swap at a given time in the future. If it is a call swaption, the holder acquires the right to pay the fixed price. In a put swaption the holder acquires the right to pay the floating price.

Consider a manufacturer bidding on a long-term supply contract. The contract is to begin in six months and last for three years. If it is signed, it will generate the need for 20,000 tons of aluminum per quarter. The current price is $1,500 per ton and the company feels that it can make a competitive bid based on this price. However, if the price rises much above $1,500, the contract will become unprofitable. The company could organize a deferred swap (a swap that begins on a future date) with its bank, but if it is not successful in its bid, the swap will not be needed. Furthermore, the price of aluminum might also fall. If it does, the company would like to take advantage of the lower price. Thus, it decides to purchase a call option on a swap on 20,000 tons of aluminum per quarter with the fixed price equal to $1,500. If the price of aluminum has risen in six months' time, the company will exercise the option and enter into the swap with the fixed price equal to $1,500. If, however, the price has fallen, the option will not be exercised and the company can negotiate a swap based on the improved market conditions.

4.5.1 Valuation of Swaptions

The swap price for a given maturity at a given time is the fixed price that would be exchanged for the floating price in a newly issued swap. Consider a swaption where we have the right to pay X and receive S on a swap that will last n years beginning in T_0 years. There are m resets per year and the amount of the swap is Q. On the exercise date at time T_0, the contracted swap price X will be compared with the swap price that could be obtained on a similar swap initiated at that time. If it is higher than X, the option will be exercised and the holder obtains a swap with the rate equal to X. If it is lower than X, the option will expire worthless and the holder will negotiate the swap at the lower swap price. Thus, the holder of the swaption owns a series of options where the payoff is calculated from the value of the variable at time T, but where the payoff is made at a later date determined by the reset dates. Let T_0 represent the date on which the payoff is calculated, $T_1, T_2 \ldots T_{mn}$ the other dates on which the payments are made (a payment may or may not be made at T_0) and X_{T_0} the swap price on the date when the payoff is calculated. The expected payoff from each call is discounted from T_i rather than T_0 and each call can be evaluated as

$$C_t^i = Q e^{-r(T_i - t)} E \max(X_{T_0} - X, 0) \tag{4.7}$$

Substituting the futures price at time t for delivery at time T_0 for $E(X_{T_0})$, $F_{t,T_0} = E(X_{T_0})$, equation (4.3) becomes

$$C_t^i = Q e^{-r(T_i - t)} [F_{t,T_0} N(d_1) - X N(d_2)] \tag{4.8}$$

$$d_1 = \frac{\ln(F_{t,T_0}/X) + \sigma^2/2(T_0 - t)}{\sigma \sqrt{T_0 - t}}$$

$$d_2 = \frac{\ln(F_{t,T_0}/X) - \sigma^2/2(T_0 - t)}{\sigma \sqrt{T_0 - t}} = d_1 - \sigma \sqrt{T_0 - t}$$

The total value of the call swaption is

$$\sum_{i=0}^{mn} C_t^i = Q[F_{t,T_0} N(d_1) - X N(d_2)] \sum_{T_i=T_0}^{T_{mn}} e^{-r(T_i - t)} \tag{4.9}$$

As an example, we can go back to the aviation company consuming 20,000 tons of kerosene per month that purchases a call swaption with a maturity date of one year. The swap involves payouts on the first day of months 14, 15, and 16 (there is no payout at T_0 = the first day of month 13). The yield curve is flat at the continuously compounded rate of 5%. The other pertinent information is as follows:

X = \$200 per ton
S_0 = the current Rotterdam spot price = \$200

Q = the amount of the contract = 20,000 tons
σ = 20%
$F_{0,1}$ = \$210.25
c = the convenience yield = 3%
k = proportional storage costs = 3%.

From equation (4.9) the total value of the call swaption is

$$\sum_{i=1}^{3} C_0^i = 20,000 \times \$21.97 \times \sum_{T_i=1.0833}^{1.25} e^{-0.05 \times T_i} = \$1,243,600$$

The equivalent price of a put swaption (the right to receive the fixed price) can be calculated in the same way. The value of each put is

$$p_t^i = Q e^{-r(T_i-t)}[XN(-d_2) - F_{t,T_0}N(-d_1)] \tag{4.10}$$

and the total value of the put swaption is

$$\sum_{i=0}^{mn} p_t^i = Q[XN(-d_2) - F_{t,T_0}N(-d_1)] \sum_{T_i=T_0}^{T_{mn}} e^{-r(T_i-t)} \tag{4.11}$$

Consider the producer of 5,000 barrels of oil per month. Suppose that he purchases a put swaption on his output with a maturity date of one year. The swap involves payouts on the first day of months 14, 15, and 16 (there is no payout at T_0 = the first day of month 13). The yield curve is flat at the continuously compounded rate of 5%. The other pertinent information is as follows:

X = \$25 per barrel
S_0 = the current spot price = \$25
Q = the amount of the contract = 5,000 barrels
$F_{0,1}$ = \$26.28
σ = 20%
c = the convenience yield = 3%
k = proportional storage costs = 3%.

From equation (4.11) the value of the put swaption is

$$\sum_{i=1}^{3} p_0^i = 5,000 \times \$1.46545 \times \sum_{T_i=1.08333}^{1.25} e^{-0.05 \times T_i} = \$14,151.58$$

4.6 EXOTIC OPTIONS

Exotic options, sometimes referred to as second-generation options, can generally be defined as standard options modified in one way or another to serve a special purpose or specific client need. There are many kinds of exotic options. Some are path dependent, such as Asian options, barrier options, lookback options, and forward start options. Others depend on correlations with other assets such as spread options, exchange options, quanto options, and basket options, to mention only a few.[3] Besides these, we have binary options, compound options, chooser options, power options, rainbow options, and many others. In this section we will look at some of the exotic options that are most pertinent to the commodity markets and show how they can be priced.

We will also make use of a more general expression of the Black–Scholes pricing formulas than we have used up to now. These formulas can refer to the spot price or the futures price of an underlying asset and include the possibility of continuous proportional payouts such as dividends on stocks or interest on foreign currency over the life of the option:

$$C = S_t e^{-\delta(T-t)} N(d_1) - X e^{-r(T-t)} N(d_2) \qquad (4.12)$$

and

$$p = X e^{-r(T-t)} N(-d_2) - S_t e^{-\delta(T-t)} N(-d_1) \qquad (4.13)$$

where δ represents the payout rate,

$$d_1 = \frac{\ln \dfrac{S_t}{X} + \left(r - \delta + \dfrac{\sigma^2}{2}\right)(T-t)}{\sigma\sqrt{T-t}}$$

$$d_2 = \frac{\ln \dfrac{S_t}{X} + \left(r - \delta - \dfrac{\sigma^2}{2}\right)(T-t)}{\sigma\sqrt{T-t}}$$

and the risk-neutral process followed by the underlying asset is

$$dS = (r - \delta)S\,dt + \sigma S\,dz \qquad (4.14)$$

We can see that if we let $\delta = r$, we obtain the formulas for the values of options on futures contracts presented in equations (3.25) and (3.26). If $\delta = 0$, we get the original Black–Scholes formulas for European options on assets with no payouts. If we let δ equal the interest rate on the foreign currency we get the Garman and Kolhagen (1983) formulas for the value of a foreign currency option. In Appendix A4 we show how to derive the call formula in equation (4.12) using risk-neutral valuation.

---

[3] Although most exotic options are the exclusive preserve of the OTC market, some are popular enough to trade on the exchanges. The American Stock Exchange, for example, trades quantos and the Chicago Mercantile Exchange trades spread options.

4.6.1 Spread Options

Spread options are options written on the difference between two indices, prices, or rates. Where commodities are concerned, for example, one popular spread option is the spread between refined and crude oil prices. It can be used by oil refiners to hedge their risks on gross profits. To hedge against the spread falling and thereby squeezing profits, the refiner could purchase puts. Alternatively, to hedge against missing out on a rise in the spread the refiner could purchase calls.

Given that some spreads can take negative as well as positive values, pricing spread options can be complicated. When the spread is liable to take on negative as well as positive values, Monte Carlo simulations or numerical methods are often used to price the spread option. However, when the spread is always positive, such as the spread on the difference between refined and crude oil prices, it is reasonable to assume that it is lognormal at the option's maturity. If this is the case, the spread can be considered as an individual asset price, albeit an imaginary one, and equations (4.12) and (4.13) can be used to evaluate the option's value. This method for valuing spread options is called the one factor model.[4]

4.6.2 Asian Options

Asian options, also called average-price or average-rate options, are options whose payoff depends on the average price of an asset, an index or rate calculated over a predetermined part of the option's life. Since an average price is generally less volatile than the price itself, Asian options are generally cheaper than corresponding vanilla options.[5] Consequently, they offer reasonably priced hedging instruments adapted to periodic cash flows resulting from purchases or sales of commodities. Airlines and refiners, for example, make regular purchases of fuel and crude oil over the year and are likely to be interested in insuring that the average cost of their inputs is below some level. An Asian call option can achieve this more cheaply and effectively than a series of vanilla call options on each cash flow.

There are basically two types of Asian options, the average price option and the average strike option. For the average price option the strike price is fixed and the payoff depends on the average price of the underlying instrument. Payoffs for average price options are $\max(S_{ave} - X, 0)$ for a call and $\max(X - S_{ave}, 0)$

---

[4] The one factor model cannot be used when the spread can become negative. It also has two other limitations. First the correlation between the two assets does not play an explicit role in the formula. Second, the volatilities of the two assets do not play an explicit role in the formula, thereby making it difficult to estimate the sensitivity of the option price with respect to the individual volatilities. To overcome these shortcomings, two factor models have been developed that use numerical methods for their solution.

[5] Because the payoff depends on an average, these options are less susceptible to possible spot price manipulation on the settlement date as well.

for a put. For the average strike option, the strike price is determined by the average price of the underlying asset. Payoffs for average strike options are $\max(S_T - S_{ave}, 0)$ for a call and $\max(S_{ave} - S_T, 0)$ for a put. Average strike calls can be used to guarantee that over a given time period the average price paid for an asset in frequent trading is not greater than the final price. Average strike puts can be used to guarantee that over a given time period the average price received for an asset in frequent trading is not less than the final price.

Kemna and Vorst (1990) have developed a pricing formula for average price options when the underlying asset is lognormally distributed and the average price in question is a geometric average. The key to the solution is that a geometric average of a set of lognormally distributed variables is also lognormally distributed. In a risk-neutral world, the probability distribution of the geometric average over a predetermined time period is the same as the distribution of the stock price at the end of the period with a growth rate equal to $1/2(r - \delta - \sigma^2/6)$ and volatility equal to $\sigma/\sqrt{3}$. Thus, average price options can be valued using equations (4.12) and (4.13) with $(r - \delta)$ and σ replaced by $1/2(r - \delta - \sigma^2/6)$ and $\sigma/\sqrt{3}$ respectively. This gives[6]

$$C = S_t e^{-(r+\delta+\sigma^2/6)(T-t)/2} N(d_{1A}) - X e^{-r(T-t)} N(d_{2A}) \qquad (4.15)$$

and

$$p = X e^{-r(T-t)} N(-d_{2A}) - S_t e^{-(r+\delta+\sigma^2/6)(T-t)/2} N(-d_{1A}) \qquad (4.16)$$

where

$$d_{1A} = \frac{\ln \frac{S_t}{X} + \left(r - \delta + \frac{\sigma^2}{6}\right)\frac{(T-t)}{2}}{\sigma\sqrt{\frac{T-t}{3}}}$$

$$d_{2A} = \frac{\ln \frac{S_t}{X} + \left(r - \delta - \frac{\sigma^2}{2}\right)\frac{(T-t)}{2}}{\sigma\sqrt{\frac{T-t}{3}}}$$

In fact, most Asian options are on arithmetic rather than geometric averages. There are no analytical pricing formulas for arithmetic averages because the distribution of the arithmetic average of a set of lognormal distributions does not have analytically tractable properties. It is, however, approximately lognormal, which makes it possible to generate an approximate analytical solution. One methodology involves calculating the first two moments of the probability distribution of the arithmetic average in a risk-neutral world and then assuming that

---

[6] The dividend payout is equal to $r - 1/2 \left(r - \delta - \sigma^2/6\right) = \left(r + \delta + \sigma^2/6\right)/2$.

the distribution is lognormal.[7] The option can then be priced as an option on a futures contract in equations (3.25) and (3.26). Another methodology involves calculating an approximation coefficient that adjusts for the difference between the arithmetic and geometric means.[8]

For the moment methodology, consider a just issued Asian option with maturity at time T based on the arithmetic average from 0 to T with n observations. The first moment M_1 and the second moment M_2 of the average in a risk-neutral world calculated between time 0 and T are equal to[9]

$$M_1 = \frac{1}{n} \sum_{i=1}^{n} F_{0,T_i} \tag{4.17}$$

and[10]

$$M_2 = \frac{1}{n^2} \left[\sum_{i=1}^{n} F_{0,T_i}^2 \, e^{\sigma_i^2 T_i} + 2 \sum_{i<j} F_{0,T_i} F_{0,T_j} \, e^{\sigma_i^2 T_i} \right] \tag{4.18}$$

The variance of the arithmetic average can thus be approximated as

$$\hat{\sigma}^2 = \frac{1}{T} \ln \frac{M_2}{M_1^2} \tag{4.19}$$

---

[7] See S.M. Turnbull and L.M. Wakeman "A quick algorithm for pricing European average options" *Journal of Financial and Quantitative Analysis*, **26**, (1991), 377–389. In this section we follow Hull (2000), pp. 468–469.

[8] See Zhang (1998), pp. 135–154.

[9] The equivalent moments for continuous sampling are

$$M_1 = \frac{e^{(r-\delta)T} - 1}{(r - \delta)T} S_0$$

and

$$M_2 = \frac{2 \, e^{[2(r-\delta)+\sigma^2]T} S_0^2}{(r - \delta - \sigma^2)(2r - 2\delta + \sigma^2)T^2} + \frac{2 S_0^2}{(r - \delta)T^2} \left[\frac{1}{2(r - \delta) + \sigma^2} - \frac{e^{(r-\delta)T}}{r - \delta + \sigma^2} \right]$$

[10] Remember that

$$V = \sum_{i=1}^{n} S_{T_i}$$

and

$$V^2 = \sum_{i=1}^{n} \sum_{j=1}^{n} S_{T_i} S_{T_j} \cdot E(S_{T_i} S_{T_j}) = F_{0,T_i} F_{0,T_j} \, e^{\rho_{ij} \sigma_i \sigma_j \sqrt{T_i T_j}}.$$

When $i < j$,

$$\rho_{ij} = \sigma_i \sqrt{T_i} / \sigma_j \sqrt{T_j}$$

so that

$$E(S_{T_i} S_{T_j}) = F_{0,T_i} F_{0,T_j} \, e^{\sigma_i^2 T_i}$$

The option can be priced using equations (3.25) and (3.26) where $F_{t,T} = M_1/n$ and $\sigma = \hat{\sigma}$.

As an example, consider the following information:

X = \$25 per barrel
S_0 = the current spot price = \$25.
r = 5%
σ = 20%
c = the convenience yield = 3%
k = proportional storage costs = 3%

The average will be calculated from two observations, one at the end of month 6 and the other at the option's expiry date at the end of month 12. Thus, $T_1 = \frac{1}{2}$ and $T_2 = 1$. From equation (2.9), we calculate the futures price as

$$F_{0,1/2} = \$25\,e^{0.05 \times 1/2} = \$25.63$$

$$F_{0,1} = \$25\,e^{0.05 \times 1} = \$26.28$$

From equation (4.16) we calculate M_1 and M_2 as:

$M_1 = 25.63 + 26.28 = 51.91$

$M_2 = 656.9 \times e^{0.04 \times 1/2} + 690.64 \times e^{0.04} + 2 \times 673.56\,e^{0.04 \times 1/2} = 2749.1$

From equation (4.18) $\hat{\sigma}^2 = \ln 2749.10/2694.65 = 0.02$. Substituting $F_{t,T} = 51.91/2 = 25.96$ and $\sigma = \hat{\sigma} = \sqrt{0.02} = 0.1414$ into equations (3.25) and (3.26) gives $C = 1.864$ and $p = 0.96$. The corresponding prices for the geometric average using equations (4.15) and (4.16) is $C = 1.39$ and $p = 0.87$.

4.6.3 Basket Options

Basket options are written on portfolios or 'baskets' of risky assets. The payoff of a basket option depends on the value of a portfolio of assets. Since the assets are imperfectly correlated, basket options have lower volatility and therefore cost less than straight options. They also make it possible to worry about the forest, so to speak, without worrying about each individual tree. Thus, they are popular with fund managers managing portfolios containing many stocks or company treasurers with cash flows in numerous currencies. They can also be useful for manufacturers and processors that use a wide range of raw materials in their products. Food processors, for example, make regular purchases of a wide range of agricultural products including corn, oats, wheat, barley, soya beans, meat, cocoa, coffee, sugar, orange juice, etc.

Basket options can be priced in a manner similar to the Asian option methodology presented in the preceding paragraph. The methodology involves calculating the first two moments of the probability distribution of the value of the basket at maturity in a risk neutral world and then assuming that the distribution is lognormal. The option can then be priced as an option on a futures contract using equations (3.25) and (3.26).

Let V represent the value of the basket. Then

$$M_1 = \sum_{i=1}^{n} F_i \qquad (4.20)$$

where F_i is the futures price of the ith asset maturing at time T. We also know that

$$V^2 = \sum_{i=1}^{n} \sum_{j=1}^{n} S_i S_j$$

From the properties of the lognormal distribution $E(S_i S_j) = F_i F_j \, e^{\rho_{ij}\sigma_i\sigma_j T}$. Using the relation $\rho_{ij} = \sigma_i\sqrt{T}/\sigma_j\sqrt{T}$, gives

$$M_2 = \sum_{i=1}^{n} F_i^2 \, e^{\sigma_i^2 T} + 2 \sum_{i<j} F_i F_j \, e^{\sigma_i^2 T} \qquad (4.21)$$

Consequently, the variance of the basket can be approximated as

$$\hat{\sigma}^2 = \frac{1}{T} \ln \frac{M_2}{M_1^2} \qquad (4.22)$$

4.6.4 Lookback Options

A lookback option is an option where the payoff depends on the maximum or minimum price of the underlying asset within the life of the option. For a call the payoff is $\max[S_T - S_{\min}, 0]$ and for a put it is $\max[S_{\max} - S_T, 0]$. For competitive purposes, it is often desirable for a manufacturer or a processor to purchase commodity inputs at the lowest price or, for commodity producers, to sell at the highest price. For this reason, the underlying asset in lookback options is often a commodity. Purchasing a lookback call option lets the holder pay the lowest price for the commodity over the life of the option. Purchasing a lookback put option lets the holder sell the commodity at the highest price over the life of the option.

Goldman, *et al.* (1979) developed a lookback pricing formula that Garman (1989) extended to currency options. The price of a European lookback call at time zero is

$$C = S_0 \, e^{-\delta T} N(d_{1LBC}) - S_0 \, e^{-\delta T} \frac{\sigma^2}{2(r-\delta)} N(-d_{1LBC})$$

$$- S_{\min} \, e^{-rT} \left[N(d_{2LBC}) - \frac{\sigma^2}{2(r-\delta)} \, e^{y_{LBC}} N(-d_{3LBC}) \right] \qquad (4.23)$$

where

$$d_{1LBC} = \frac{\ln\left(\frac{S_0}{S_{min}}\right) + \left(r - \delta + \frac{\sigma^2}{2}\right)T}{\sigma\sqrt{T}} \qquad d_{2LBC} = \frac{\ln\left(\frac{S_0}{S_{min}}\right) + \left(r - \delta - \frac{\sigma^2}{2}\right)T}{\sigma\sqrt{T}}$$

$$d_{3LBC} = \frac{\ln\left(\frac{S_0}{S_{min}}\right) + \left(-r + \delta + \frac{\sigma^2}{2}\right)T}{\sigma\sqrt{T}} \qquad y_{LBC} = -\frac{2(r - \delta - \sigma^2/2)\ln(S_0/S_{min})}{\sigma^2}$$

and

$$p = S_{max}\,e^{-rT}\left[N(d_{1LBp}) - \frac{\sigma^2}{2(r - \delta)}\,e^{y_{LBp}}N(-d_{3LBp})\right]$$

$$+ S_0\,e^{-\delta T}\frac{\sigma^2}{2(r - \delta)}N(-d_{2LBp}) - S_0\,e^{-\delta T}N(d_{2LBp}) \qquad (4.24)$$

where

$$d_{1LBp} = \frac{\ln\left(\frac{S_{max}}{S_0}\right) + \left(-r + \delta + \frac{\sigma^2}{2}\right)T}{\sigma\sqrt{T}} \qquad d_{2LBp} = \frac{\ln\left(\frac{S_{max}}{S_0}\right) + \left(-r + \delta - \frac{\sigma^2}{2}\right)T}{\sigma\sqrt{T}}$$

$$d_{3LBp} = \frac{\ln\left(\frac{S_{max}}{S_0}\right) + \left(r - \delta - \frac{\sigma^2}{2}\right)T}{\sigma\sqrt{T}} \qquad y_{LBp} = -\frac{2\left(r - \delta - \sigma^2/2\right)\ln(S_{max}/S_0)}{\sigma^2}$$

The foregoing formulas assume that the asset price is observed continuously. In fact, as with Asian options, the price is sensitive to how frequently the price is observed for computing the maximums and minimums. To account for this, the foregoing formulas can be adjusted to take the observation frequency into consideration.[11]

4.6.5 Binary Options

Binary options, also known as digital options, are options with discontinuous payoffs. In general, the payoff is either a fixed amount of cash (cash or nothing option), an asset (asset or nothing option), or the difference between the price of a given asset and a prespecified level which can be different from the strike price (gap option). Binary options can be useful for hedging ordinary commodity swaps or 'exotic' commodity swaps, which possess knock-in or knock-out properties that depend on whether the price of the underlying commodity exceeds a prespecified level on some prespecified date.

[11] See Broadie et al. (1998).

Cash or Nothing Options   As the name implies, cash or nothing options pay a fixed amount of cash if the price of the underlying ends up above the strike price for a call or below the strike price for a put. If it ends up below the strike price for a call or above the strike price for a put, it pays nothing. From Chapter 3 and Appendix A4 we know that in a risk-neutral world, the probability that the asset price ends up above the strike price is $N(d_2)$. The probability that it ends up below the strike price is $N(-d_2)$. Thus, if the cash amount is equal to Q, the value of a cash or nothing call is $Q\,e^{-r(T-t)}N(d_2)$ and the value of a cash or nothing put is $Q\,e^{-r(T-t)}N(-d_2)$.

Asset or Nothing Options   Asset or nothing options pay an amount of cash equal to the price of the underlying security if the price of the underlying security ends up above the strike price for a call or below the strike price for a put. If it ends up below the strike price for a call or above the strike price for a put, it pays nothing. Again from Chapter 3 and Appendix A4, we know that in a risk-neutral world $N(d_1)$ is the factor by which the present value of contingent receipt of the asset price, contingent on exercise, exceeds the current value of the asset. Thus the value of an asset or nothing call option is equal to $S_t N(d_1)\,e^{-\delta(T-t)}$. For puts the value is $S_t N(-d_1)\,e^{-\delta(T-t)}$.

Gap Options   Gap options pay the difference between an asset price and a prespecified level (the level is different from the strike price), if the asset price is above the strike price for a call and below the strike price for a put. Otherwise it pays nothing. At maturity, the payoff of a gap option is equal to $\max[S_T - G, 0]$, where G is the prespecified level, called the gap parameter. With this in mind it is easy to value a gap option. The factor by which the present value of contingent receipt of the asset price, contingent on exercise, exceeds the current value of the asset is $N(d_1)$, the same as for the asset or nothing option. The probability that the asset price ends up above the strike price is $N(d_2)$, the same as for the cash or nothing option. Putting these two together along with the payoff at maturity gives the value of the call as

$$S_t N(d_1)\,e^{-\delta(T-t)} - G\,e^{-r(T-t)}N(d_2)$$

and the value of the put as

$$G\,e^{-r(T-t)}N(-d_2) - S_t\,e^{-\delta(T-t)}N(-d_1).$$

Comparing these formulas with equations (4.12) and (4.13), we can see that they are the same as those for straight calls and puts with X replaced by G.[12]

---

[12] $N(d_1)$ and $N(d_2)$ are unchanged, i.e. G does not replace X.

Correlation Binary Options   Correlation binary options involve two assets or indices.[13] One is called the measurement instrument and the other is called the payment instrument. In our notation, S is the payment asset and M is the measurement asset. At maturity, the payoff of a European-style correlation binary option is $[S_T - G]$ if $M_T \geq X$ and 0 otherwise. It is obvious that the correlation binary has the same payoff as the ordinary gap option if the measurement instrument is the same as the payment instrument.

Suppose that both S and M follow risk-neutral geometric Brownian motion

$$dS = (r - \delta)S \, dt + \sigma S \, dz \tag{4.25}$$

$$dM = (r - \delta_M)M \, dt + \sigma_M M \, dz_M \tag{4.26}$$

and the correlation between the two processes is $\rho \, dt$. Applying the joint lognormal probabilities to the payoff function and discounting at the riskless rate gives

$$C_{CB} = S_t \, e^{-\delta(T-t)} N_2(d_1, a_1, \rho) - G \, e^{-r(T-t)} N_2(d_2, a_2, \rho) \tag{4.27}$$

where d_1 and d_2 are defined above and

$$a_1 = \frac{\ln \dfrac{M_t}{X} + \left(r - \delta_M + \dfrac{\sigma_M^2}{2}\right)(T-t)}{\sigma_M \sqrt{T-t}} \qquad a_2 = \frac{\ln \dfrac{M_t}{X} + \left(r - \delta_M - \dfrac{\sigma_M^2}{2}\right)(T-t)}{\sigma_M \sqrt{T-t}}$$

This pricing formula in equation (4.27) is very general. As mentioned, if the payoff and measurement instruments are the same, it gives the formula for an ordinary gap option. If $S = M$ and $G = X$, it gives equation (4.12), the formula for an ordinary European call option. If $S = M$ and $G = 0$, it gives the formula for an assets or nothing option. When we let $G = 0$, we get the value of an asset or nothing option where the payoff is the other asset. This is called 'another asset or nothing' option.

4.6.6   Other Popular Exotics

The range of exotic instruments is so vast that anything more than a sketch of the most popular and useful types is outside the scope of this book.[14] Up to now we have tried to present the best known and most widely used instruments. We end this chapter with a brief description of some other popular instruments that could be useful to active participants in the commodities markets.

Forward Start Options   Forward start options become effective some time after they are bought or sold. They start sometime in the future with the strike

---

[13] See Zhang (1998), pp. 410–422 for a complete discussion of correlation binary options.

[14] For an in-depth, comprehensive treatment of exotic options in general, see Zhang (1998).

price set to be the underlying asset price at the time that the option starts. Thus, they begin life at-the-money and the payoff is $\max\lfloor S_T - S_{t_1}, 0\rfloor$ for a call and $\max\lfloor S_{t_1} - S_T, 0\rfloor$ for a put, where t_1 is the time in the future when the option becomes valid. Since they start at-the-money we can substitute S_{t_1} for X in equations (4.28) and (4.29) to get the value of the option at t_1.

$$C_{t_1} = S_{t_1}\, e^{-\delta(T-t_1)}N(d_{1FS}) - S_{t_1}\, e^{-r(T-t_1)}N(d_{2FS}) \qquad (4.28)$$

and

$$P_{t_1} = S_{t_1}\, e^{-r(T-t_1)}N(-d_{2FS}) - S_{t_1}\, e^{-\delta(T-t_1)}N(-d_{1FS}) \qquad (4.29)$$

where δ represents the payout rate and

$$d_{1FS} = \frac{\left(r - \delta + \dfrac{\sigma^2}{2}\right)(T-t_1)}{\sigma\sqrt{T-t_1}} \qquad d_{2FS} = \frac{\left(r - \delta - \dfrac{\sigma^2}{2}\right)(T-t_1)}{\sigma\sqrt{T-t_1}}$$

In a risk-neutral world $E(S_{t_1}) = S_{t_0}\, e^{(r-\delta)t_1}$. The value of the option at t_0 is the present value of the option at t_1 discounted at the riskless rate, $e^{-rt_1}C_{t_1}$. Substituting this information into equations (4.30) and (4.31) gives the price of the start forward as

$$C_{t_0} = S_{t_0}\, e^{-\delta t_1}\left\lfloor e^{-\delta(T-t_1)}N(d_{1FS}) - e^{-r(T-t_1)}N(d_{2FS})\right\rfloor \qquad (4.30)$$

and

$$P_{t_0} = S_{t_0}\, e^{-\delta t_1}\left\lfloor e^{-r(T-t_1)}N(-d_{2FS}) - e^{-\delta(T-t_1)}N(-d_{1FS})\right\rfloor \qquad (4.31)$$

Barrier Options   Barrier options are options where the payoff depends on whether the price of the underlying asset reaches a prespecified level over a given time period. In fact, barrier options are one of the oldest types of exotic options, having traded in the USA as far back as 1967. One advantage of these options is that they are cheaper than corresponding standard calls and puts. Another advantage is that the barriers make it possible for users to restrict their hedging to price ranges that they consider feasible. Thus, risk managers can hedge their exposures without paying for price ranges that they believe are unlikely to occur.

Barrier options can be classified as either knock-out or knock-in. A knock-out option ceases to exist when the price of the underlying asset reaches a barrier. A knock-in option comes into existence when a barrier is reached. The standard knockout option entitles its owner to receive a rebate when a barrier is hit and a European option payout if it is not hit. The standard knock-in option entitles its owner to receive a European option if a barrier is hit and a rebate at expiration, if it is not hit. The price of the option depends on whether the barrier is hit from above or below. Depending on whether the price of the underlying asset is above or below the barrier, there are basically four kinds of barrier options for calls and for puts: down-and-outs, down-and-ins, up-and-outs, and up-and-ins.

Barriers can be added to almost any kind of option. Thus, besides the standard barrier options, there are Asian barriers, forward start barriers, dual barriers, correlation binary barriers, spread barriers, lookback barriers, and so on. The common feature of all these barrier options is that their payoffs depend on whether or not one or more barriers are breached during the life of the option. The diversity of this family of options makes it impossible to go into much detail on pricing formulas.[15] However, to get an idea of how the barriers and rebates can affect the price of the option, we can look at a standard down-and-out barrier European call option with no yield, where R represents the rebate and H represents the barrier with $H < X$.[16]

$$
C_B = S_t N(d_{1B}) - X e^{-r(T-t)} N(d_{2B})
$$

$$
- \left[S_t \left[\frac{S}{H} \right]^{-2\varepsilon} N(d_{3B}) - X e^{-r(T-t)} \left[\frac{S}{H} \right]^{-2\varepsilon+2} N(d_{4B}) \right]
$$

$$
+ R \left[\left[\frac{S}{H} \right]^{-2\varepsilon+1} N(d_{5B}) + \left[\frac{S}{H} \right] N(d_{6B}) \right] \tag{4.32}
$$

where

$$
d_{1B} = \frac{\ln \frac{S_t}{X} + \left(r + \frac{\sigma^2}{2} \right)(T-t)}{\sigma \sqrt{T-t}}
$$

$$
d_{2B} = \frac{\ln \frac{S_t}{X} + \left(r - \frac{\sigma^2}{2} \right)(T-t)}{\sigma \sqrt{T-t}}
\qquad
d_{3B} = \frac{\ln \frac{H^2}{S_t X} + \left(r + \frac{\sigma^2}{2} \right)(T-t)}{\sigma \sqrt{T-t}}
$$

$$
d_{4B} = \frac{\ln \frac{H^2}{S_t X} + \left(r - \frac{\sigma^2}{2} \right)(T-t)}{\sigma \sqrt{T-t}}
\qquad
d_{5B} = \frac{\ln \frac{H}{S_t} + \left(r + \frac{\sigma^2}{2} \right)(T-t)}{\sigma \sqrt{T-t}}
$$

$$
d_{6B} = \frac{\ln \frac{H}{S_t} + \left(r - \frac{\sigma^2}{2} \right)(T-t)}{\sigma \sqrt{T-t}}
\qquad
\varepsilon = \frac{r}{\sigma^2} + \frac{1}{2}
$$

We can see that the down-and-out call has been written as the sum of three terms: (1) the value of a standard European call, (2) minus the reduction in value due to the early cancellation feature of the barrier, (3) plus the value of the rebate.

---

[15] See Zhang (1998), pp. 203–335 for an in-depth treatment of barrier options.
[16] See Cox and Rubenstein (1985), 410–411.

4.7 SUMMARY

Exotic options are standard options modified in one way or another to serve a special purpose or specific client need. Consequently, they are more complicated to price than standard options. There are many kinds of exotic options. In this section we have looked at a relatively small sample: spread options, Asian options, basket options, lookback options, binary options, forward start options, and barrier options. Although the sample is relatively small, it is representative of the exotic options that are the most popular and potentially the most useful for hedging on the commodity markets. Some of the options we have considered can be priced using straightforward extensions of the methods developed in Chapter 3 and Appendix 4A of this chapter. Others can be priced analytically using more complicated formulas and techniques. Finally, others require Monte Carlo simulations or numerical techniques.

BIBLIOGRAPHY

F. Black (1976) The pricing of commodity contracts, *Journal of Financial Economics*, **3**, 167–179.

M. Broadie, P. Glasserman and S. G. Kou (1998) Connecting discrete and continuous path-dependent options, *Finance and Stochastics*, **2**, 1–28.

J. Cox and M. Rubenstein (1985) *Options Markets.* Prentice-Hall, Englewood Cliffs, NJ.

J. Cox, S. Ross and M. Rubenstein (1979) Option pricing: a simplified approach *Journal of Financial Economics*, **7**, 229–264.

M. Garman (1989) Recollection in tranquility, *Risk*, **2**(3), 16–19.

M. Garman and S. Kolhagen (1983) Foreign currency options values, *Journal of International Money and Finance*, **2**, 231–237.

B. Goldman, H. Sosin and M.A. Gatto (1979) Path dependent options: buy at the low, sell at the high, *Journal of Finance*, **34**, 1111–1127.

J. C. Hull (2000) *Options, Futures and Other Derivatives.* Prentice-Hall International, London.

A. Kemna and A. Vorst (1990) A pricing method for options based on average asset values, *Journal of Banking and Finance*, **14**, 113–129.

R. C. Merton (1990) On the mathematics and economic assumptions of continuous time models, in *Continuous Time Finance*. Basil Blackwell, pp. 57–93.

S. N. Neftci (1996) *An Introduction to the Mathematics of Financial Derivatives.* Academic Press, San Diego, CA.

P. J. Zhang (1998) *Exotic Options*, 2nd edn. World Scientific Publishing Co. Pte., Singapore.

APPENDIX 4A

Derivation of the value of the call option on an asset with a continuous yield

In this appendix we derive the expected expiration value of the call option on an asset with a continuous yield. We follow the procedure in Appendix 3B. This involves solving the equation

$$C = e^{-r(T-t)}E[\max(S_T - X, 0)] \tag{A4.1}$$

Going through the steps of setting up a riskless portfolio as in Chapter 3, we know that the return on S is r. It pays a dividend equal to δ so that the risk-neutral growth rate of S is equal to $r - \delta$. Thus the risk-neutral process of the price of S is

$$dS = (r - \delta)S\,dt + \sigma S\,dz \tag{A4.2}$$

We know that S is lognormally distributed. Applying the lognormal distribution to equation (A4.1) gives

$$C = e^{-r(T-t)} \int_{\ln X}^{\infty} \frac{1}{\sqrt{2\pi\sigma^2(T-t)}} \frac{1}{S_T} e^{-(\ln S_T - m)^2/2\sigma^2(T-t)}[S_T - X]\,dS_T$$

$$= e^{-r(T-t)} \left[\frac{1}{\sqrt{2\pi\sigma^2(T-t)}} \int_{\ln X}^{\infty} e^{-(\ln S_T - m)^2/2\sigma^2(T-t)}\,dS_T \right.$$

$$\left. -X\frac{1}{\sqrt{2\pi\sigma^2(T-t)}} \int_{\ln X}^{\infty} \frac{1}{S_T} e^{-(\ln S_T - m)^2/2\sigma^2(T-t)}\,dS_T \right] \tag{A4.3}$$

where m is the mean of $\ln S_T$.

First we evaluate the second interval on the RHS of equation (A4.3). Let

$$\varepsilon = \frac{\ln S_T - m}{\sigma\sqrt{T - t}}$$

and make the change of variable, knowing that

$$\frac{d\varepsilon}{dS_T} = \frac{1}{S_T\sigma\sqrt{T - t}}$$

This gives

$$-X\frac{1}{\sqrt{2\pi}}\int_{\frac{\ln X-m}{\sigma\sqrt{T-t}}}^{\infty} e^{-\varepsilon^2/2}d\varepsilon \tag{A4.4}$$

Equation (A4.4) is X multiplied by the probability that $S_T > X$. This probability can be visualised as the area under the standard normal curve to the right of the cut-off point. As we know, the convention in option pricing is to use areas to the left of the cut-off point. Thus, since the standard normal curve is symmetrical around zero, the probability that

$$\varepsilon > \frac{\ln X - m}{\sigma\sqrt{T-t}}$$

is the same as the probability that

$$\varepsilon < -\frac{\ln X - m}{\sigma\sqrt{T-t}}$$

Making this transformation gives

$$-X\frac{1}{\sqrt{2\pi}}\int_{\infty}^{\frac{m-\ln X}{\sigma\sqrt{T-t}}} e^{-\varepsilon^2/2}d\varepsilon \tag{A4.5}$$

To find the parameters for $\ln S_T$, let

$$y = \ln S_T \tag{A4.6}$$

Apply Ito's lemma to equation (A4.6) and substitute from equation (A4.2)

$$dy = \frac{1}{S_T}dS_T - \frac{1}{2S_T^2}dS_T^2$$

$$dy = \frac{1}{S_T}[(r-\delta)S_T\,dt + S_T\sigma\,dz] - \frac{1}{2S_T^2}\sigma^2 S_T^2\,dt$$

$$dy = \left(r - \delta - \frac{\sigma^2}{2}\right)dt + \sigma\,dz \tag{A4.7}$$

Integrate equation (A4.7)

$$y_T = y_t + \left(r - \delta - \frac{\sigma^2}{2}\right)(T-t) + \sigma\varepsilon\sqrt{T-t} \tag{A4.8}$$

Since $E(dz) = 0$, the mean of $\ln S_T$ is

$$y_t + \left(r - \delta - \frac{\sigma^2}{2}\right)(T-t)$$

and the variance is $\sigma^2(T - t)$. Substituting the mean as

$$\ln S_t + \left(r - \delta - \frac{\sigma^2}{2} \right) (T - t)$$

for m in equation (A4.5) means that equation (A4.5) is evaluated at

$$d_2 = \frac{\ln \dfrac{S_t}{X} + \left(r - \delta - \dfrac{\sigma^2}{2} \right) (T - t)}{\sigma\sqrt{T - t}} \tag{A4.9}$$

which gives

$$-XN(d_2) \tag{A4.10}$$

To evaluate the first integral on the RHS of equation (A4.3) we proceed as before. Let

$$\varepsilon = \frac{\ln S_T - m}{\sigma\sqrt{T - t}}$$

and make the change of variable, knowing that

$$\frac{d\varepsilon}{dS_T} = \frac{1}{S_T \sigma\sqrt{T - t}}$$

This gives

$$\frac{1}{\sqrt{2\pi}} \int_{\frac{\ln X - m}{\sigma\sqrt{T-t}}}^{\infty} S_T \, e^{-\varepsilon^2/2} \, d\varepsilon \tag{A4.11}$$

Substituting from equation (A4.8) for S_T in the first integral on the RHS of equation (A4.3) gives

$$\frac{1}{\sqrt{2\pi}} S_t \, e^{(r-\delta-(\sigma^2/2))(T-t)} \int_{\frac{\ln X - m}{\sigma\sqrt{T-t}}}^{\infty} e^{\sigma\varepsilon\sqrt{T-t}} \, e^{-\varepsilon^2/2} \, d\varepsilon \tag{A4.12}$$

Add

$$\frac{\sigma^2(T - t)}{2} - \frac{\sigma^2(T - t)}{2}$$

to the exponents in the integral to complete the square.
This gives

$$\frac{1}{\sqrt{2\pi}} S_t \, e^{(r-\delta-(\sigma^2/2))(T-t)+(\sigma^2/2)(T-t)} \int_{\frac{\ln X - m}{\sigma\sqrt{T-t}}}^{\infty} e^{-(1/2)(\varepsilon^2 - 2\sigma\varepsilon\sqrt{T-t}+\sigma^2(T-t))^2} \, d\varepsilon$$

$$\tag{A4.13}$$

Make the change of variables $\omega = \varepsilon - \sigma\sqrt{T - t}$

$$\frac{1}{\sqrt{2\pi}} S_t e^{(r-\delta)(T-t)} \int_{\frac{\ln X - m}{\sigma\sqrt{T-t}} - \sigma\sqrt{T-t}}^{\infty} e^{-\omega^2/2} \, d\omega \qquad (A4.14)$$

Substituting the value for m and translating from the right of the cut-off point to the left gives

$$\frac{1}{\sqrt{2\pi}} S_t e^{(r-\delta)(T-t)} \int_{-\infty}^{d_1} e^{-\frac{\omega^2}{2}} \, d\omega \qquad (A4.15)$$

where

$$d_1 = \frac{\ln\frac{S_t}{X} + \left(r - \delta + \frac{\sigma^2}{2}\right)(T - t)}{\sigma\sqrt{T - t}} \qquad (A4.16)$$

Thus the first integral on the RHS of equation (A4.3) is equal to

$$S_t e^{(r-\delta)(T-t)} N(d_1) \qquad (A4.17)$$

$$C = S_t e^{-\delta(T-t)} N(d_1) - X e^{-r(T-t)} N(d_2) \qquad (A4.18)$$

5
International commodity markets: the management of information

5.1 MANAGING COMMODITY MARKET INFORMATION: AN INTRODUCTION

Chapters 1–4 have been devoted to the description and the theoretical analysis of commodity markets, including spot and derivative markets. An important concern from the practical point of view, especially from the point of view of practitioners working on commodity markets for producers, trading companies, and industrial end-users as well as for various financial intermediaries, is *managing information* concerning these markets. Information concerning commodity markets comes in many different forms from many different sources. It can be in the form of a telephone conversation between a trader and his/her client. It can be a computer screen with a graph of historical spot prices. It can be an article in an economic or financial journal, or it can be a database about past prices, demand, supply, and inventory data available to a corporate economist.

Some information can be used immediately. A marketing manager who is receiving an order from a client for 10,000 oz of refined silver will immediately check the available information about spot prices and futures prices. He/she will just get an idea about the price that can be quoted and proposed to the client. As we will see later in this chapter, different information is needed to address different corporate objectives and activities.

Thus, information gathering is not an end in itself. It is gathered to be used and in order to be used it must be processed. The next problem that arises, then, is processing market information. Of course, some information can be processed informally by the executive or the trader who needs it for an immediate decision. More generally, however, given the variability of prices, various people in companies have to *forecast* market information. Forecasting can be carried out at various time horizons corresponding to different needs. The day trader on an organised market or the trader wanting to hedge a physical position immediately might be interested in the very short term of a few days or even less. The short term (anything less than a few months) is the time horizon of the physical trader who concludes a forward contract for delivery between one month and three months ahead. Executive officers in charge of investments or of long-term corporate policy are interested in the medium term to long term (one year or more). As we will see, different time horizons require different forecasting methods.

This chapter will therefore be organised as follows. In the next section, we will discuss information concerning commodity markets. Our discussion will involve the various market variables and parameters that are useful to various commodity market operators. It will also be concerned with the various forms of information that address these needs as well as with the main principles of its management. The third section will analyse the main approaches to forecasting commodity markets at different time horizons. It will also discuss the economic principles that are useful in these forecasting exercises. The fourth section presents the specific problems of price forecasting.

5.2 COMMODITY MARKET INFORMATION AND ITS MANAGEMENT

5.2.1 Various Types of Information for Various Purposes

The management of information is a key element of forecasting and decision-making with regard to commodity markets. There are, of course, some basic pieces of generally available commodity market information that may be of interest to a large number of decision-makers in a company. There are also various corporate concerns and objectives that require distinct and more specialised information.

Marketing or selling its products is, of course, the firm's essential activity. In the case of producers and trading companies, the volatility of commodity prices makes quoting a fixed price to a potential client a difficult and risky exercise. Whatever the level of current prices, trading companies must be able to buy commodities and resell them at a higher price, usually with a narrow profit margin. This implies accurate and up-to-date information, day-to-day, and even minute-to-minute, on current spot prices. It also requires accurate information on futures prices because quoting a forward price to a client implies immediate hedging on a futures market. For producers and industrial end-users of commodities, the situation is similar. Their profit margins depend on the prices at which they sell, in the case of producers, or purchase, in the case of end-users.

In all these cases, reliable, short-term information on spot and futures market prices must be available to the company. It has to be constantly monitored and updated every day, even every hour and every minute of the day, usually through online databases sold by data vendors and available on computer screens in market rooms and/or in marketing or purchasing departments. Short-term news on supply and demand and other short-term news about commodity markets are also of interest and should be made available to commodity market operators.

Adequate information on commodity markets is an essential element for the analysts, investors, shareholders, and other stakeholders of firms active on the commodity markets. This information involves all aspects of the markets and is usually processed to allow for forecasting and scenario building that can range from a horizon of a few days to several years. The relevant information is available from many sources, the most important of which will be presented below. Processing and forecasting is handled by the services of corporate economists and other specialised agencies and consultants.

5.2.2 Different Sources of Information

There are several kinds of information. First, *private information* is specific to a firm and confidential. This is the case for much, if not all, of the information involving a firm's commercial transactions. The contents of the commercial contracts that the firm has concluded, including prices, the level of its commodity stocks and of the detail of the quantities supplied and purchased are usually confidential data. Other private information concerns capital and investment operations planned by a company, including take-overs. However, the company's outstanding positions on futures and derivatives markets are usually disclosed in the case of quoted companies with an indication of what fraction of physical positions has been hedged. This information is important for shareholders for assessing the risk level of company stocks.

Public information is either free or available at a price. The usual case is information sold by specialised data vendors or data suppliers. Data suppliers are companies that supply data at a price, often a very high price, but they are quite useful and even indispensable in the practice of trading and commercial activities involving commodities. Many of these data vendors are recognised as supplying 'fair' prices, which are used as reference prices in commercial contracts. This is the case, for instance, of Platt's, who supplies reliable spot market data for oil and refined oil products.

There are many data vendors that supply short-term products suitable for commodity trading, whether on physical or on derivative markets. These data vendors usually offer online and real-time data on commodity markets and indexes with suitable charts giving the evolution of prices over various periods of time from anywhere between one day and several years. Most of these data vendors also supply data on financial and foreign exchange markets as well as real-time market news and analyses. Charts may be processed using simple statistical and mathematical methods, such as moving averages.

Reuters, a British company specialised since its inception[1] in the supply of real time financial data, is one of the most important of these data vendors. As far as commodities are concerned, Reuters supplies online and real-time data and charts on both physical and derivative markets for a large number of commodities, including energy, metal, and agricultural commodities. It also publishes news concerning all these markets. Bloomberg, an American company, is another vendor that supplies similar services. Some information and access to databanks for subscribers are provided on the web sites of these data suppliers, which are respectively *www.reuters.com* and *www.bloomberg.com*. The Bridge Commodity Research Bureau (Bridge/CRB) is more specialised in commodities and in forecasting. It also publishes one of the most important commodity indexes, the Bridge/CRB commodity index (see e.g. Chapter 6) (*http://www.crbindex.com*). These commercial data sources are supplemented by a host of financial journals. The *Wall Street Journal* and the *Financial Times*, for example, supply both physical and derivative commodity market prices along with financial market prices in their daily issues.

In addition to these general data sources, there are a number of other data sources concerning specific commodities and/or groups of commodities. These data sources are more specialised and usually correspond to specific commodities or specific commodity groups. They come in the form of professional journals and publications, including specialised databases. Table 5.1 gives some examples.

Besides the foregoing sources of data, it is worth while mentioning here the existence of some web sites specialising in commodity and commodity market data and information. In particular, all major commodity exchanges have web sites, which give a wealth of usually free information and pertinent data, including general information on the exchange, contracts, prices and charts, educational information, and other topics. The most important sites in the United States are those of the Chicago Board of Trade (*http://www.cbot.com*), the Chicago Mercantile Exchange (*http://www.cme.com*), and the NYMEX/COMEX (*http://www.nymex.com*). In the UK, they are those of the London International Financial Futures Exchange (LIFFE) (*http://www.liffe.com*), the London Metal Exchange (*http://www.lme.co.uk*) and, finally, the International Petroleum Exchange (*http://www.ipe.com*).

Several official US sites supply free information of great interest for operators on physical and derivative markets. We can mention in particular the site of the USDA (*http://www.usda.gov*). This site gives detailed information on agricultural commodity markets, such as crop reports, weather, agricultural statistics, supply and demand, foreign trade information, satellite imagery and periodic reports on specific commodity markets. Similarly, the site of the US Geological Survey (USGS) (*http://minerals.cr.usgs.gov*) provides very useful material for forecasting

---

[1] Reuters was founded in 1851 by Paul Julius Reuters, a German immigrant in London who specialised in supplying telegraphic stock exchange data.

Table 5.1 Examples of sources of information concerning various classes of commodities (non-exhaustive list; source: field survey)

Commodity groups	Data and statistical sources
Energy commodities	
Oil and gas	Reuters, Bloomberg, *Oil and Gas Journal, Petroleum Economist*, Platt's, Raw Materials Group, US Department of Energy, IPE, NYMEX/COMEX
Petrochemicals	*Oil and Gas Journal, Petroleum Economist*, Chemical Data, Chemical Industries Services, Morgan Stanley, Goldman Sachs
Coal	Coal Week, Raw Materials Group, US Department of Energy, NYMEX/COMEX
Electricity	Reuters (USA), NYMEX/COMEX
Metals	
Iron and steel products	International Iron and Steel Institute (IISI), US Geological Survey
Non-ferrous metals	Reuters, Bloomberg, *Metal Bulletin*, Mineral Commodity Summaries, US Geological Survey, Raw Materials Group, LME, NYMEX/COMEX
Precious metals (gold, silver, PGM metals)	Reuters, Bloomberg, Gold Institute, Johnson Matthey, Minemet, Raw Materials Group, CBOT, NYMEX/COMEX, TOCOM
Agricultural commodities	
Cereals	Reuters, Bloomberg, International Wheat Council, Topfer, USDA, CBOT, LIFFE, MATIF
Oilseeds and edible oils	Reuters, Bloomberg, *Oil World*, CBOT
Coffee	Reuters, Bloomberg, International Coffee Organization, LIFFE, NYBOT
Cocoa	Reuters, Bloomberg, ED & F Man, LIFFE, NYBOT
Natural rubber	Reuters, Bloomberg, IRSG, Safic Alcan, FAO
Sugar	Reuters, Bloomberg, ED & F Man, International Sugar Organisation, LIFFE, NYBOT

metal commodity markets, including leading index forecasts of primary metal market variables (prices and demand).

Finally, there are informal information sources that can be either private or public. They usually go with judgmental approaches to forecasting, or with judgmental aspects of quantitative and econometric forecasting. These informal sources can be important since they complement and complete other formal data sources.

5.3   FORECASTING COMMODITY MARKETS

5.3.1   Various Approaches to Commodity Market Forecasting for Management

As we pointed out in the introduction to this chapter, managers and traders with different corporate concerns require different prices and market forecasts about the commodities that interest them. There are several types of such forecasts. First, we have *judgmental forecasting*, involving intuitive hypotheses and little or no use of mathematical or statistical techniques. A second group of methods consists of *technical analysis or charting methods*, in which the evolution of prices, as visualised through charts, is taken in consideration. More sophisticated *time series modelling* can also be applied to historical data for forecasting. Most technical and time series approaches do not assume any economic behavioural hypothesis. However, some of these methods, which attempt to find the leading indicators of the variables of interest, have more economic content than others. Finally, a third group of methods consists of so-called *econometric modelling*. In these methods, behavioural hypotheses are formulated in the form of mathematical equations, which are estimated by various techniques and can be used for forecasting.

Charting methods or some of the time-series modelling may be considered as *technical analysis* in a broad sense, meaning that they do not take into consideration any economic hypotheses. On the other hand, other econometric models give *fundamental approaches* to forecasting, meaning that they take into account analytical hypotheses about the behaviour of market agents. More precisely, fundamental approaches rest on an analysis of the evolution of the markets, taking into account supply, demand and inventories. In so doing, fundamental approaches make use of the results and the relationships supplied by economic analysis. Leading indicator methods represent an intermediate case.

Judgmental approaches are usually associated with both attitudes. They can involve technical analysis and/or taking into consideration fundamental analysis of market data. But, as already mentioned, they involve little or no use of formalised mathematical or statistical techniques.

Along the lines developed in the introduction to this chapter and following Jacques *et al.* (1988), we can formulate a 'three levels rule' whereby there are three main levels of corporate concern which correspond to three time horizons.

The *first level* of management corresponds to what can be done in the short term and without capital investment. This is the level of the marketing and purchasing of commodities on international markets with a time horizon of the order of three months or less. At this time horizon, one has to manage the negotiation and the implementation of commercial commodity contracts, which will be discussed in Chapter 7. This implies working out strategies to minimise commodity risks and, in particular, price risks, which very often means using suitable hedging techniques, as discussed in the previous chapters. At the three month or less time horizon, we need short-term forecasts that help the traders involved in physical marketing, hedging, or purchasing in their task.

The *second level* of management involves what can be done through medium-term and long-term real investments by the firm. This level corresponds to the planning of such investments, with a time horizon of the order of one to five years, or even more.

The *third level* of management involves both capital investments and techno-logical changes with possible product changes and/or diversification. This level corresponds to the long-term strategy of the firm. It can imply complete changes in technology and/or take-overs. The time horizon implied at this level might be anything above a few years.

Commodity market forecasts at the second and third levels typically use funda-mental approaches, possibly with econometric models. These models supply demand and price forecasts that are used for the financial assessment of the planned investments. However, in the case of long-term technological forecasting, qualitative and judgmental approaches based on the opinion of experts rather than quantitative approaches are usually of interest.

What are the variables and elements that should be forecast? In the case of commodity markets, quantitative forecasts may involve *market prices*, whether spot or futures and *market quantities* produced, under order or inventoried. In addition, forecasts of other related variables, such as quantities and prices of production factors may also be useful. Furthermore, qualitative forecasts are also very important for some applications, especially at the third level of management described above. At this level, qualitative assessments of the new technologies and/or the new products that will emerge may typically be of interest. We start our survey of forecasting methods with judgmental forecasting approaches.

5.3.2 Judgmental Forecasting

Jacques *et al.* (1988) point out that judgmental forecasting[2] is 'one of the most widely used' approaches to forecasting, especially at the first level of short-term management actions. But it is also used at the two longer-term levels of management that we have defined. As already noted, it is at this level and at a short-time horizon that trading actions take place, whether on physical or on derivative markets. Clearly, much of the forecasting carried out by traders on commodity markets rests on their judgmental assessment of market situa-tions, market changes, and the influence of external events on markets. This is, of course, true of traders in producing companies, trading companies and in industrial end-consumer companies as well. A judgmental approach to fore-casting is comparatively less expensive than a quantitative approach. It does not require costly specialised skills and/or the services of costly external consul-tants. Neither does it require econometric or quantitative expertise (Jacques *et al.*, 1988), although it might be useful to combine the conclusions of judgmental forecasting with those provided by quantitative analyses.

---

[2] Little has been published on judgmental forecasting, except perhaps in the case of specific methods such as the DELPHI method. However, our work owes much to a detailed discussion of the topic in the case of energy markets by Jacques *et al.* (1988), (eds). Kress and Snyder (1994), Hanke and Reitsch (1997), and Wolton Wilson and Keating (1998) are recent works which also cover this topic.

Judgmental methods do, however, require precise, complete and real-time information. One of the skills required for judgmental forecasting techniques is the ability to verify data, criticise it, and assess its pertinence. Short of errors that might occur even in reputable databases, some of the data provided, although factually exact, might be meaningless or of little importance.

Example   Assume that the futures price of wheat on the CBOT opens at 2.34 US $/bushel on some day of year 20**. Later in the day, it goes up sharply to 2.38, but this price might be meaningless if it corresponds to a very small transaction. An experienced trader in a market room of a trading company would know that and he/she would wait until the market comes back to a price of, say, 2.35, which effectively happens later in the day. Conversely, after opening at 2.32, an abnormal price of 2.38 might have been reached at some time later in a day because of a large buying order from a pension fund. The trader who intends to go long might know that this does not really correspond to the state of the market on that day. In this case, he/she will wait until market forces restore a price more related to the actual state of the market, which effectively happens the day after, with an opening at US$2.31/bushel. This having been said, much caution is in order since it is well known and documented many times over that even an experienced trader often gets it wrong.

As shown by Jacques *et al.* (1988), the success of judgmental approaches is in line with the analytical skills and the experience of the corporate expert and it is also related to his/her familiarity with a given market. Access to reliable private or informal sources of information is also important. A trader experienced in wheat markets might be less effective if he/she starts to work on the soybean markets. Although our previous examples focus on short-term forecasting in the context of trading, it must be emphasised that judgmental techniques are used at all time horizons. Finally, the success of judgmental approaches to forecasting relies on the operational experience and the intuition of corporate experts using them. It also owes much to the ability of these experts to work in teams and/or to confront their views with those of outside experts. The DELPHI method, for instance, is among the most successful long-term judgmental forecasting techniques (Dalkey, 1967; Masini, 1993). Its success is based on interactions among the opinions of experts within a group of several experts.

Another advantage of judgmental and subjective approaches to forecasting is that they can be tailored to the specific needs of a given situation in a given company. Conversely, judgmental approaches are 'frequently criticised because they apparently lack the exactness of quantitative approaches' (Jacques *et al.*, 1988). But this argument is not fully relevant. Judgment can be a substitute for a formal model. But, in so doing, it uses an implicit, informal model of the market that is constructed in the analyst's mind owing to his/her experience. Furthermore, even in the actual implementation of sophisticated econometric models, there is a lot of judgment, which is usually hidden and unknown to an external observer.

The analyst will usually sharpen his/her forecast by discussing his/her judgmental and subjective aspects of his/her work with other staff members or with a senior executive officer. And this is true whether he/she uses an informal judgmental approach or a quantitative method. Anyway, this means, again, that teamwork is essential to the success of judgmental forecasting. But this also applies to quantitative and analytical techniques.

The informal models underlying judgmental forecasts also have the advantage of being easily adaptable to change. Conversely, if market conditions change in such a manner that the formal model underlying an econometric model becomes irrelevant, it usually is much more difficult to adapt the model to this new situation. Econometric models have to be maintained and eventually discarded if they are no longer adapted to the state of the market. Another point is that econometric models and/or their results are often used by several experts. Furthermore, an informal judgmental model is a personal or firm-specific model. This means that judgmental forecasts are often private. In that case, they are not available, even at a price, to the public and they are not published, except perhaps internally. This situation is adapted to the confidentiality requirements that prevail in commodity trading companies (see e.g. Chapter 8). As mentioned by Jacques *et al.* (1988), many judgmental forecasts about commodity markets are nevertheless available every day in financial and professional publications and contribute to the understanding of these markets by corporate managers and traders. Furthermore, judgmental approaches to forecasting are often used along with other methods, such as technical analysis, charting methods and elementary time-series statistical analysis. Of course, they go together with detailed and real-time information.

5.3.3   Technical Analysis and Time-series Forecasting Models

Forecasting models may be either informal or formal mathematical, econometric models, validated by the analyst's intuition or judgment about market fundamentals. The question is whether one can forecast commodity prices and other commodity market data using time series of their past values. It is a difficult exercise because of the economic complexity and the wide range of events that influence markets and that cannot be foreseen. However, econometric and other long- or medium-term economic or mathematical models (such as computable general equilibrium models) may have some validity if combined with some fundamental analysis that comes from the analyst's intuition.

In the short run, or in the very short run (a few minutes to a few days or a few months), many stochastic elements in demand and/or in supply make forecasts difficult and risky, and, except in particular circumstances, fundamental prices are not necessarily a useful guide. Charting, or more sophisticated time-series methods are often used in this context along with the analyst's intuition. Other, more fundamental econometric models can still be derived, using, for instance, the fact that futures prices may be the market estimate of the effective spot prices that will prevail at the end of the futures contract.

Technical analysis or charting is a technique which attempts to forecast future prices from the study of a series of future quotations. The same is true of econometric time-series methods, which use mathematical and statistical techniques to forecast time series. To detail these methods would be impossible within the framework of this chapter. They are not specific to commodities and such a detailed development is outside of the scope of our book. They have, furthermore, been the object of a number of exhaustive reference books (Hanke and Reitsch, 1997; Makridakis *et al.* 1998; Ferris, 1997) in the specific case of agricultural commodities.

Another interesting and appealing forecasting technique for managers is based on leading indicators, defined as variables, or composite variables or indexes, the values of which are statistically correlated with some series of interest, such as prices. This method has been developed by the NBER in the USA. Its development follows the pioneering works of Burns and Mitchell (1938, 1961).

Although there is no such thing as perfect correlation and perfect forecasting, the use of such methods is often useful. These methods are not contradictory to market efficiency, inasmuch as we are dealing with statistical correlations such that arbitrage, if any, is more or less risky. They are of special interest in attempting to forecast *turning points* of variables that are *leading indicators* of other variables. The variable, x, is defined as a *leading indicator* for y, the variable of interest, if y_t and $x_{t-\tau}$ are correlated:

$$y_t = ax_{t-\tau} \tag{5.1}$$

It is defined as a *coincident indicator* for y, if there is a correlation between y_t and x_t:

$$y_t = ax_t \tag{5.2}$$

Finally, x is defined as a *lagging indicator* of y, if there is a correlation between y_t and $x_{t+\tau}$:

$$y_t = ax_{t+\tau} \tag{5.3}$$

Leading indicators are of special interest in forecasting, especially in capturing turning points in short-term forecasting. In this book we cannot develop the econometric details of the method. Stock and Watson (1992) provide a detailed methodological survey. As far as commodities are concerned, the US Geological Survey maintains and publishes periodically (in particular on its web site: *http://www.minerals.cr.usgs.gov/minerals/pubs/mii*) a number of leading indicators for the prices of non-ferrous metals and for the demand of metal commodities, including iron and steel products.

Where cycles are concerned, one can doubt the existence of perfectly predictable price cycles, because one could then respond in a countercyclical fashion and earn larger than 'normal' arbitrage profits over time. Countercyclical riskless arbitrage would then dampen price fluctuations at the market level, causing the cycle to disappear. Thus, predictable price cycles would be incompatible with rational behaviour.

This is true only of perfectly predictable cycles. In the real world, if we are talking about medium-term cycles, they are not perfectly predictable and arbitrating on forecasts of up to one or two years is risky. It is nevertheless useful to attempt such forecasting. In our case, a peak is defined as following a trough and is preceded by a fixed number of months of prices that are lower than at the peak and are followed by at least an equal number of months of lower prices. A trough follows a peak and is preceded by the fixed months of higher prices which are followed by the fixed months of higher prices than at the trough. An expansion is the period following a trough until the next peak, whereas a contraction or recession follows a peak and lasts until the next trough. Irregularities, of course, exist in that a price series may not proceed continuously upward or downward. However, the recognition of a distinct turning point is governed by the peak and trough rules stated above. These rules establish criteria to recognise the more significant turning points. In addition, a turning point cannot be established until some time after it has occurred. Some recent work on this approach to commodity cycles has been carried out by Davutyan and Roberts (1994) and by Labys *et al.* (1988).

5.3.4 Commodity Market Models

Although there are examples of commodities that are not storable, most commodities have some material basis and are storable. This is the case of energy commodities like fuels, metal commodities, and agricultural commodities. However, other goods that may be considered as commodities and are traded on efficient spot and futures markets, such as electricity, or services, such as freight, are not storable.

The storable character of most commodities has several implications. It means that commodity inventories are, as already mentioned, *capital* in the form of running assets, so that there is some cost of capital attached to them. We have seen in Chapter 2 that this cost has two components. First of all, there is the opportunity cost, i.e. the income, either interest or profit, that could be obtained from an equivalent investment in a purely financial asset with an equivalent level of risk that is lost because that capital is invested in inventories. The second cost associated with commodity inventories is the physical cost of storage, which can be very large. Therefore, holding commodity inventories can be justified for two reasons. First, a minimum precautionary stock may have to be held in order to meet clients' orders without delay. The optimal level of such a stock is a traditional problem in operations research, which is outside of the scope of this work. In this problem, one has to balance the cost of losing an order due to insufficient stocks with the cost of reordering. Secondly, some physical stocks may be held for speculative reasons because the operator expects the price of the commodity in question to increase.

Clearly, as will be discussed in more detail in the next section, along with supply and demand, the level of inventories is a key determinant of commodity prices. If the level of industrial stocks is high, this will tend to push prices downward because operators will cut their prices in order to reduce excess stocks. Conversely, if the level of industrial stocks is low, prices might rise as operators seek to rebuild depleted stocks. Consequently, market equilibrium, or market clearance, is not simply obtained through equating supply and demand as would be the case with non-storable goods. Thus, the following section, devoted to the basic features of commodity market modelling, will take into account, not only supply and demand functions, but also an inventory variation function as determinants of the price of any commodity.

The economic modelling of commodity markets and its econometric and forecasting applications have been discussed in a number of synthetic works, especially by Labys and Pollak (1984) and Güvenen *et al.* (1991). We will limit ourselves to the modelling of markets for storable commodities, by far the most general case. Let S represent market supply by producers, D the demand from end-users for the commodity, and ΔI the increase in inventories I. $\Delta I > 0$ means that demand for inventories exists, so that there is some oversupply by producers. $\Delta I < 0$ means that there is excess demand, so that sellers are obliged to sell part of their stocks to meet that excess demand. The accounting equation that expresses market clearance is therefore:

$$S = D + \Delta I \qquad (5.4)$$

Although in econometric modelling, much more complex formulations could be retained, we express S, D, and ΔI as, respectively, a supply function, a demand function and an inventory function. These functions involve prices, so that price determination for market clearance results from equation (5.4) if we choose suitable functions for S, D, and ΔI. Since in the practice of forecasting, one wants to model (in econometric and other dynamic models) the evolution of the market over time, dynamic formulations with lagged variables are chosen, rather than static formulations that stem from equilibrium theory. Furthermore, this sort of modelling is well adapted to competitive conditions and to medium-term to long-term analyses where the time horizon of the operator must be at least one or two years.

In this case, we write the demand function at time t as

$$D_t = d(D_{t-1}, p_t, q_t, Y_t, T_t) \qquad (5.5)$$

In this equation, D_{t-1} stands for lagged demand at time $t - 1$, with d usually being an increasing function of D_{t-1}; p_t for the price of the commodity at time t, with

d being a decreasing function of p_t; q_t for the vector of the prices of substitute commodities at time t, with d being an increasing function of q_t; Y_t for a vector of activity-related indexes in the industries that use the commodity. Finally, T_t is a vector of technological dummy variables that influence demand.

A second equation describes the supply function as

$$S_t = s(S_{t-1}, p_{t-\theta}, q_t, N_t, Z_t) \qquad (5.6)$$

In this equation, S_{t-1} stands for lagged supply at time $t-1$, with s usually being an increasing function of D_{t-1}; $p_{t-\theta}$ for a lagged price of the commodity at time $t - \theta$, with being an increasing function of $p_{t-\theta}$; N_t for agronomic or geological variables that may influence the supply of the commodity. Finally, Z_t is a vector of dummy policy and technological variables that influences supply.

A third equation relates the variation of inventories ΔI_t to the dynamics of prices, with ΔI_t being a decreasing function of the first difference in prices:

$$\Delta I_t = \phi(P_t - P_{t-1}) \qquad (5.7)$$

Finally, the model is closed by the identity expressing equation (5.4):

$$S_t = D_t + \Delta I_t \qquad (5.8)$$

As already mentioned, the model can be made much more complex by breaking down the supply function into separate functions for each supplier or each group of suppliers. Similarly, the demand function can be broken down into separate functions for each class of demand and/or each geographical area. All these theoretical formulations require some explanations and examples that illustrate their practical utility.

One of the most important relationships in the above formulations is the equation relating the variation of stocks to the dynamics of prices. It is essential in capturing the short-term price dynamics. If stocks are low or falling, this means that prices tend to be high because the current demand is higher than current supply. In this case, traders or other operators holding stocks may supply the market from stocks. If, on the other hand, stocks are high, this might be because of an oversupply resulting in low prices.

The equation governing demand stems from the fact that for a given commodity or raw material, demand results from the installed capacity of industries that use the commodity as an intermediate input. Demand is, of course, related to variables describing the activity of these industries and hence from a vector Y_t that describes this activity. In the case of materials, their demand depends upon the renewal of equipment that use the commodity as an input. It also depends upon the production of new equipment that uses the commodity as an input. Demand for a given commodity is therefore directly related to the demand for products requiring the commodity for their production. At the same time, the demand for a given commodity is negatively related to its price. Of course, the demand for various commodities will, in general, depend strongly on the prices of their substitutes. In the case of perfect substitutes, the relative prices of the substitutes will generally be the main variable influencing demand. In the case of imperfect substitutes, requiring different equipment, and/or having various quality differences, the situation is generally more complex.

Example The demand for natural rubber depends on (1) the demand for tyres from existing vehicles (renewal demand) and from new vehicles (including cars and industrial vehicles). It also depends on the demand for other rubber appliances, and (2) on the relative prices of artificial rubber, which in turn depends on the price of crude oil.

In the longer term, the demand for a given commodity depends heavily on technological trends and on the general social and economic environment. In general, there is a long-term trend in OECD countries with a marked decrease in the intensity of demand for most commodities, including energy, and 'traditional' materials, such as steel products, copper, cement, etc. On the other hand, emerging economies such as the 'dragons' of South East Asia (South Korea, Singapore, Taiwan, Hong Kong, and Thailand) are still in a period of increasing demand for such materials. There are also very long-term technological trends that affect the use of many commodities because, due to advances in the technologies that use the commodity, substitutes might be used much more effectively. For demand analysis, all this can be captured either in prices or in the technological dummy variables (T_t).

Example Copper is a metal whose main uses stem from the fact that it is a good conductor of electricity. Hence, the demand for copper will depend heavily upon the demand for all electrical and electronic equipment. However, there are technological trends that tend to affect the demand for copper. In particular, electronic components are smaller and smaller, and include materials other than copper. For applications in telecommunications, glass fibre has become a major substitute for copper, being more effective in technical terms and, hence, cheaper for a given telecommunication service.

The supply of commodities can also be analysed in terms of price, because producers' supply will react positively to any increase in price. Their reaction to the price of substitutes may be positive or negative, depending upon market and technological conditions.

In the medium and long-term, the theory of rent has been a useful guide to capture some of the fundamental price movements for some basic commodities. This theory dates back from Ricardo (1817) who formulated it for agricultural commodities. It implies both a constant market price such as the price of wheat, for instance, and the existence of variable costs (capital costs, labour costs, energy, and fertilisers, except for land rent costs). Since variable costs cannot exceed the market price (except perhaps in the short term), because this would mean, in a market economy, that producers would lose money in their activity, one has:

$$\text{Market price} = \text{variable costs} + \text{rent on land}$$

In the case of the producer(s) on the least fertile land, there is no rent and the market price is just equal to variable costs, called the marginal cost:

$$\text{Market price} = \text{marginal cost}$$

This analysis in terms of rent, in spite of its historical interest, is no longer adapted to assessing the fundamental price of agricultural commodities. This is because technological progress has been the key determinant of the long-run evolution of costs, the scarcity of land being only a secondary cost factor nowadays. In the case of non-renewable resources, the problem is the same as in the case of agricultural products, but there is an added exploration cost, which enables the producer to maintain the capital he owns in terms of reserves. In this case, we can write:

$$\text{Market price} = \text{variable costs} + \text{exploration costs} + \text{rent}$$

The exploration costs express the fact that, at least in the long run, exploration in order to add to reserves will be necessary to meet the demand for exhaustible resources. However, they may be omitted in a medium-term analysis. Again, for the producer with the largest cost, i.e. the marginal producer:

$$\text{Market price} = \text{marginal cost} + \text{exploration costs}$$

For many mineral commodities, it can be argued that, as in the case of agricultural commodities, technical progress is the key factor, which has led to a real-term decrease in costs and in prices. Furthermore, for recyclable materials (such as most industrial metals) recycling is a source of supply that is increasing and pushes prices downward. However, the theory of rent is still useful for non-recyclable and exhaustible commodities such as energy commodities and, in particular, crude oil, a very important commodity indeed. Table 5.2 gives some

Table 5.2 Long-term costs of production of crude oil for some specific production areas

Area	Production cost (average, US$/barrel)
USA	18
Canada	15
Latin America	5
Western Europe	14
Middle East	2
Far East	3

estimates of long-term costs of production of crude oil for some specific areas of production.

The knowledge of these costs of production is useful in short-term and medium-term forecasting inasmuch as it gives some idea of the medium-term 'fundamental' price of oil. If there is a marked discrepancy, especially in terms of low prices, between fundamental and observed prices, the situation will sooner or later result in higher prices that correspond better to the actual market situation. At the end of 1998 and the beginning of 1999, for instance, the price of oil reached a comparatively very low value of around US$10/barrel. This value clearly was not in line with the fundamentals, except perhaps for a short-term effect of the Asian crisis that had occurred a few months before. This meant that the price of crude oil had to rise, which it did later in 1999 and in 2000. Conversely, if the price of oil were to increase strongly, substitution effects would play a role in pushing it downward, as happened after the 'oil shock' of 1973–74. Since 1974, the industrial consumption of energy per unit of output has steadily decreased, at least in the OECD area, thereby contributing to keep prices at a comparatively moderate level. With 100 as the base in 1974, energy consumption in 1995 was about 60 in the 'heavy' industries (steel, chemistry, cement, metal industries, glass, pulp and paper industries...) and about 85 in the secondary and less energy-intensive industries. Technological advances, energy-saving investments, and the substitution of coal and of natural gas for oil products in the heavier industries have been the principal causes of the reduction.

Long-term trends, such as technological trends, can be observed. In many cases, commodity prices decrease in real terms due to technological progress; this is true, for instance, in the case of aluminium. In other cases, real prices fluctuate, in the long term, around a constant value. Finally, the supply of some commodities may depend upon policy variables (expressed as Z_t) in the above equation, such as subsidies to agriculture, which still prevail in many countries.

Example   The supply of sugar depends upon two main sources, which are sugar cane in the tropical world and sugar beet in some OECD countries. However, sugar is in oversupply, as are most agricultural commodities, due to the subsidies in many developed countries such as the USA and the European Union. Furthermore, the demand for sugar is threatened by other general trends in OECD countries: for medical reasons, several substitute products, known as artificial sweeteners, have become popular.

Monopolies or cartels, although less frequent than in the past, also play a role in the medium and long-term analyses that one can make, pushing the prices upward. Models suitable for a cartel or monopoly supply have been developed (see e.g. Labys and Pollak, 1984). However, an analyst who feels that a market will become more competitive may rightly deduce from this situation that, at least in the medium term, prices will be pushed downward.

Examples The 'seven sisters' (seven large oil companies: BP, Exxon, Shell, Gulf Oil, Standard Oil of California, Texaco and Mobil Oil) dominated the international oil market until 1973, after a near-monopoly situation by Standard Oil that prevailed until 1911. The OPEC, a group of 13 countries, including Saudi Arabia, UAE, Iraq, Iran, Kuwait, Qatar, Algeria, Gabon, Libya, Nigeria, Ecuador, Venezuela, and Indonesia, dominated the market until 1979–80 through posted prices maintained by the cartel. This lasted until a more competitive market emerged. It certainly was one of the factors that led oil prices to decrease during the 1980–90 period, after a peak in 1980.

Commodity prices can often be analysed in terms of seasonal variations. Agricultural and energy commodities are a case in point. There are also some medium-term cycles that last for about four to five years. These cycles can be observed for all commodities (the case of oil, for instance, is clear, although the cycles in question are irregular). Long-term trends, such as technological trends, can also be observed.

We have only discussed here the most common forecasting techniques. These techniques are judgmental, charting, econometric statistical and econometric modelling. In the context of this book, they are the most interesting techniques. However, there are a number of other methods, which are described by several authors, such as Labys and Pollak (1984) and Güvenen *et al.* (1991). Among these methods, one can mention balance-sheet methods, which are accounting methods based on the equilibrium of demand, supply and inventories. There are also computable general equilibrium models, in which general equilibrium equations are computed in order to introduce economic optimisation behaviour into the model. These models may be similar to the econometric commodity models described above. However, the parameters of a computable general equilibrium model are calibrated instead of being estimated from statistical regressions. The model can then be used for forecasting, especially in long-term applications. Similar models in which optimisation behaviour is taken into account are programming models. In these models, optimisation results from linear or non-linear programming. Finally, there are technological models in which relationships taken from the underlying technology are taken into account. The reference book of Güvenen *et al.* (1991) gives examples of almost all these approaches to modelling commodity markets.

5.4 COMMODITY PRICE FORECASTING FOR TRADERS AND MARKET PARTICIPANTS

In the case of price forecasts, an important issue is whether it is possible to use forecasts estimated on the basis of an analysis of past prices. This issue is important for trading purposes, since trading is defined as buying for reselling at a profit. As emphasised throughout this book, trading is especially important on commodity markets. This issue is related to the question of the efficiency of commodity markets (Fama, 1970, 1991) and was discussed in Chapter 1. If markets are weakly efficient, prices should fully reflect all information contained in past market data. This does not mean exactly that one cannot make forecasts, but rather that forecasts that are made on this basis cannot lead to abnormal speculative or trading profits. The semi-strong efficiency hypothesis extends this property to all publicly available information. In the case of financial markets, it is generally recognised that both the weak and semi-strong efficiency hypotheses are usually met with few exceptions. Kolb (1997) gives some empirical evidence in the case of both financial and commodity derivative markets, but contends that the strong hypothesis is certainly not true. This means that prices do not reflect private information and that it is possible to make profits from private information.

What is the situation then on the commodity markets? Let us first consider the case of commodities with organised futures and options markets. As mentioned in the previous section, all operators are professionals that trade on the basis of online and real-time price data supplied by data vendors such as Reuters and Bloomberg. These operators also have practically all the pertinent information supplied by professional publications and journals concerning the commodity they are interested in. All this information, and the information supplied by data vendors, constitutes public information on these markets. This means that their situation is very similar to the situation prevailing on organised financial markets. The only differences are that these markets are OTC markets and that public information differs from the information available on financial assets such as shares. Up to these differences, we can conclude that the semi-strong and weak efficiency hypotheses are true on these markets. Inasmuch as commodity futures markets are closely related to physical markets, one can also conclude that they are also weak and semi-strong efficient. The only limit to the validity of these hypotheses should be the existence of non-competitive situations, but we have seen that they have become the exception. Finally, it might even be argued that on some commodity markets with efficient derivative markets, strong efficiency is valid in some sense. All operators have at least some imperfect perception of private information that will make abnormal profits difficult to come by. It can be argued, at least, that the meaning of speculative or trading profits resulting from private information is quite different from what it is on stock markets.

In the case of commodities with no organised derivative markets, however, the situation may be different. Many of these markets, including, for instance, markets for minor rare metals and some markets for minor precious metals, are under a monopoly or cartel situation with one or a few dominant suppliers. They are less liquid than the markets for commodities with efficient organised futures markets. They are also less transparent and the elasticities of supply and demand with respect to price are quite small, meaning that a comparatively small change in both supply and demand can completely upset the market in terms of price. This means that a dominant operator can cause enormous price variations by holding a comparatively small amount of stock. For instance, rhodium, one of the metals of the PGM group, has no organised futures market and appears to be very volatile with prices of about US$900/oz during the third quarter of 1999 going up to US$2340/oz in February 2000. On such markets, the concept of strong efficiency is very far from valid because large or dominant operators can make abnormal profits based on their private information. It is likely that on some of these markets even the efficiency concept in the weak and semi-strong sense are not valid. Prices do not fully reflect even the information contained in past prices. Some large operators can take advantage of this situation to make abnormal speculative profits.

Regarding the strong efficiency hypothesis, it should be stressed that the status of private information is quite different from what it is in the case of capital assets. We have already developed some aspects of that point in Chapter 1. Another aspect of this question is the implications that it has for trading profits. As already noted in Chapter 1, the only utility of financial assets to their owners is the income they provide in the form of dividends and/or capital gains. In particular, in the case of shares, fundamental financial information is indispensable for assessing their value. Hiding such information is tantamount to hiding the share's essential characteristics. If financial information is not disclosed, the stock market is not transparent and cannot function. Therefore, in the case of stock markets, there are regulations that impose disclosure requirements on quoted companies. Conversely, insider trading, meaning using private information to make abnormal profits, is prohibited. The situation is completely different in the case of physical commodity markets. The utility of physical commodities is related to their physical characteristics, not to their economic fundamentals. In their case, the use of private information for trading on physical markets is not an unfair way of trading. Private information comes, for instance, as cost information to commodity producers. Here, the situation is close to the situation for any other industrial good. Conversely, industrial end-users purchase commodities on the basis of private information on their costs, which of course include commodity costs. They may shift to substitutes of a given commodity if its price is too high. Finally, trading companies use everyday private information to perform profitable trading. They may in some cases buy commodities for speculative inventories. This can be after a judgmental or a quantitative forecast obtained by processing both publicly available and private information. In other cases, for pure trading activities, they make profitable arbitrage or basis arbitrage, thereby contributing to market efficiency. They are not necessarily making abnormal speculative profits because, as shown by Kolb (1997) in the case of day traders on recognised futures markets, these trading profits are commensurate with certain production costs (traders' salaries, investments in databases, other risky investments, etc.). In any case, as emphasised several times in this book (see in particular Chapter 8), trading is a risky activity. Traders minimise the risks through various techniques and strategies. They often hedge their positions and they are often vertically integrated.

Producers of commodities also use price forecasts when selling their commodities. Given their costs and their expected sales prices, they decide whether or not to hedge. This means that they should have at least a judgmental or crude forecast of an expected sales price. They can also use forecasts based on more quantitative methods. These forecasts should be able to assess the risk that the price will go down below production costs. On that basis, the producer will decide whether or not to hedge, or to negotiate a forward price. As will be seen in Chapter 6, producers do not systematically hedge all their positions.

Commodity purchasing in the case of industrial end-users is based on similar principles. Here, the operators also use a judgmental price forecast or a forecast based on an analytical quantitative approach. The risk that the price of the commodity goes up too much is also systematically assessed for hedging.

5.5 CONCLUSION

In this chapter, we have shown the importance of suitable information for playing the commodities markets. Given the volatility of the prices of most commodities, operators need accurate and real-time information on prices, especially for marketing, trading, and purchasing purposes. They also need some longer-term market information and market analyses to address other corporate needs, such as investments and long-term strategy.

There are a number of commodity market forecasting methods, of which we have presented only the most important. Price forecasts are the most useful and the most important types of forecasts, even if market efficiency precludes making abnormal trading or speculative profits on the basis of these forecasts. However, demand forecasts are also very important for many producers.

Of course, all forecasts contain a large dose of uncertainty: forecasters, whatever their professional skills, are not prophets. This uncertainty is relatively moderate in the case of quantity variables, such as demand, but, as discussed in the previous chapters, it is high in the case of commodity prices. Hence, using price forecasts for trading and speculation purposes is very risky. This is why the use of derivative markets for hedging commodity transactions is so important. Chapters 2–4 have developed theoretical and practical analyses concerning commodity futures, options, and OTC derivatives markets. Chapter 6 will provide some covering of the residual risks involved in the operational aspects of hedging, especially in terms of cash flows. It will also discuss some longer-term implications in terms of corporate finance. In addition to these short-term and long-term implications for corporate finance, Chapter 7 will also discuss the use of commodity derivative instruments as investment vehicles by managed futures and hedge funds. These market finance developments are useful in completing our previous discussion of derivative markets with a discussion of the actors of commodity derivative markets other than participants in physical markets.

BIBLIOGRAPHY

A. F. Burns and W. C. Mitchell (1938) *Statistical Indicators of Cyclical Revivals*, NBER, Cambridge, MA., republished as Chapter 6 of G. H. Moore (ed.) (1961), *Business Cycle Indicators*. Princeton University Press, Princeton, NJ, 1961.

N. Dalkey (1967) *Delphi*. Rand Corporation, Santa Monica, CA.

N. Davutyan and M. Roberts (1994) Cyclicality in metal prices, *Resources Policy*, **20**, 49–57.

E. Fama (1970) Efficient capital markets: A review of theory and empirical work, *Journal of Finance*, **25**, 383–417.

E. Fama (1991) Efficient capital markets, II, *Journal of Finance*, **46**, 1575–1617.

J. E. Ferris (1997) *Agricultural Prices and Commodity Market Analysis*. McGraw-Hill, New York.

C. W. J. Granger (1980) *Forecasting in Business and Economics*. Academic Press, New York.

O. Güvenen, W. C. Labys and J. B. Lesourd (eds) (1991) *International Commodity Market Modelling. Advances in Methodology and Applications*. Foreword by R. Duncan (World Bank); Introduction by L. R. Klein, Nobel Laureate. Chapman & Hall, London, 330 pp.

J. E. Hanke and A. G. Reitsch (1997) *Business Forecasting*. Prentice-Hall, New York.

R. Kolb (1997) *Understanding Futures Markets*. Blackwell, Oxford.

G. J. Kress and J. Snyder (1994) *Forecasting and Market Analysis Techniques*. Greenwood Publishing Group, Westport, CT.

J. K. Jacques, W. C. Labys and J. B. Lesourd (1988) The energy manager's methods for forecasting and data analysis, Chapter 3 in J. K. Jacques, J. B. Lesourd and J. M. Ruiz (eds), *Modern Applied Energy Conservation. New Directions in Energy Conservation Management*. Ellis Horwood/Halsted Press — Wiley, Chichester/New York, pp. 84–105.

W. C. Labys and J. B. Lesourd (1988) *The New Energy Markets*, Chapter 2 in J. K. Jacques, J. B. Lesourd and J. M. Ruiz (eds), *Modern Applied Energy Conservation. New Directions in Energy Conservation Management*. Ellis Horwood/Halsted Press — Wiley, Chichester/New York, pp. 37–83.

W. C. Labys and P. K. Pollak (1984) *Commodity Models for Forecasting and Policy Analysis*. Croom Helm/Nichols Publishing, London/New York.

W. C. Labys, J. B. Lesourd and D. Badillo (1988) The existence of metal price cycles, *Resources Policy*, **24**, 147–155.

S. Makridakis, S. G. Wheelwright and R. Hyndman (1998) *Forecasting*. Wiley, New York.

E. Masini (1993) *Why Futures Studies?* Grey Seal, London.

D. Ricardo (1817) *On the Principles of Political Economy and Taxation*, recent edition: D. Ricardo (P. Sraffa, ed.) (1990) *On the Principles of Political Economy and Taxation*, Cambridge University Press, Cambridge, UK.

J. H. Stock and M. S. Watson (1992) *A Procedure for Predicting Recessions with Leading Indicators: Econometric Issues and Recent Experience*. NBER, Cambridge, MA., published as J. H. Stock and M. S. Watson (1993) *Business Cycles, Indicators and Forecasting*, Studies in Business Cycles No. 28, University of Chicago Press, Chicago.

J. Wolton Wilson and B. Keating (1998) *Business Forecasting*. Irwin, Columbus, OH.

6
Commodities, market finance, and corporate finance

6.1 INTRODUCTION

In the first part of this book, we discussed the various aspects of commodity markets. In particular, this involved futures and derivative markets, whether they are organised markets (Chapters 2 and 3), or OTC markets (Chapter 4). The second part of this book is devoted to actors on various commodity physical and derivative markets and to corporate management issues concerning these actors. It opened with Chapter 5, which was still devoted to a market-related corporate management issue and is, so to speak, a transition chapter between the first and the second parts of the book. This chapter dealt with the commodity market forecasting techniques that are used for corporate management and commodity trading. These methods concern various market attributes and variables on the physical and derivative commodity markets.

The present chapter is still interested in commodity derivative markets, but under investor-specific and firm-specific financial aspects that have not been discussed in Chapters 2–4. Its main purpose is to discuss the specific aspects of commodity derivatives in terms of both market finance and corporate finance at the respective microeconomic levels of portfolio management and corporate finance. The issues that are dealt with in this chapter are seldom discussed in standard presentations of commodity futures markets. The first issue is developed in the second section of this chapter. It concerns actors on commodity derivative markets that usually are not actors on physical markets. More precisely, these actors are speculators and more generally purely financial actors such as various types of investment funds whose essential activity is managing portfolios. These actors are useful from an economic point of view in providing price discovery and liquidity to the community of corporate actors involved in physical commodity trading. These services are risky, but risks may be controlled through careful portfolio management and diversification. In this respect, commodity futures are useful as diversification instruments in financial portfolios. This is because they are financial assets that are not correlated with traditional financial assets, such as bonds, stocks, and the derivative instruments related thereto. There are even purely financial commodity-related instruments, such as commodity index futures, which may be used for portfolio diversification just as financial futures on stock market indexes.

The first objective of this chapter, to be dealt with in section 6.2, is therefore to discuss how commodity-related financial assets are used as investment vehicles. This next section thus deals with the role of commodity-related assets in market finance.

But there are also important issues that link commodity-related assets, not only to market finance but also to corporate finance. One of the services provided by investors or speculators to physical commodity market actors is liquidity. Liquidity is closely related to corporate financial issues that are important for physical commodity market participants. As discussed previously, these participants often hedge their physical positions to protect against adverse market price variations. But hedging requires a counterparty, which is provided by speculators in a broad sense. Hedging also requires a careful management of cash flows and of liquid working assets. These short-term corporate financial aspects of hedging have not been studied extensively, in our opinion. They are discussed in section 6.3 of this chapter.

Finally, section 6.4 is devoted to commodity-specific aspects of the medium-term and long-term financing of firms, which are involved in the production of basic commodities.

6.2 COMMODITIES AND MARKET FINANCE

6.2.1 Commodity-related Instruments

In some cases, physical commodities as such are also used as investment instruments. This is the case especially for precious metals, which may be held in a portfolio as receipts for physical metal (under the form of bullion or coins) kept in the vaults of a financial institution. Other physical commodities may be held as warehouse receipts. Direct investment in physical commodities implies facilities for physical storage, which are usually in the hands of professionals of the industries and of the trading of these commodities (see e.g. Chapter 8).

While direct investment in physical commodities is awkward and costly to manage, it is also disappointing in terms of long-term performance. The prices of many commodities have been decreasing in real terms over time because of technological advances that have been driving costs downward in the long run. However, investment in physical commodities may have been a hedge against inflation during periods of strong inflation, such as much of the 1980s. Priovolos

(1991) studied the possibility of investing in physical commodities over a long period (1921–86). His calculation of optimal Markowitz commodity portfolios found an expected return of 8.5% over that long period under the most favourable hypothesis, to be compared to a 4.3% expected return for an investment in a portfolio of US treasury bonds, which are riskless assets.

The stocks of commodity-producing companies usually perform better than physical commodities as such. They provide a gearing effect with respect to commodity price increases and with respect to commodity cost decreases. The price of the stocks of a gold mining company with a cost of production of US$250/oz will provide a profit margin of US$25/oz if the current price of gold is at an average of US$275/oz. If, of course, the price of gold goes up to US$300/oz, this will approximately double the value of expected profits and hence the market value of the stock of the company. If the company decreases its costs down to US$225/oz, for instance through technological advances in its process, the profit margin will again double at a constant market price of gold. This will of course double the price of the stock of the company if investors believe that this will be a durable effect. We thus may expect that commodity stocks provide a gearing effect over the prices of physical commodities, thereby amplifying any increase of the price of the commodity produced. Conversely, however, the effect might also be that, if the price of a commodity were decreasing, this would severely hit the price of the underlying stock. Commodity-related stocks, such as the stocks of mining companies or oil companies holding crude oil reserves, will usually be speculative assets. They leverage the price of the underlying commodities, just as futures and options will do, but in a less systematic manner.

But the most useful commodity-related financial assets that are directly available for investors as investment instruments are derivative instruments, including commodity futures and options and commodity OTC derivatives. Of course, these derivative instruments, especially when quoted on a large organised market, are leveraging price increases until the maturity of the contract. This is just what commodity stocks do over a different (usually longer) period of time. In the case of tradable futures and options, this is done in a more systematic and organised manner. The investor may choose the time horizon he/she is interested in. He/she can also choose, to some extent, the magnitude of the leverage effect provided and hence the degree of risk inherent in the instrument. Combinations of futures, options, and other instruments also enable one to work on the risk profile. They lend themselves to the constitution of diversified portfolios. Furthermore, many of the derivative instruments traded on large organised international markets are liquid instruments, which is useful in terms of cash flow and portfolio management. OTC derivatives are less liquid and in some ways more risky; they often enable investors to hedge and to invest in more or less risky contexts for longer time horizons.

Finally, there are *commodity indexes*, some of which are underlying futures and hence are investment instruments. Indexes of asset prices, such as stock indexes, are useful in several ways. Firstly, they provide an indication of the evolution of the price of a diversified portfolio invested in a particular class of assets. Stock indexes such as the Dow-Jones indexes for US stocks, the FTSE 100 index for UK stocks, and other indexes such as the CAC 40 for French stocks provide *benchmarks* which are useful to assess the performance of diversified portfolios in various classes of stocks. Secondly, they lend themselves to building up index-tracking portfolios, some of which are replications of the composition of the index. The development of stock index-based futures and derivative instruments has been very useful in that they enable investors to easily build up portfolios that will, in the long run, match the performance of the representative index chosen with lower transaction costs than a direct replica of the index. This is usually achieved by holding a fully collateralized long position on an index futures. Index derivatives also enable investors to hedge diversified stock portfolios.

A commodity index is a suitable aggregate function of the (spot and/or futures) prices of commodities, which belong to a group of commodities. There are a number of commodity indexes available, a few of which are underlying futures, that can be used directly as investment instruments with more diversification, less volatility and hence less risk than many other portfolios. Provided it is suitably collateralised or corresponds to suitably collateralised futures positions, a commodity index can match, in the long run, the performance of a diversified investment in physical commodities.

The Bridge/CRB Futures Index, first developed in 1957, is the oldest of the investor-directed commodity indexes. It has served as the underlying commodity for the oldest commodity index futures and options contracts that were established in 1986 on the New York Futures Exchange (now on the NYBOT). It is an equally weighted commodity futures price index which is calculated as a geometric mean of the individual futures price indexes of 17 underlying commodities (which are given in Table 6.1) divided by the base value of the index which is the average for the base year (1967). Each component futures price is calculated as an arithmetic mean of the nearby futures prices over the next nine months. Then, these arithmetic means are geometrically averaged. The resulting value is divided by 30.7766, the base-year average value of this geometric mean for the same 17 commodities. An adjustment factor of 0.8486 is applied and the result is multiplied by 100, giving a base value of 100 in 1967.

The Bridge/CRB Futures Price Index serves as the underlying commodity for index futures and options currently quoted on the NYBOT (see e.g. Chapter 1). The contract is valued at $500/Bridge/CRB index point. Futures are available for January, February, April, June, August, and November. The contract implies, as is usual with futures on indexes, cash settlements only, with daily cash payments corresponding to differences in the index futures, and a final cash settlement on the basis of the spot index at maturity. Options are treated in a similar manner, with immediate payment of the premium by the buyer. Daily cash differences

Table 6.1 Current composition of the Bridge/CRB Futures Index (2000)[a]

Energy commodities (3)
Crude oil (NYMEX/COMEX)
Heating oil (NYMEX/COMEX)
Natural gas (NYMEX/COMEX)
Base metals (1)
Copper (NYMEX/COMEX)
Precious metals (3)
Gold (NYMEX/COMEX)
Platinum (NYMEX/COMEX)
Silver (NYMEX/COMEX)
Agricultural commodities and livestock (10)
Wheat (CBOT)
Cocoa (NYBOT)
Coffee (NYBOT)
Corn (CBOT)
Cotton (NYBOT)
Lean hogs (CBOT)
Live cattle (CBOT)
Orange juice (NYBOT)
Soya beans (CBOT)
Sugar No 11 (NYBOT)

[a] Bridge/CRB® is a registered trademark of Commodity Research Bureau.

are paid by the option seller in case of a detrimental evolution of the index. This makes margin deposits available to the buyer if the option is exercised, which can be done at any time.

The Goldman Sachs Commodity Index (GSCI) is one of the most important of the representative commodity indexes. It consists of a weighted combination of the prices of 26 commodities from all commodity sectors, including energy commodities, metal commodities, and agricultural commodities. Stock indexes are usually arithmetic means of individual stock prices, weighted by the number of stocks outstanding, divided by the value of the same aggregate at some reference date, at which the index is defined as 100 or 1000. They are, therefore, arithmetic means of market capitalisations of the individual stocks composing the index. One may therefore define such an index as

$$\frac{u^t \cdot y_1}{V^t \cdot X_1} \rightarrow I(t) = B \frac{\sum_i N_i(t)\pi_i(t)}{\sum_t N_i(0)\pi_i(0)} \tag{6.1}$$

In this equation, $N_i(t)$ is the number of outstanding stocks of company i, of price $\pi_i(t)$ at time t, and B is the base index at time 0, usually 100 or 1000.

In the case of commodities, the economists of Goldman Sachs argue that market capitalisation is meaningless, which is the case for most commodities for which there are no large outstanding inventories. They propose an annual production-weighted index called the GSCI index. The GSCI index is an aggregate of the prices of 26 commodities with the most liquid dollar-denominated markets, weighted by annual productions. There is first a GSCI spot index which consists of a combination of production-weighted nearby long futures positions on each of these 26 commodities, fully collateralized with short-term riskless assets in an amount equal to the full positions, with reinvestment of the gains and of the interest on the riskless asset. The calculation of this index requires somewhat complex rolling forward of the contracts. It is thus comparable to an index in physical positions on the 26 commodities, thus reflecting an aggregate evolution of the spot prices of these commodities. Table 6.2 indicates the weighting of the individual commodities that was effective on 22 September 2000. The base date, for which the index is normalized as 100, is January 2, 1970.

In addition to the GSCI spot index, there are two further GSCI indexes, which aim at describing returns of GSCI futures rather than the actual prices.

Since 1992, the GSCI spot index has been the underlying for futures and options quoted on the Chicago Mercantile Exchange. The contract is valued at $250/GSCI spot index point. Futures are available for 12 consecutive months. Cash settlements and margin payments are similar to what has been described for the Bridge/CRB futures and options.

Commodity futures contracts have been shown to provide a hedge against inflation, with an average return larger than the return on riskless assets. In addition, a long position in these futures has the useful property of being negatively correlated with usual financial assets. Thus, in terms of risk-return combination (Sharpe ratio) it improves the properties of a traditional financial portfolio, at least if held in a reasonable proportion (between 2.5% and 20% of the portfolio).

A number of other commodity futures and spot price indexes are available, but with no derivatives (except perhaps OTC derivatives) using them as underlying assets. One of the most interesting of them is the Dow-Jones AIG Commodity Index, which is supplied by Dow-Jones Indexes and AIG International Inc.

We now come to discussing the investment vehicles that use commodity-related instruments as possible investments, including, of course, all categories of investment funds.

6.2.2 Investment Funds and Commodity-related Instruments

Individual investors may invest in physical commodities and in commodity futures, and often do so. However, except in the case of gold and of other precious metals (which, in the USA, may now be included in tax-free pension

Table 6.2 Composition and weighting of the GSCI[a] index (22 September 2000)

Dollar weights for individual commodities and groups of commodities

Energy commodities: 67.97%
American crude oils: 27.47%
Brent crude oil: 12.53%
Unleaded gasoline: 5.13%
Heating oil: 8.21%
Gasoil: 3.52%
Natural gas: 11.11%

Base metals: 6.91%
Aluminium: 3.38%
Copper: 1.89%
Lead: 0.22%
Nickel: 0.61%
Tin: 0.10%
Zinc: 0.70%

Precious metals: 2.02%
Gold: 1.62%
Platinum: 0.21%
Silver: 0.19%

Agricultural commodities and livestock: 23.10%
Wheat: 3.09%
Red wheat: 1.19%
Corn: 3.33%
Soya beans: 1.85%
Cotton: 2.14%
Sugar: 1.96%
Coffee: 0.82%
Cocoa: 0.18%
Orange juice: 0.52%
Live cattle: 5.63%
Lean hogs: 2.39%

[a] GSCI® is a registered trademark of Goldman, Sachs and Co.

plans such as 401 (k) plans), holding positions in physical commodities and in commodity derivatives is risky and requires professionalism.

Thus, much of commodity-related investment is carried out through public or private investment funds and public pension and life insurance funds. There are a number of public *investment funds* and investment vehicles that are either available to the public as public companies or public partnerships or, in some cases, as private companies or partnerships. Table 6.3 gives a summary of the main categories of these saving and investment vehicles.

Among the most important of these saving and investment vehicles are money-market funds, bond and equity funds, derivative funds, hedge funds, pension and life insurance funds. Commodity-related investment mainly takes place through

Table 6.3   The main categories of investment funds

Risk[a]	Types of funds	Characteristics
0	Money market funds (EU, USA, etc.)	Portfolio of money market positions, of short-term bonds and other fixed-interest instruments, such as repurchase agreements; regulations: no borrowing, limited uncovered positions on futures and option markets
1	Bond-oriented mutual funds (Canada, USA); regulated bond-oriented investment funds under the UCITS[b] directive in all EU member countries, including bond-oriented unit trusts (UK, Ireland, etc.).	Diversified portfolio of bonds quoted on organised markets; regulations: minimum diversification of portfolio, no borrowing, limited uncovered positions on futures and option markets, transparency and disclosure rules (publication of portfolio and of various elements of performance); regulations for UE member countries: UCITS directive of 1985
2	Regulated mutual funds (Canada, USA); regulated investment funds under the UCITS directive in all EU member countries, including unit trusts (UK, Ireland, etc.).	Diversified portfolio of bonds and shares quoted on organised markets; regulations: minimum diversification of portfolio, no borrowing, limited uncovered positions on futures and option markets, transparency and disclosure rules (publication of portfolio and of various elements of performance); regulations for EU member countries: UCITS directive of 1985
3[b]	Commodity pools (USA); regulated funds of futures throughout the EU, including FOF and GFOF (UK), and FIMT (France, Luxembourg)	Diversified portfolios of derivative positions quoted on organised markets; regulations: minimum diversification of portfolio, no borrowing, limited uncovered positions on futures and option markets, transparency and disclosure rules (publication of portfolio and of various elements of performance); publicity submitted to strict regulations or even forbidden. Submitted to the control of national market authorities. Minimum value of shares provided for in some countries.
4	Hedge funds (USA and elsewhere)	Diversified speculative portfolios (often of derivative positions that are either quoted on organised or OTC derivative markets, of arbitrage positions); regulation (USA): Private companies or partnerships (which are not public companies), borrowing and uncovered derivatives possible, some disclosure rules (information for investors). Access restricted 'accredited' investors (financial institutions and high net worth investors, etc.).

Table 6.3 *(continued)*

Risk[a]	Types of funds	Characteristics
1–2	Pension funds and life insurance funds (in most countries)	Diversified portfolio of bonds and shares quoted on organised markets; other investments such as real estate, commodities and, in some cases, positions on futures markets possible in some countries; regulations: minimum diversification of portfolio, no borrowing, limited uncovered positions on futures and option markets, transparency and disclosure rules (publication of portfolio and of various elements of performance). Available to employees and self-employed people as pension-oriented saving instruments or as life insurance products.

[a] Risk classes: 0 = riskless asset; 1 = moderate risk; 2 = important risk, but very little risk of bankruptcy; 3 = more important risk, with significant but still low risk of bankruptcy; 4 = very important risk, significant risk of bankruptcy.
[b] UCITS = undertakings for collective investment in transferable securities; FOF = funds of futures; GFOF = geared funds of futures; FIMT = Fonds d'intervention sur les marchés à terme.

commodity derivatives that are part of the portfolios of managed futures funds and of hedge funds.

However, a new generation of commodity-invested investment funds appeared more recently, in which commodity derivatives are used, together with other derivatives such as financial derivatives, providing a gearing effect with more diversification and thus a better risk-return profile.

Clearly, commodity futures and options are risky and speculative assets. In a number of countries, there are regulated speculative investment funds (commodity pools in the USA, futures and options funds and geared futures and option funds in the UK, and similar investment vehicles in other EU and OECD member countries). The activity of these funds is to manage portfolios of positions on futures and option markets under reasonable diversification and prudential rules. Regulated funds of futures are subject, in most countries in which they are allowed and regulated, to specific diversification and collateralization rules that minimise their risks, while providing a gearing effect.

Hedge funds are defined as investment funds managing diversified portfolios of derivative instruments under minimal regulation. They represent a relatively new financial innovation. According to historians of finance, the first hedge fund was established by Alfred Winslow Jones in 1949[1] (Ledermann and Klein, 1995). But hedge funds really took off in terms of the volume of assets managed only at the end of 1980–90 (Chandler, 1998; Nicholas, 1999). While famous funds such as

---

[1] Whereas ordinary investment funds date back from the end of the eighteenth century.

George Soros' quantum funds are invested in various financial assets, including currency and financial futures, they also often use commodity derivatives as portfolio assets.

Futures funds and hedge funds alike will benefit from asset allocation including several categories of assets (financial futures, currency futures and commodity futures). As mentioned in Chapter 2, Elton *et al.* (1990), over a shorter period, show evidence that the performance of public commodity funds has been quite disappointing. But, as noted previously, the inclusion of diversified commodity assets in existing portfolios with other categories of assets will usually improve the characteristics of a portfolio.

Finally, the economic utility of derivative markets is manifold, and derivative markets play at least three roles.

Firstly, they are used for *hedging* physical operations, price risk in particular, by firms involved in the physical trading of commodities, producers, industrial operators, or trading companies. They are used as an insurance system for physical traders, for whom it may be highly desirable to protect themselves, or to *hedge*, against the risk of adverse price variations.

Secondly, organised derivative markets and in particular futures markets also serve the purpose of providing *information* on prices and prices on futures markets are often used as reference prices for commercial commodity contracts. They provide reference prices that are recognised internationally and thus provide an invaluable service in supplying 'fair' prices that may be used in physical purchasing contracts on OTC markets. This service rendered to actors of the physical trading community is a positive externality because, except for the (usually comparatively small) cost of information, this is a *free* service.

Thirdly, they are used as vehicles for *speculation*. As discussed in previous chapters, and in particular in Chapter 2, speculation may be defined as leveraged investment in risky assets, such as derivative instruments. Speculators defined in this sense are usually members of the financial community, or financial intermediaries. They use commodity derivatives as risky (sometimes highly risky) investments in portfolio management with investment vehicles such as funds of futures and hedge funds, as described above.

Although speculators are often demonized in the media and in the general public, efficient futures markets are indeed an indispensable complement to efficient physical and global trading. They lead to significant gains for end-consumers as well as to constant liquidity for producers and physical traders on markets which are highly competitive. More precisely, speculators contribute to price discovery on derivative markets as well as to the competitive character, efficiency, and liquidity of commodity derivative markets.

This means that they contribute to the second mission of derivative markets, which is to provide fair pricing with recognised prices that may be used as reference prices in the negotiation of physical commercial commodity contracts.

As far as the first role is concerned, speculators on derivative markets, by accepting the market risks that the hedgers want to avoid, contribute to the *transfer and dilution of market risks*. In return, they expect to make a profit as the reward for the risk they are taking. This is the main function of actors of the financial community, such as banks, investment companies (such as mutual funds) and insurance companies. We are dealing here with risks that are higher than the usual risks taken by banks or ordinary investment companies or insurance companies. However, these risks can be pooled by suitable diversification, just as any other financial risks are, under the portfolio management theory that was first developed by Markowitz (1959).

Speculators also provide liquidity for physical traders hedging on these markets. They are the necessary counterparties of hedgers on commodity derivative markets. In his historical normal backwardation model (see e.g. Chapter 2) Keynes (1931) was one of the first authors to notice this. In Keynes' approach, the net position of hedgers was short, because they were mainly commodity producers. However, this is not generally true. Depending on the general level of commodity prices, the net position of hedgers can be short if prices are currently low and decreasing, with a high risk for commodity producers. In that first case, as will be discussed in section 6.3.3, many industrial end-users face a low risk and do not hedge. But this net position of hedgers may be long if prices are currently high and increasing, with a high risk for commodity end-users. In the second case, as will be discussed in section 6.3.3, many producers face a low risk and do not hedge. During the depression of the 1930s, when Keynes developed his well-known normal backwardation theory, commodity prices were low and decreasing, so that the hypothesis that hedgers were net short was probably true.

6.3 HEDGING AND CASH FLOW MANAGEMENT

6.3.1 Hedging Positions or Hedging Cash Flows?

Standard presentations of futures and derivative markets neglect a number of risks, which, in the practical management of commodity marketing, purchasing, and trading, are quite important and may be enormous. Hedging a position on a physical market by taking an opposite position on a futures market, as discussed in Chapter 2, amounts to creating a riskless portfolio except for the basis. Consequently, there remains the risk attached to the evolution of the basis. This risk is usually much smaller than the risk inherent in a cash or futures position on the same quantity of a commodity. But it is not negligible and may be important in some cases. In any case, it must be managed. Furthermore, the basic presentations of optimal hedging, although they rest on portfolio theory, are valid only in *accounting terms, not in cash flow terms*. They do not consider the cash deposits that are actually required for any position on any organised futures market. Neither do they take into consideration margin calls and other negative cash flows that the operator may be charged on the cash market in the event of a suitable price variation for the underlying commodity (price increase for a seller and price decrease for a purchaser). If the operator is either a producer or a trader selling a physical commodity on the cash market, these cash flows usually occur before the operator's client has paid for the physical commodity. If the operator is an industrial end-user, these cash flows will add to the final settlement that is due, usually before that final settlement. In the case of options bought on an organised market, the premium is a negative cash flow which occurs when purchasing the option and before the final payment of the physical commodity, whether received or due.

In terms of cash flows this situation can be illustrated by a simple example. INTCO, a large international copper smelting company, receives an order for 6000 metric tonnes of cathode grade copper on 2***, June 10 to be sold at the prevailing LME spot price by the end of September 2***. INTCO intends to complete the production of these 6000 tonnes on 25 September, 2***, at a production cost of US$1290/tonne. The company's market room operator wishes to hedge against the risk that the LME spot price, which is US$1520.00 / tonne on 16 September, goes down by 30 September. He/she therefore *sells* futures on LME contracts for 6000 tonnes for 30 September, 2***, at US$1577 / tonne: he/she is 'short', his/her position is opposite to the equivalent buying position he/she is forecasting for 25 September. This position amounts to $9,462,000. The operator will bring the hedging action to an end on 25 September when he has produced the 6000 tonnes of copper that are then sold at the LME spot price prevailing at that date.

Assume now (in the unfavourable case in which the spot price of copper goes up) that the LME spot price of copper goes up to US$1625 per tonne at that date and that the corresponding LME futures price for 30 September on 20 September is US$1641. This is again close to the spot price. Then, the operator sells 'spot' his 6000 tonnes, for US$9,750,000; he will also *offset* his futures position by an opposite operation, which is buying futures for 6000 tonnes at US$1641, for US$9,846,000 (see Table 6.4 below).

Table 6.4 Selling futures for hedging: example 1

Spot	Futures	Basis
Spot price on 10.6.2***	Futures price on 10.6.2***	US$57
US$1520 (objective for 30.9.2***)	US$1577(settlement on 30.9.2***)	
Spot price on 20.9.2***	Futures price on 20.9.2***	US$16
US$1625	US$1641	
	US$64 (Loss)	US$41

The result of this operation is usually represented on a *T-account*. Result per tonne (exclusive of brokerage commissions):

Cash selling price: US$1625 − futures loss of US$64

= net selling price of US$1561

= price objective of US$1520 + basis gain of US$41

This T-account is, however, only a partial accounting representation of the situation, as it does not describe fully INTCO's operational cash flows. First of all, the operator is requested a deposit which might be 10% of its position at the beginning of the operation. This means a deposit of US$946,200, which adds to INTCO's working capital requirements. This deposit is usually under the form of riskless assets. It may consist in cash or treasury bonds. It may also be an irrevocable letter of credit (see e.g. Chapter 7). This means that some additional low-return working capital has to be used for hedging. This working capital is, however, quite risky in terms of the returns that one may expect for it in terms of the cash flows it generates either in the case of adverse price evolution, or in the case of favourable price evolution. Of course, these cash flows have to be balanced by almost equal reduction in the risks concerning the cash flows observed on physical markets. In our example, the fact that the price of copper has increased by US$41/tonne implies a cumulative negative cash flow of US$ − 384,000 to be taken from INTCO's deposit. This cash flow will add to the other operational cash flows (labour costs, other capital costs, costs for energy and raw materials, etc.) which amount to US$1290/tonne; hence, these operational cash flows are negative and amount to US$ − 7,740,000. All these negative cash flows occur *before* INTCO is paid by its client, thus giving a positive cash flow of US$9,750,000 which might take place by the end of September, once the client has received the copper. These successive cash flows are summarised in Table 6.5.

Table 6.5 Successive cash flows in a hedged sale: example 1

Dates and nature of cash flows	Amounts of cash flows (US$)	Balance of brokerage account (US$)
10.6.2***: futures deposit (if in cash)	−946,200	946,200
10.6.2*** to 20.9.2***: Operational cash flows	−7,740,000	—
20.9.2***: margin payments	−384,000	562,200
20.9.2***: Brokerage commission	−2,000	560,200
20.9.2***: Refund of deposit	560,200	0
30.9.2***: payment of commodity by client	9,750,000	—
Net profit	1,624,000	—

Clearly, in this example, the unfavourable evolution of prices on futures markets is more than compensated by the increase in the payment of the commodity by the client. It is not exactly compensated here because of the basis and because of the US$2000 brokerage commission. Here, the basis even plays a favourable role, since it decreases the margin payment by US$246,000. But commodity price volatilities may be higher than in this example, leading to much more adverse cash flows. Assume, for instance (Example 2), that the spot price of copper goes up to US$1960 by 20 September, 2***, an evolution which might effectively be observed in some cases. The new T-account in that case is given in Table 6.6. Result per tonne (exclusive of brokerage commissions):

Cash selling price: US$1960 − futures loss of US$408

= net selling price of US$1552

= price objective of US$1520 + basis gain of US$32

This second example assumes increases of the spot and futures prices of copper that are strong, but not altogether unlikely. Here, in order to maintain a minimum amount for the deposit, several margin calls before the maturity of the futures contract are necessary. Assume, for instance, that the evolution of the futures price for copper runs as given in Table 6.7. The dates correspond to the margin calls that INTCO is requested to pay. In this second example, the cash flow evolution is much less favourable than in the first example (Table 6.8).

In this second example, we can see that the cash flows resulting from margin payments are huge (US$2,460,000); they are significantly higher than the profit expected from the sale of copper. The first example shows that, if the price evolution is either flat or moderately increasing, the cash flows due to margin payments are reasonable. But, if the price evolution is strongly increasing, the cash flows due to margin payments become of the order of magnitude of the

Table 6.6 Selling futures for hedging: example 2

Spot	Futures	Basis
Spot price on 10.6.2*** US$1520 (objective for 30.9.2***)	Futures price on 10.6.2*** US$1577 (settlement on 30.9.2***)	US$57
Spot price on 20.9.2*** US$1960	Futures price on 20.9.2*** US$1985	US$25
	US$408 (LOSS)	US$32

Table 6.7 Assumed evolution of the futures prices for copper: example 2

Date	10.6.2***	30.6.2***	10.7.2***	28.7.2***	14.8.2***	21.8.2***	3.9.2***	12.9.2***	20.9.2***
Price	1577	1602	1670	1755	1846	1836	1902	1940	1985

Table 6.8 Successive cash flows in a hedged sale: example 2

Dates and nature of cash flows	Amounts of cash flows (US$)	Balance of brokerage account (US$)
10.6.2***: futures deposit (if in cash)	−946,200	946,200
10.7.2***: margin call	−578,000	946,200
28.7.2***: margin call	−510,000	946,200
14.8.2***: margin call	−546,000	946,200
12.9.2***: margin call	−554,000	946,200
10.6.2*** to 20.9.2***: operational cash flows	−7,740,000	—
20.9.2***: margin payment	−270,000	676,200
20.9.2***: brokerage commission	−2,000	674,200
20.9.2***: refund of deposit	674,200	0
30.9.2***: payment of commodity by client	11,760,000	—
Net profit	1,560,000	—

expected profit. Clearly, however, at least *if the hedging position is matched to the expected cash flows*, the cash flows due to margin payments and the operational cash flows should *be of the order of magnitude of the expected positive cash flows from sales*. They should even lead to a profit. The conclusion to be drawn from these examples concerning a producer's hedge are that *one should hedge cash flows, not accounting positions*. Similar conclusions could be drawn by examining the case of a purchaser. We will examine later the case of traders, in which hedging is both more crucial and more risky. This is an important point which should be stressed, as many of the disasters that might occur are due to a mismatch and/or an excessive time lag between hedging positions and physical positions that lead to short-term cash flows. For instance, still in the case of producers, some mining companies are tempted to hedge their reserves, which are long-term accounting positions, rather than only their shorter commercial positions that will lead to immediate or short-term cash flows. This is not a good practice. While hedging gold reserves, for instance, theoretically stabilizes the value of an essential asset of the company, the negative cash flows that might occur to the firm in the case of a price increase may simply become much higher than the operational cash flows. This might lead the firm to serious financial problems. Therefore, if the company decides to hedge, the following hedging rules are appropriate:

1. A company should hedge cash flows, not accounting positions.
2. There should be no mismatch, and no excessive time lag, between the physical positions resulting in the foregoing expected cash flows and the hedging position adjusted to it (which should be the optimal hedge as described in Chapter 2).
3. An unfavourable evolution of the basis should be taken into account.

These conclusions are valid in the case of both producers and purchasers, and are even more important in the case of traders. An example of the pertinence of these rules is the case of the disaster that happened to the well-known German trader, Metallgesellschaft.

6.3.2   A Case Study: Metallgesellschaft

The case of the hedging disaster that happened to MGRM, a US oil trading subsidiary of Metallgesellschaft, has been the object of several academic studies (Culp and Miller, 1994; Edwards and Canter, 1995; Mello and Parsons, 1995; Pirrong, 1997; Gilbert, 2000). At the end of 1992 and in the beginning of 1993, the German commodity trader Metallgesellschaft incorporated MG Refining and Marketing as a US subsidiary specialised in the trading of oil and oil products. Inasmuch as MGRM was a newcomer on that market, it tried to attract clients by granting them long-term (5-year and 10-year contracts), fixed price forward contracts for very large amounts. At that time, the spot price of crude oil was about some US$20/barrel. Pirrong (1997) shows that these physical contracts amounted to a huge short position of 160 million barrels. Therefore, MGRM as a trader expected to supply on the spot market, so that the company had to take a long hedge against any price increase above US$20/barrel. It decided to hedge on a one-for-one basis, using three-month futures and planning 'rolling' the futures over every three months. This meant an (enormous) long position of 160 million barrels and, for any marginal oil price decrease of US$1, margin payments of US$160 million.

This hedging position was initially harmless to MGRM, but at the end of 1993, the price of crude oil fell down to US$12/barrel, implying enormous cash flows (of the order of magnitude of US$1 billion) in order to meet margin payment requirements.

An additional problem was that the three-month futures price of crude oil, which was initially in backwardation and hence beneficial to MGRM, shifted to contango. This meant that the basis played an unfavourable role, adding to negative cash flows.

At the end of 1993, the management of MGRM's parent company decided to stop any further hedging on futures markets. This decision was taken at a time when the price of crude oil and oil products were rather low and therefore strongly exposed to upward price risks. The decision to give up any hedging thus left MGRM with no protection whatsoever against this heavy risk. It led the company to a final disaster, when eventually the price of crude oil went above the level required for break even of the forward contracts concluded with MGRM's clients. MGRM thus suffered heavy losses on its unhedged physical operations this time: no hedge under these conditions amounts to a very risky short speculative position.

Several hefty management errors can be found in the case of MGRM. The first point is that the hedging positions were disconnected from the firm's cash flows, leading to huge negative cash flows that were not covered by nearby positive cash flows. This phenomenon was aggravated by the fact that these hedging positions were well over optimal hedging, which has been estimated by Pirrong (1997) as 0.5 to 0.6 as a proportion of the total position, rather than as one to one. But, more importantly, following Edwards and Canter (1995) one can ask whether concluding long-term forward contracts with its clients was the first and the largest of MGRM's mistakes because hedging these physical contracts was almost impossible.

A second point (Pirrong, 1997; Gilbert, 2000) is that the basis risk was neglected by MGRM, because the futures prices of crude oil were initially in backwardation, a favourable but rather abnormal situation. As could have been expected and taken into account, the basis later shifted back to contango, leading this time to an unfavourable situation. According to Pirrong, this basis risk was also very high.

A third point is that in the Metallgesellschaft group, there was a lack of communication between the management of the parent company and MGRM's financial management. As noted by several authors, including Culp and Miller (1994), the decision of MGRM's parent company to stop any hedging at the end of 1993 was a disastrous one. While it is somewhat difficult in the absence of further information to establish the responsibilities, some general lessons can be drawn from this case study. A clear strategy concerning the management of forward contracts and the hedging of price risks appears to be necessary, with the financial management being left with clear guidelines. Furthermore, specific training of management in the issues related to forward contracts and hedging appears as indispensable in the light of what happened with MGRM.

Following this rather negative example, we are going to discuss some basic strategies and management issues concerning hedging.

6.3.3 To Hedge or not to Hedge? A Few Strategies and Management Principles

The examination of actual situations of both commodity producers and purchasers is the key to some conclusions that can be drawn with respect to the hedging strategies that are optimal for each case, including no hedging at all if the exposure to commodity price risk is small. The specific case of traders, for which hedging is usually more necessary, is also worth discussing, but even in their case, some strategies such as vertical integration may contribute to offsetting commodity price risks on both sides of the markets.

In the case of commodity producers, the overall cost of production and the logistics costs (in the case of a FOB delivery contract, these should be comparatively small) is a crucial parameter. If the current spot price is much higher than this cost, an assessment of the risk that the price goes below a certain level that ensures a minimum profit must be undertaken by the management of the firm. If, on the one hand, forward fixed-price contracts are concluded on the basis of the current spot price or on the basis of the current futures price at the date of delivery, with either a discount or a premium according to the situation of the market in some cases, no hedging at all is usually necessary. If, on the other hand, contracts are concluded on the basis of the current spot price at the time of delivery, hedging might not be necessary again if the current price when concluding the contract is well above the cost applying to the producer. However, it might be safer in that case to buy an in-the-money put at a strike price which is still well above the cost of production. A more sophisticated approach might be selling an out-of-the-money call at a price that is well above the current spot price, as this will cover the price of the put or part of it. The possible negative cash flows resulting from margin payments due to selling a call will be entirely covered by positive cash flows resulting from the physical sale of the commodity.

Example   Derris Mining is an Australian mining company. In September 2***, the company receives an order from a large British client for 44,000 oz of fine gold, to be delivered FOB at London Heathrow airport at the end of November 2000. The cost of production and the logistics costs of Derris Mining are estimated at US$240/oz. The current spot price is US$270.61/oz; the current futures price at COMEX for November 2*** delivery is US$271.40/oz. Call options with November 2*** expiration are currently priced at US$1.50/oz for a strike price of US$280/oz, and put options with November 2*** expiration are currently priced at US$0.90/oz for a strike price of US$260/oz.

Derris Mining has several possibilities. First, it may choose not to hedge at all, with the (rather small) risk that the price of gold goes down below US$240/oz. But there still is a significant probability of a price going down to some US$250/oz, thus cutting the profit margin to unacceptable levels. One of the solutions might be to buy puts with a strike price of US$260, thus securing a minimum profit of US$19.10/oz. A second strategy would be to sell a covered call at US$1.50/oz, and to buy the put still at US$0.90/oz, leaving a profit of US$0.60/oz, which can give Derris further possibilities in the negotiation of its contract if the market is very competitive. In this case, the profit margin will be between a minimum of US$19.70 and a maximum of US$40.60.

If, now, the cost of production of the commodity is lower than its market price, but comparatively close to it, so that there is a significant price risk, the seller can do either of two things. A first approach is to negotiate a suitable fixed forward price. This is usually a rather effective way of protecting oneself through suitably negotiating the commercial contract (see e.g. Chapter 7). If we assume that there is a clear profit edge between the spot price and the operating costs for the commodity, the spot price may be used as the basis of pricing, with either a premium or a discount if the state of the market justifies it. If there is an efficient futures market that can serve for reference pricing, the futures price is usually close to the spot price and may be accepted by both parties as an acceptable forward price. However, the pricing basis has to be corrected if delivery occurs at a place that is not the futures market warehouse.

If a fixed forward price is provided for in the contract, giving the seller a clear margin profit, no hedging is necessary. If the price risk is significant, a second strategy, which requires hedging, is to negotiate the pricing clause of the commercial contract on the basis of the spot price at the time of delivery. Then, a short hedge is indispensable and it is an easy operation if there exists an efficient and liquid futures market. The short hedge should take into account the optimal hedge ratio, so that it usually occurs on a less than one-for-one basis. If there is no efficient futures market, a suitable OTC derivative, usually a swap, will have to be negotiated. But in this case, it will usually be better to negotiate a fixed forward price.

A short hedge on an organised market implies a residual cash flow risk if the price of the commodity goes up sharply. To limit this risk, the producer can buy an out-of-the-money call provided it is available on the market at a reasonable price.

Example Imagine, now, that Kerpel Mining, a Canadian competitor of Derris Mining, receives an order for 38,000 oz from an American client in Chicago for delivery in November 2*** under the same market conditions as previously. However, the operational costs of Kerpel Mining are US$262/oz, leaving the company with a significant price risk. In addition to previous figures, call options with November 2*** expiration are currently priced at US$1.10/oz for a strike price of US$285/oz.

Kerpel Mining is left with several possibilities. First, it can negotiate a fixed forward price, such as US$271.40/oz and in this case will not have to hedge at all. This leaves the company with a profit margin of US$9.40/oz on this sale. A second strategy would be to negotiate the contract at the spot price prevailing at the date of delivery. This implies going short for 38,000 oz on Comex at US$271.40/oz, also leaving a profit of US$9.40/oz. If the company wants to limit its cash flow risk, it can buy a call with a strike price of US$285 for US$1.10/oz, but this will decrease the profit margin by US$1.10/oz.

Table 6.9 gives a summary of the hedging strategies available to commodity producers.

Industrial end-users also have several possible strategies that are opposite to the strategies of producers. A first case is when the price risk is low, because the commodity is integrated in an industrial good and its cost share is small, so that even a large increase in the price of the commodity will not threaten the profit margin. Similar situations will occur even if the cost share of the

Table 6.9 Hedging strategies available to producers

Market price vs operational costs	Price risk	Pricing	Hedging strategy	Residual risk
Much higher	Small	Fixed forward price	No hedging	None
		Spot price at time of delivery	Buying in-the-money put (and selling covered call)	Small, minimum profit
Small difference	High	Fixed forward price	No hedging	None
		Spot price at time of delivery	Short hedge	Cash flow risk

commodity is large, but if the profit margin is large enough not to be threatened again by an increase in the price of the commodity. In this first case, the industrial purchaser will have two possible pricing strategies. The first strategy is to conclude a purchasing contract with a fixed forward price. In that case, no hedging is necessary. The second strategy is to conclude the purchasing contract with pricing at the spot price that will prevail at the time of delivery. The price risk being small, no hedging may still be required. But our purchaser may also buy a call (and possibly sell a covered put) to limit the risk.

If the price risk is significant, the purchaser will have to take a long hedge on the commodity bought. This leaves small basis and cash flow risks. The cash flow risk may be addressed and limited through buying an in-the-money put.

Hedging strategies for purchasers are thus symmetric to the strategies available to sellers (Table 6.10).

Thus, we can see that producers and industrial purchasers alike have a number of strategies at their disposal. They can either not hedge at all, or hedge only if the price risk is large. In all situations, the effect of possible price variations has to be assessed with respect to the profit margin.

In practice, many producers and even more purchasers will not hedge at all or hedge only partially, because the effect of adverse price variations on their

Table 6.10 Hedging strategies available to industrial end-users

Commodity cost share vs profit margin	Price risk	Pricing	Hedging strategy	Residual risk
Much smaller	Small	Fixed forward price	No hedging	None
		Spot price at time of delivery	Buying in-the-money call (and selling covered put)	Small, minimum profit
Same order of magnitude	High	Fixed forward price	No hedging	None
		Spot price at time of delivery	Long hedge	Cash flow risk

profit margins is small. In other cases, if this effect is large, they will have to hedge if the price provided for in the forward contracts is the spot price at time of delivery or close to delivery.

The case of traders or trading companies is quite different because they usually have profit margins that are smaller than the profit margins available to producers and industrial end-users.

As will be discussed in Chapter 8, traders often keep and manage stocks for various commodities, including agricultural commodities, metals, oil products and other energy commodities such as coal. It is indeed one of their industrial activities. They ideally purchase commodities that are inventoried whenever prices are low, selling from their stocks when prices are higher. This requires short hedging in order to protect the value of inventories, especially if commodities are sold forward and priced on the basis of spot market prices at the time of delivery. As a rule, profit margins of traders are small, because there usually is a small difference between the selling price and cost of the physical commodities under storage, including storage and logistic costs. Thus, no hedging in the case of a trader keeping inventories can be very risky. If markets are in contango, which is usual, traders will play on the basis in order to maintain their profit margin. As shown in Chapter 2, the basis may be thought of as the price that futures markets ascribe to carry over costs and to the industrial management of stocks. Traders running their stocks in a competitive manner may expect to sell at a profit, however small it may be, especially if market prices are increasing. In that case, traders can also often sell forward at fixed prices and at a small premium over spot prices, which in principle does not require hedging. But in general their activity is still quite risky, as will be emphasised in Chapters 7 and 8. Risks can nevertheless be kept under control and lowered if the trader is vertically integrated and especially when trading companies are present in commodity production. In that case, their situation is similar to that of producers described above.

Example   Westgrain is a large American trading company running elevators. On 20 November, 2***, it has purchased 750,000 bushels (21,150 tonnes) of wheat (soft red) on the spot market. The spot price of wheat is US$2.28/bushel. A few days later, the company receives an order for 20,000 tonnes of wheat to be delivered FOB New York in early January and concludes a sales contract on the basis of the spot price at the time of delivery, plus a premium of US$0.02/bushel to take into account logistics costs given the place of delivery. The futures price for the January delivery is US2.40\frac{3}{4}$/bushel. The physical costs of storage are estimated to be US$0.095/bushel. The trader also expects several orders that will account for the rest of the quantity that has just been bought on 20 November.

In this case, the trader will take a short hedge to protect its stock. The profit margin that can be expected is only a few cents and the price risk is enormous. If, for instance, the spot price goes down to US$2.10/bushel at time of delivery and if the basis is at $2\frac{1}{2}$ cents, so that the January futures trade at US2.12\frac{1}{2}$/bushel, offsetting the trader's position leads to a profit of US$0.2825/bushel. Thus, the net selling price is US$2.4025/bushel, leaving the trader with a profit of 2.75 cents/bushel.

In other cases, to meet clients' orders, traders will buy on the spot market just before selling. If so, they may hedge their purchase by a long position on futures markets, and sell forward at a fixed price.

Example   Assume, for instance, that a trader of Westgrain, a few days after having sold the 20,000 tonnes of wheat mentioned above, is asked to quote a fixed forward price for 12,000 tonnes of wheat, for delivery at the end of January. This is an order that cannot be met out of company stocks. The spot price has gone up to US$2.32/bushel and the futures price for the January delivery has gone up slightly to US2.41\frac{1}{4}$/bushel. The company will thus have to buy the wheat on the spot market about two weeks before delivery.

Estimating the basis to be about 4 to 6 cents/bushel at that time (through statistics concerning the historical basis at that time of the year), and the transportation costs to the FOB destination to be 2 cents/bushel the trader will quote a forward price of US$2.45/bushel. In the worst possible situation in which the basis is of 6 cents/bushel, this will leave him/her with a profit of about 5 cents/bushel.

If there are no organised futures, traders have an even more risky activity. In this case, they can protect themselves against adverse price variations by using fixed forward pricing on both sides of the market, or by using OTC derivatives.

Table 6.11 below gives some examples of hedging strategies available to traders.

The influence of the physical counterparty risk, which concerns the purchaser, on the price risk is important and deserves some discussion. We are interested in the case where the seller partially defaults, being late in delivering the commodity. In this case, there is the additional risk that the purchaser, under a spot pricing clause in the commercial contract and having taken a long hedge, will no longer be hedged because delivery occurs after maturity of the hedge, which might be very risky. This problem requires a careful choice of the suppliers on the basis

Table 6.11   Examples of hedging strategies available to traders

Pricing on supply side	Pricing on demand side	Price risk	Hedging strategy	Residual risk
Spot price at time of supply	Spot price at time of delivery	High	Short hedge (if contango)	Basis risk
Spot price at time of delivery	Fixed forward price on the basis of futures price + commission or spread	High	Long hedge	Basis risk

of their ability to deliver in time. A systematic choice of a hedge expiring a little later than the delivery date (two weeks to one month) should be made. Generally speaking, the penalties in case of late delivery should take into account this situation. In this case, the seller or trader should roll the long hedge after expiration of a previous futures contract. This can be costly in terms of basis risk, and adequately provided for by imposing adequate penalties to the seller in the contract.

6.3.4   Hedging: Corporate Control and Organisation Aspects

The example of Metallgesellschaft shows, among other things, that some problems occurred in terms of the internal organisation of the group with respect to hedging. As has been shown by this case and by other discussions, mismanaged hedging can be disastrous. Hedging can be very useful in protecting the firm against undesirable price risks, provided a clear and harmless hedging strategy is fully defined and implemented, under adequate control and monitoring of derivative markets activities.

First of all, price risks, hedging and the safe use of derivatives should be fully understood by all the executives of a company at a responsible level that are concerned with these issues. This concerns of course the chief executive officer (CEO) and other top management executives, such as, in particular, the financial officer of the company. This means that a *hedging strategy should be carefully defined and implemented for the company or for the group, with full commitment of the CEO*. The next step is to define responsibilities at the level of the company or of the group and its subsidiaries. Teams of individual traders that are in charge of hedging physical positions on organised derivative markets should be carefully trained. Their activity should be carefully controlled and carried out in close connection with the physical positions taken by the marketing department. These traders should work to imposed detailed trading rules and a code of conduct excluding speculation. This means that the positions that they take are to be limited in quantity and time and that traders should be made to report to some responsible executive. In addition, some risky speculative actions, such as rolling contracts, taking uncovered positions on futures markets and selling uncovered options, should be prohibited. Traders should be trained into responsibly assessing the price risk of any physical position and into suitably hedging all significant exposures to price risk, no more and no less. As mentioned earlier, this might mean that some positions would not be hedged. This can be left to the traders' appreciation. The negotiation and use of OTC derivatives should be the responsibility of carefully trained persons and some responsible executive should approve any OTC derivative contract.

Control, auditing, and monitoring structures, implying detailed and precise accounting documents, should be implemented in order to be able to assess at any time the company's exposure to price risk.

A detailed discussion of company control and management structures with respect to hedging has been provided by UNCTAD (1996).

6.4 COMMODITIES AND CORPORATE FINANCE

We have just discussed hedging in terms of cash flows. Hedging is also important with regard to market finance. First of all, well-managed hedging increases the shareholder value of a company, especially in the case of producers. It eliminates most of the price risk and thus decreases the risk premium that capital markets associate with a company. Thus, companies such as mining companies will usually disclose their hedging policy in their financial reports aimed at investors, thereby giving indications of how much of their production is hedged, if any.

A second and important aspect of the topic is medium-term and long-term commodity-related finance, which mainly concerns commodity producers. During the 1970s and the 1980s, commodity-related finance, especially in the case of commodity producers such as mining companies, developed steadily as this was generally a bullish period on commodity markets. Commodity-related finance was available mainly in the form of bonds with commodity (call) warrants attached (Priovolos and Duncan, 1991) or with commodity-indexed interest or principal. Commodities with efficient organised international spot and derivative markets such as gold, silver, nickel, copper, and crude oil were involved. The fact that warrants with a suitable exercise price were attached to the bonds enabled borrowers to obtain better interest terms. For instance, Duncan and Priovolos (1991) mention the example of a bond issued by Echo Bay Mines, a well-known Canadian mining company. Each bond of Swiss francs 5000 was issued with a 3.875% coupon and a gold call warrant was attached to it, enabling the bearer to buy 6 oz of gold at an exercise price of US$560/oz, between 30 November 1986 and 30 September 1991.

Similar bonds were common in the 1970s and in the 1980s, but they disappeared later, due to the fact that commodity prices such as the price of gold were generally decreasing during the 1990s.

Other financial innovations for commodity producers came in the form of asset-backed finance (UNCTAD, 1998; Matringe, 2000). Asset-backed finance refers to loans with a collateral that is related to commodities held by the producer or cash flows related to commodity sales. For instance, a comparatively simple form of asset-backed finance consists of a loan from a bank in a developed country to a mining company in a developing country. The loan is backed by cash flows due to periodic payments that stem from the sales of the commodity to an industrial end-user from a developed country (Figure 6.1). This scheme makes it possible to shift repayment cash flow risks from a risky area to a less risky area. This is achieved by transferring some of the payments from an industrial end-user to an escrow account which is used by the bank granting the loan (or by the syndicated

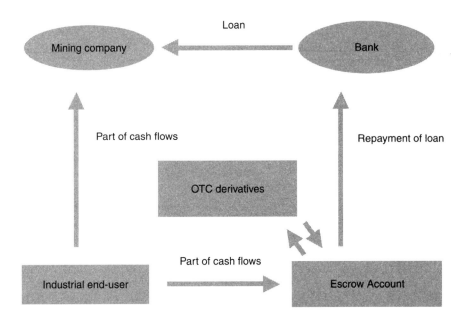

Figure 6.1   General arrangement of asset-backed finance to a mining company

banks granting the loan) to cover loan payments. The industrial end-user is under a medium or long-term supply contract with the mining company. The loan payments are secured by payments by the mining company's client based on the quantities of the commodities stipulated in the contract. Since these payments are subject to commodity price risk, they should be hedged. The medium to long-term nature of the contracts (5 to 10 years is common) means that there are usually no organised market instruments for hedging these cash flows. Consequently, they are usually hedged on OTC markets.

Mexicana de Cobre, a leading Mexican copper company, is an example given by Matringe (2000) of a company that has used asset-backed finance for its activities. Matringe (2000) also describes other more sophisticated asset-backed finance techniques.

6.5   CONCLUSION

Throughout this chapter, we have discussed specific financial problems related to commodities. There are indeed commodity-related market finance problems that concern derivative markets as well as physical markets. Commodity derivatives and, to a lesser extent, physical commodities, are of interest to many types of investors including funds of futures and hedge funds as well as pension funds and insurance companies.

Although individual commodity derivatives are very risky and speculative assets, they can be of interest to investors because of their specific risk-return profiles that contribute to portfolio diversification. Futures based on commodity indexes are also important as financial instruments in this respect, although they are less liquid than futures on financial indexes.

Physical commodity market participants such as commodity producers, commodity industrial end-users, and commodity trading companies do face a number of specific *corporate finance* problems. They must often hedge their physical positions to offset price risk. We have shown that commodity hedging positions on derivative markets and especially on futures markets should be matched by equivalent opposite positions on physical markets in terms of *cash flows*. In addition, there are basis risks that should not be overlooked. Any hedging position that is not in line with operations on the physical markets is speculative. Cash flow risks for mismanaged and speculative hedging positions can be enormous, as shown by the MGRM case. In the discussion of hedging strategies concerning all commodity physical market participants we have also shown that, especially in the case of commodity producers and industrial end-users, it is often not necessary to hedge. Hedging, however, is more prevalent in the case of commodity traders. Where commodity-based finance is concerned, asset-backed finance can be useful for commodity producers.

In the next chapter, we discuss commercial contracts on physical commodity markets, which imply risks other than the price risk. As we shall see, these risks can be addressed by some other short-term financial techniques such as the letter of credit and require careful negotiation of the contract.

BIBLIOGRAPHY

B. Chandler (1998) *Investing with the Hedge Fund Giants. Profit Whether Markets Rise or Fall*. Financial Times–Pitman Publishing.

C. Culp and M. Miller (1994) Metallgesellschaft and the economics of synthetic storage, *Derivatives Quarterly*, **1**, 7–25.

F. R. Edwards and M. Canter (1995) The collapse of Metallgesellschaft: unhedgable risks, poor hedging strategy or just bad luck?, *Journal of Futures Markets*, **15**, 211–264.

E. J. Elton, M. J. Gruber, and J. Rentzler (1990) The performance of publicly offered commodity funds, *Financial Analyst*, July, 23–30.

M. Fox-Andrews and N. Meaden (1995) *Derivative Markets and Investment Management*. Prentice-Hall, London.

C. L. Gilbert (2000) *'Derivatives: Use and Abuse'*. Invited Lecture, International Conference of the Applied Econometrics Association on Industrial Econometrics, University of Luxembourg, 6 July.

J. Ledermann and R. A. Klein (1995) *Hedge Funds. Investment and Portfolio Strategies for the Institutional Investor*. Irwin Professional Publishing, Chicago.

J. Markowitz (1959) *Portfolio Selection. Efficient Diversification of Investment*. Wiley, New York.

O. Matringe (2000) *'Asset-backed Finance for the Metal and Mining Industry.'* Invited Lecture, International Conference of the Applied Econometrics Association on Industrial Econometrics, University of Luxembourg, 6 July.

A. Mello and J. Parsons (1995) The maturity structure of hedge matters: lessons from the Metallgesellschaft debacle, *Journal of Applied Corporate Finance*, **8**, 106–120.

J. G. Nicholas (1999) *Investing in Hedge Funds. Strategies for the New Marketplace.* Bloomberg Press, Princeton.

C. Pirrong (1997) Metallgesellschaft: a prudent hedger ruined, or a wildcatter on NYMEX?, *Journal of Futures Markets*, **17**, 543–578.

Th. Priovolos and R. C. Duncan (1991) *Commodity Risk Management and Finance.* Oxford University Press, Oxford.

Th. Priovolos (1991) La frontière efficace des profits sur les matières premières. Une approche par le modèle CAPM, in O. Güvenen, W. C. Labys and J. B. Lesourd (Editors), *Politiques économiques et marchés internationaux de matières premières. Analyses économétriques.* Economica, Paris, 35–44.

UNCTAD (1996) *Company Control and Management Structures. The Basic Requirements for a Sound Use of Market-based Risk Management Instruments.* UNCTAD, Geneva.

UNCTAD (1998) *New Strategies for a Changing Commodity Economy. The Role of Modern Financial Instruments.* Selected papers, 'Partners for Development' Summit, Lyons, France. UNCTAD, Geneva.

7
The management of physical commodity contracts

7.1 INTRODUCTION

Raw materials and more generally commodities (for instance, grains, tropical commodities, non-ferrous metal, oil products, meat and dairy products, etc.) are most often produced in specific geographical areas. Their consumption, however, generally involves all continents, and is therefore linked to global international markets. Furthermore, the industries that consume basic commodities usually form a very complex vertical transformation network with several stages of production using the commodity under more and more elaborate forms up to the final retail product. A retailer eventually sells the final product to an end-consumer with several commercial intermediaries between the production of the commodity and its final consumption. This means that the relationship between the production of a basic commodity and its consumption in the form of an elaborate consumption good is not straightforward and that, in addition to the geographical imbalance between supply and demand, there may also be a quantitative imbalance between the supply of a basic commodity and its consumption when incorporated in a consumption good. The reasons for this imbalance will be analysed in detail in section 7.2. However, due to this situation, some actors on international commodity markets have to provide for adjustment between supply and demand from various countries and geographical areas. This means in particular that, because of this adjustment problem between supply and demand, fundamental participants in these markets, which are mainly commodity producers and industrial end-users, must use the services of commercial intermediaries such as trading companies or merchants. The activity of these intermediaries is to optimise physical transfers of these products from one place to another as well as from seller to purchaser.

The legal environment of commercial contracts where these various actors come together in a deal is very complex and the wording of these contracts is extremely precise. The meticulous work of working out such contracts is clearly not only a matter of legal formalism. It also addresses, as will be discussed later, very precise economic and financial problems. The commercial contract on physical commodity markets may be defined as a written statement which describes precisely the rights and obligations of each of the parties to the commercial exchange of a commodity. The parties might include one or several producers, one or several industrial consumers or purchasers and/or one or several merchants or trading companies. The latter act as commercial intermediaries and may be either on the supply side, or on the demand side. The roles and the characteristics of these different actors will be developed in Chapter 8.

Drawing up physical commodity contracts generally amounts to formalising negotiations between the purchasing and selling parties. These negotiations are often lengthy and difficult in large part because the contracts must define precisely the nature and the quality of the goods as well as their price. These are essential elements of the agreement that must also stipulate the general conditions of the sale, which must be very carefully considered and prepared.

There are two essential reasons for requiring both conciseness and precision in defining the terms of the contract, first of all, because the commercial contract creates reciprocal obligations between the parties and, secondly, because of the risks pertaining to any international physical trading operation, which necessarily implies risk sharing between the parties.

More precisely, the risks related to international trading operations are manifold, including price risks, exchange rate risks, counterparty and default risks, logistic risks, freight-related risks, etc. Considering the physical quantities and the financial amounts in question, each of the parties has a vested interest in reducing the impact of each of these risks. In terms of price risk, which clearly is a crucial risk, if the commercial contract is an agreement which aims at a division of the risk between actors, it is clear that each actor, whatever his role in the operation, very often has to hedge on derivative markets. We have shown how the derivative markets are essentially financial contracts to be used for hedging or speculation. The commercial contract clearly differs from the derivatives contract in that it corresponds to commitments concerning a physical good. These commitments can only be fulfilled with the physical delivery of the goods by the supplier and their payment by the purchaser.

In this chapter we focus on the physical contract. In section 7.1, we discuss the specific characteristics of commodity contracts. International commercial contracts, whether they concern basic commodities, industrial goods or various services such as engineering services in the context of large projects, require diverse provisions and clauses. We address the question of the specific characteristics of commodities that require specific attention in the negotiation of commercial contracts.

In section 7.2, we discuss the nature and the role of the various actors who take part in commercial operations, together with the specific risks to which each of them is subjected in the particular case of commodity markets.

Section 7.3 is devoted to an analysis of the essential attributes of commercial commodity contracts. This section will attempt to analyse as clearly as possible the reciprocal obligations that the parties accept, and pinpoint which obligations are most important in the case of commodity contracts. These attributes of commercial contracts will be presented and discussed from the point of view of the safeguards that are indispensable in drafting the contract in the context of international commodity markets.

In section 7.4, we propose an analysis of the financial instruments that can be used by the actors of commercial operations in order to optimise them. These instruments include of course derivative instruments that we have already dealt with in depth. There are, however, other important instruments and clauses regarding prices that may be inserted into the contract in order address price risks, and other essential risks such as the risk of default on either the supply or the demand side, among others.

We start by comparing the international commodity markets with other types of markets in order to bring out the particular characteristics that require specific features in the negotiation of commercial contracts.

7.2   THE SPECIFIC CHARACTERISTICS OF COMMODITY MARKETS

Joan Woodward (1965) developed a useful categorisation of production systems in which there are four types of production. This classification may be modified in order to introduce commodities, allowing for their specific characteristics. Without introducing commodities, a slightly modified version of Woodward's categorisation gives the following classes of production systems.

1. *Mass production*, defined as industrial production in large series with a standard quality of the product which is not divisible. Here, production is an integer, which may be very large.
2. *Process production*, which is an industrial process with a standard product quality, which is indivisible. This sort of production may be either continuous, if the output is continuous over time, obtained on a 24-hour basis, or batch production, if the output is discontinuous over time.
3. *The production of craft industries*, which is a production in small series with non-standardised product quality.
4. And, finally, *project production*, in which, contrary to what happens in all other types of production, the product is unique with unique quality norms, derived from the client's specifications.

While the production in large series of various identical objects which cannot be divided, such as automobiles, may be described as mass production, the production of divisible outputs, such as products of the chemical and of the food industries, may be described as continuous or process production. There are indeed borderline cases: milk, which in bulk is a divisible input, must be conditioned for retailing into suitable packages or bottles such as 1-litre bottles. Such production is therefore mass production if we consider the production for clients in the retailing business, and continuous production for industrial clients, such as dairies. By contrast, project productions and, to a lesser extent, the productions of the craft industries miss most of the aspects of mass and process production. In project production, such as building an oil refinery, an airport, or a highway, the product is unique and usually constitutes a single element.

How does the production of commodities fit into this classification? It is quite clear that the production of most, if not all, commodities can be described as continuous production with usually a standard quality. This is true of energy commodities, of mineral and metal commodities. Agriculture, and therefore the production of agricultural commodities, used to be production with features akin to those of craft industries. However, its evolution has led in most cases to something that is very close to process production[1] in industry.[2] In general, the production of commodities cannot be described as project production and it usually has all the characteristics of industrial process or mass production.

This is not the end of the story, however, because the production of commodities also differs widely from industrial production through a number of economic features. Woodward's classification, useful as it may be, is a technical classification that misses economic characteristics of commodities. Another categorisation that will be more useful to us is distinguishing between the following:

1. *Basic commodity products*, which are upstream products used mostly for industrial demand, which can be the products of both industry and agriculture and are produced through production techniques that are akin to process production.
2. *Elaborate industrial products*, which are all downstream industrial products using basic commodities, among other resources, for their production.
3. *Elaborate products of the craft industries*, which are also downstream products also using basic commodities, among other resources, for their production.
4. *Products of project production*, whether physical products (buildings, infrastructures, etc.) or immaterial services.

A first group of characteristics that is important for us is related to the way *market clearance, or equilibrium between supply and demand*, occurs on the markets for these various products, and, in particular, for commodities. This issue is closely related to the importance of inventories or stocks as an industrial practice on these markets. Clearly, market clearance for project production is guaranteed by the market itself because products are produced only upon order, so

---

[1] Most agricultural productions being seasonal, they are discontinuous, so that they can be classified more precisely as batch productions.

[2] Except, perhaps, in traditional products such as fine wines.

that their supply always meets their demand. Moreover, project production does not hold inventories, because it is technically impossible. Its products either have no physical basis because they are immaterial services or cannot be inventoried because the products are unique with complex characteristics on a made-to-order basis.

Contrary to upstream commodities, industrial mass or process production of elaborate downstream products also tends to produce only upon demand, keeping stocks as low as possible. For these products, stocks are a costly use of capital because of the opportunity cost in the form of lost interest and storage costs and because these products usually deteriorate rapidly. Downstream industrial products are characterised by prices which are usually fixed in the short term and are much less flexible than is the case for basic commodities. This situation reflects the fact that a large part of the costs of such industrial products consists of costs that are fixed in the short term, such as the cost of labour and the cost of capital.

A different situation altogether occurs with commodities with flexible prices that can be inventoried. In this case, as we mentioned in Chapters 1 and 2, profits can be made by holding inventories for speculation, if the price of a commodity is expected to rise beyond the cost of carry — the opportunity cost together with other costs of physical storage. As shown in Chapter 5, the demand for stocks of a given commodity will thus occur whenever the prices of this commodity are low and are expected to increase. This means that current supply, not including the quantities that are inventoried, is exceeding demand. Conversely, whenever demand exceeds supply and prices are high and expected to decrease, stocks will decrease. The imbalance between supply and demand for most basic commodities is often a consequence of a time lag between the act of production and the final demand. An act of production will usually be planned ahead of time because, for technical reasons, it takes some time, sometimes a very long time, between planning and the time at which output will be physically available for marketing. Agricultural commodities, for instance, by their nature require some time between sowing the seeds and harvesting the actual crop. This time can be up to nine months for annual crops such as wheat, and several years for perennial crops such as coffee, cocoa, natural rubber, etc. The price volatility of agricultural commodities stems from the random effects of weather and climate that affect output as well as forecasting errors about supply and demand. The resulting imbalance between supply and demand causes price fluctuations as the price adjusts to the imbalance through speculative stocks. The same is true in the case of mineral and energy commodities, usually with an even longer time lag. In this case, exploration for mineral and oil deposits must be undertaken many years before the output of a marketable commodity comes onstream. For example, oil exploration takes several years. Once a possible deposit has been found, test wells must be drilled. Most come up dry. Thus, it will take several years before an exploration campaign or programme is fruitful in the sense that actual deposits of the resource have been detected. An additional time lag of several months to several years will evolve between detection of commercially exploitable deposits and actual production, the time necessary to implement investments in the oil wells. Thus, the volatility of mineral commodity and crude oil or natural gas prices is a consequence of the time lag resulting from the very duration of the exploration–investment cycle. This time lag results in long-term volatility of supply, which adds to both long-term and short-term volatility of demand.

In the very short term — anything between a few weeks and a few months — price volatility will usually be a consequence of fluctuations in demand with respect to supply, which is relatively inelastic in the short term. This means that some agents will keep short-term speculative stocks to be able to meet demand if it increases suddenly. Hence the importance of traders on physical commodity markets. The economic role of commodity traders is to balance supply and demand from end-consumers and, therefore, it is fundamental. Traders do this business at a price in the form of a spread between purchasing and selling prices. This means a very risky business because their commissions are comparatively small compared to the potential price fluctuations resulting from the imbalance between supply and demand. Thus, a number of clauses of commodity contracts aim at controlling risks due to price volatility. Other clauses and conditions are aimed at other business risks such as counterparty default risk and other physical risks (often insurable) that, because of price volatility and the nature of the product, are more acute than in other types of international trade. The need to control these risks will be reflected in commodity contracts.

Another specific characteristic of commodities, which is also reflected in the negotiation of commodity contracts, is *quality*. While the quality of a downstream industrial good or a project production good is most often a very complex array of several quantitative and qualitative variables, which makes the comparison of different otherwise substitutable goods a difficult exercise, the quality of a commodity is a comparatively simple combination of variables that makes comparison of different qualities in terms of price an easier task. The price of a commodity that is an almost perfect substitute for another reference commodity of the same kind will be at a discount with respect to the price of the reference commodity if its quality is technically lower than in the case of the reference commodity. Conversely, the price of a substitute commodity with respect to a reference commodity will be at a premium with respect to the price of the reference commodity if its quality is technically higher than that of the reference commodity. In many cases, quality is comparatively such a simple attribute that there is only one reference quality for the commodity. In this case, substitutions are still possible between commodities with different countries of origin or up to very minor quality variations. This situation can be contrasted with that of downstream industrial goods that are substitutes for each other. They are usually protected by proprietary brands or registered trademarks, which can make it difficult or impossible to substitute one brand for another within the commercial contract. Different qualities of commodities are usually not protected by proprietary brands and a commercial commodity contract may even allow for optional quality, meaning that the supplier may have the choice of the quality that will be delivered. For instance, under such a clause, in a soft wheat contract, European soft wheat may be substituted for American soft wheat with a slightly different quality at either a discount or a premium. In the case of metals and of other commodities, there is often only one quality available, such as electrolytic copper in the case of copper. An optional clause is still possible even in this case, leaving the supplier with the possibility of any country of origin or with the possibility of supplying the commodity under very minor differences in its chemical composition and/or in its physical properties.

The fact that standard qualities may be obtained easily and are usually in small number, together with the fact that quality differences with respect to a reference standard quality may easily be accounted for makes trading on global spot and futures markets much easier. In fact, the prices observed on these markets are very often recognised as reference prices. This is a further feature of commodities that is often reflected explicitly in contracts. This means that in commercial commodity contracts the price provided for might be a reference price. Clearly, such is not the case for downstream industrial products and the concept of a reference price is meaningless for these products. In the case of project production, price indexes for a standard type of project, such as an oil refinery, may serve as an implicit reference in the negotiation of contracts.

Table 7.1 Specific characteristics of commodity markets in comparison with other types of markets

Characteristics	Classes of productions			
	Commodities	Industrial products	Products of craft industries	Products of project production
Market clearance	Not guaranteed. Existence of stocks	Usually guaranteed. Minimal stocks	Usually guaranteed. Minimal stocks	Guaranteed
Price volatility	High	Low	Low	Moderate to low
Quality	Comparatively simple	Complex	Complex	Complex
Intermediaries	Trading companies, merchants	Trading companies, wholesalers	Trading companies, wholesalers	Little or none
Importance of intermediaries	Fundamental	Moderate	Moderate	Small
Reference pricing in commercial contracts	Common	Indirect	Indirect	Price indexes may serve as implicit reference

Table 7.1 above describes the various features whereby commodities differ fundamentally from other types of products. As we will show in the following sections of this chapter, these characteristic differences are reflected in commercial commodity contracts.

7.3 PHYSICAL COMMODITY CONTRACTS: THE ACTORS

7.3.1 Physical Commodity Contracts and Commodity-related Actors

The specific activities related to the international physical trade in basic commodities are manifold. As will be discussed in detail in Chapter 8, these include producers, trading companies or merchants, brokers, forwarding agents, switchers, and end-users of physical commodities. Enacting a commercial operation may indeed imply several actors, but the commercial contract in itself will concern, in terms of reciprocal obligations, two main parties.

As a simplified presentation, we can describe a commercial contract as an agreement concluded between a purchaser and a seller, either of which can be a physical producer, a consumer, an end-user, or an intermediary such as a trading company.

7.3.2 Preparation of a Sale Proposal

In a commercial operation on commodities markets, preparation of the sale proposal is extremely important. Producers and merchants alike recognise this step as the key step. It requires high professional qualities, including both technical and human skills.

The commercial proposal must be carefully prepared by the seller, it must take into account the potential client's needs and it must also be adapted to his/her culture. A well-prepared proposal will make the negotiation and the conclusion of a draft agreement for a final offer much easier.

Unlike some other classes of products, such as the products of engineering services or, more generally, of project production, the selection of suppliers in the case of basic commodities is seldom submitted to formal tenders. Formal tenders for commodities are usually reserved for large markets and to official contractors such as governments and other public bodies. They also tend to be less frequent than they were in the past, owing to the trends towards deregulation and privatisation in the commodity industries and to the transition of formerly command economies, such as the USSR and other Eastern European countries, towards market economies.

It is at the preparation of the sale proposal that the technical questions related to the conclusion of the commercial agreement are treated. This is because the preparation of the proposal is the step during which personal and professional links between the counterparties and their agents are forged.

The commercial proposal usually takes the form of a letter of intent (LOI) that is sent to the potential purchaser, expressing a firm proposal from the producer–seller. An example of a letter of intent is provided in Annex 7B. The LOI is not merely an informal statement or a document issued just for the sake of information. It expresses the irrevocable commitment of the selling party who legally binds itself to respecting the terms of its offer if accepted. Any such firm offer must stipulate the period over which it is valid. Besides this validity delay, the LOI may also require, in case of acceptation by the purchaser, presentation of a performance bond.

The LOI may take the form of a proforma which enables the potential buyer to know the amount and the various conditions of the order. The LOI, or this proforma, may also be useful to the buyer in order to apply for authorisations, such as import licences and/or to apply for documentary credit, should the seller impose this as the payment method. Completion of this first step will enable the two parties to continue their negotiation towards the final commercial contract.

7.3.3 Producers

Commodity producers typically arrange to sell their output before it is available. There are two reasons for this situation:

1. First of all, the producer wants to avoid suffering from any market imbalance, whether it experiences an over-supply or an under-supply. An over-supply is costly in terms of holding inventories and an under-supply is costly in terms of losing clients to competitors.
2. Secondly, our producer also wants to avoid an adverse price evolution.

These reasons are closely related to each other and are specific to commodity markets. Thus, forward selling at a fixed price (as defined in Chapters 1 and 2), implying deferred delivery and payment, is a very frequent practice on commodity markets. Of course, forward contracts are also concluded on the markets for downstream industrial goods but their negotiation is less crucial and a mispricing is less risky and easier to avoid on these markets where delays for delivery might be shorter.

7.3.4 Industrial End-users

On commodity markets, an industrial end-user is usually not involved in direct negotiations with a producer, and, as already noted, a commercial intermediary such as a trading company is very often the supplier of an industrial end-user.

Besides the reasons that have been analysed in the previous section, the reasons for this situation are related to the end-user client's joint specific management requirements that correspond:

1. To the technical specifications of the goods that are requested, which might not be easily found without using the services of a market intermediary.
2. To the quantities that are necessary for the end-user's activities knowing that zero-defect and zero-inventory management have led to in-depth modifications of the behaviour of industrial users. The producer's concern for liquidity of its production may not be compatible with the end-user's manufacturing schedule.
3. To purchasing management's concerns. Purchasing management today is an important function with a strong potential for reducing costs. Moreover, the evolution of purchasing practices leads purchasing officers to negotiate forward contracts, taking into account their expectations for the prices of commodities that are of concern to them.
4. To corporate risk management concerns. If the client end-user concludes, for instance, a fixed-price forward contract with a trading company, this means that it is protected against commodity price and market risks, which are thus transferred to the physical trader, and may concentrate on the risks inherent to the markets for its own products.

We can therefore conclude that matching the respective constraints to which the producer and the end-user are subject require, as a rule, the action of intermediaries, in effect the trading companies.

7.3.5   Merchants or Trading Companies

As already noted, merchants or trading companies, although they are encountered on other markets, such as the markets for downstream industrial products, have acquired a special importance on commodity markets. Their function as intermediaries on these markets consists of reconciling the producer's needs with the requirements and objectives of a final purchaser.

Thus, a trading company fills four major roles:

1. Firstly, to conduct separate negotiations with the producer–seller on the one hand, and with the final purchaser on the other hand, in such a manner that all parties are satisfied with the negotiated terms for their commercial contracts.
2. Secondly, to manage the physical goods that are the object of transactions. This means that the trader bears a number of risks that are related to the goods themselves, such as price risks as well as the risks for damages and inventory losses.
3. Thirdly (in many cases) to maintain and manage stocks of the commodity and/or to effect an industrial transformation of the commodities. For instance,

large trading companies (such as Cargill) started their business in the management of grain elevators in the US Middle West and are still running elevators. Others are in transformation activities such as grinding oil seeds (Tradigrain) or refining edible oils (Bunge y Born).

4. Fourthly, to match the operational timing of both the producer and the purchaser inasmuch as there is some time lag between them. This means that, in addition to keeping stocks, physical traders have to conduct ongoing hedging programmes on futures and derivative markets in order to control the price risks inherent in their business.

Owing to these various roles, the trading company bears a number of risks that are specific to commodity markets, which are:

1. The risk of price mismatch between selling and buying.
2. The physical risks related to the conditions of delivery of the goods with respect to the date of delivery to the final end-user, in particular in the case of freight risks.
3. Financial risks other than the price risk such as payment-related risks and exchange rate risks.

These features and risks that are specific to commodity markets are reflected in the attributes of commodity contracts and in the financial instruments corresponding to the legal terms of these commodity contracts.

7.4   THE ATTRIBUTES OF COMMODITY CONTRACTS

7.4.1   The Commodity Contract: Basic Features

For every physical transaction, the commercial actors sign a purchasing/selling contract giving the precise details of the agreement. Although physical commodities markets are OTC markets with contracts adapted to the needs of each supplier and purchaser, an individual contract is often the adaptation of a standard contract issued by one of the professional trading associations. For example, in the case of grains, we can mention the standard contracts issued by the British Grain and Feed Trade Association (GAFTA). Thus, most of the time individual contracts follow standard contracts, the terms of the contract are freely negotiated and are adjusted to the particular context of each transaction. Each commercial operation is indeed unique with respect to the nature of the good, the degree of confidence that has been established between the parties (experience, professionalism, creditworthiness, and overall reputation), as well as with respect to the amount of the transaction.

Each contract must specify the legal and regulatory environment for settling disputes. For this environment most commercial contracts refer to RUU 500 which are uniform rules and specifications issued by the International Chamber of Commerce (ICC). This reference is internationally recognised and makes it easier to handle clauses related to letters of credit, for instance, or clauses related to risk transfers in the case of incoterms. International regulations are not sufficient for solving all the interpretation problems that may appear during the execution of a contract. To this end, national legislations are not very helpful either. Thus, most commercial contracts provide for an arbitration procedure, which may be more costly than using national legislation, but is more generally accepted by the parties as it leads to much quicker settlement of disputes. Disputes may then be submitted to reference arbitration courts (ICC in Paris, GAFTA in London, or the Geneva Arbitration Court, etc.). It is customary in commercial contracts to distinguish between general clauses referred to as contractual, and more specific clauses that are linked to the settlement of disputes between parties (see the example of the sugar contract presented in Annex 7A).

7.4.2 Legal Features as Tools for Solving Economic Problems

We now move on to the analysis of commercial contracts in the trading of commodities, especially on international markets. Clearly, the legal presentation of the contract aims at addressing economic and financial problems that are concerns in most markets. In economic terms, one will have to answer the following questions:

1. What are the quantities of the commodity that the purchaser needs?
2. What are its particular quality specifications?
3. At what price and under what pricing principles are the seller and the purchaser going to agree on entering into a transaction?
4. What are the schedule and other conditions for delivery (place of delivery) that may suit both parties?

Financial terms of contracts enable both parties to address problems such as method of payment, as well as taking into account the various risks that may occur in the execution of any commercial operation in addition to the price and exchange rate risks which are normally covered through derivative instruments and which have been discussed in Chapters 2–4. In financial terms, therefore, the following questions can be asked:

1. How can the risk of default by the seller be addressed, i.e. the risk that the seller does not deliver the good?
2. How can one ensure that the seller delivers at the right time and at the right place the right quantity and adequate quality of the good?
3. How can one deal with the risk of default by the buyer, i.e. the risk that the buyer will not pay for the good?

4. How can one treat other miscellaneous risks such as freight risks and transportation risks?

All these risks may be addressed by using financial and insurance instruments that will be discussed in the next section. Finally, in any contract there are other non-economic and non-financial clauses that determine other rules of conduct on which the two parties agree. These may answer questions such as:

1. What are the rules applicable to the disputes and differences that may arise between the parties due to events beyond the control of the parties, usually termed a *force majeure* or an *act of God*?[3]
2. What are the other miscellaneous rules applicable?

7.4.3 The Economic Attributes of a Commercial Commodity Contract

The economic attributes of the contract are market-related variables such as quantities, quality specifications, prices, date of delivery, and other conditions of delivery. *Quantities* are, of course, an essential part of a contract. They are expressed in some unit of measurement (weight, volume, energy), which may be a metric unit (metric tonne, cubic metre, kWh), an Anglo-Saxon unit (ounces, pounds, bushels and tons)[4] or in some traditional measurement unit (barrel of oil, 1 barrel = 0.159 m^3 = 136.05 kg, bag of coffee = 60 kg, but which traditionally is less than 60 kg in some Latin American countries ...). The physical unit used may be ambiguous if the quality is not specified precisely. Tolerances with respect to exactness may be traditional for some products. Typical tolerances may range between ±1% and ±5%. The seller up to these tolerances usually guarantees the quantity. Contracts will usually provide for verification of quantity shipped by a third party on which both the seller and the buyer agree. Independent and reputable companies that supply these specialised services such as Société Générale de Surveillance (SGS, whose headquarters are in Geneva) are very often mentioned in commercial contracts.

For medium or long-term contracts, clauses such as 'take or pay' provisions guarantee the buyer against the risk of supply disruption while ensuring the seller a minimum revenue. In the case of ongoing or renewable supply contracts, more flexibility may be advantageous for both parties.

---

[3] Owing to innovations in financial instruments, risks that were previously considered as beyond the control of economic agents, such as weather-related risks, tend to lend themselves to the development of new marketable hedging instruments, weather derivatives, for example. These instruments may become important in the future and they have important implications for the markets of a number of commodities — agricultural commodities because crops are submitted to climatic hazards, but also commodities such as heating oil, the demand for which varies according to the temperature.

[4] 1 lb = 453 g, short ton = 2000 lb = 900 kg, troy ounce = 31.103 g, for precious metals such as gold, silver, and platinum group metals; bushel of wheat = 27.218 kg; millions of BTU: 1 MBTU = 0.252 thermie, for natural gas.

Incoterms (international commercial terms) are defined as clauses of a commercial contract which refer to how a number of costs, including transportation costs, freight-related costs, and other logistic costs, conditions, and responsibilities are shared between the two parties. In the case of maritime transportation, liner-terms must also be covered in commercial contracts. Some usual incoterms in international commodity contracts are for instance FOB, CFR, and CIF, which are summarily described in Table 7.2. An in-depth analysis of incoterms is beyond the scope of our work.

Clauses regarding *prices* are obviously very important in commodity contracts and, as noted previously, given the volatility of the prices of most commodities, they are specific to commodity markets. Prices in commodity contracts are often specified as fixed within the framework of a forward transaction[5] or for the duration of the contract if it involves several deliveries over a short period of time. Thus, for short-term contracts, prices are usually fixed on an absolute basis, at least for a given period of time. Most commodity contracts are *forward* contracts, inasmuch as they refer to some delivery at some future date. A fixed price in a particular forward contract protects both the buyer and the seller against adverse price variations. If there is an efficient futures market for the commodity, the futures price for contacts with expiration at the contemplated delivery date or a nearby date can be used as the reference price which is used for calculation of the forward price. In ongoing long- and medium-term contracts, this fixed price may be revisable periodically — quarterly, every six months, or every year — according to some suitable index, which may be another price or a price index with either a premium, or a discount.[6] Other more complex schemes involve a fixed part and an indexed part with optional possibilities for the seller, the buyer, or both.

Commodity prices can also be specified as *spot prices* or producers' prices at the date of delivery or at some related date close to delivery. More precisely, they may be calculated at a given date of delivery on the basis of a *reference price* that is accepted as such by both parties. Some examples of reference prices are: aluminium at LME price, first ring of quotations, cash price at the date of delivery, or copper at LME second ring of quotations, cash price, or white sugar

Table 7.2   Examples of incoterms of special interest in the case of commodity markets

Incoterms	Summary definitions
FOB (free on board)	Property transfer becomes effective at the embarkation port
CFR (cost and freight)	The seller is responsible for costs and international freight
CIF (cost, insurance and freight)	The seller is responsible for costs, insurance and international freight

[5] Examples: coal of specified quality at US$30/tonne or the sugar contract given in Annex 1.

[6] This is the case in long-term natural gas supply contracts.

at the end of July, LIFFE price for delivery on 15 August 20**. This implies a significant price risk, which may be high and which is not addressed by the clauses of the commodity contract. This risk has to be managed outside of the contract itself by hedging on organised or OTC derivative markets.

More complex pricing clauses imply a combination of pricing on the basis of spot prices at the date of delivery with either a floor or a ceiling price, or both. Below the floor price and above the ceiling price, the profit resulting from the evolution of the price is shared between the two parties (UNCTAD, 1998). For instance, if the price of silver is US$4.60/oz, the forward pricing clause may provide for a price floor of US$4.40/oz and a price ceiling of US$4.80/oz. The spot price at the time of delivery will be the price applying to the sale if it still is beween these two limits. If the spot price becomes higher than US$4.80/oz, the profit will actually be shared between the seller (who will benefit from an increase by US$0.20/oz of the spot price) and the buyer (who will benefit from the fact that the price is limited to US$4.80); for instance, if the spot price goes up to US$5.00/oz, the buyer will make an opportunity gain of US$0.20/oz). The profit will be shared in the opposite direction between the seller and the buyer if the price goes down below US$4.40/oz.

For forward operations and for ongoing longer-term contracts as well, commodity contracts may also specify that the price applicable to the operation in question will be the *average of some reference price*, usually the average of a spot price recognised as a reference price by both parties, over a specified period of time. Under such terms, price risks will usually be significantly reduced because upward and downward fluctuations in price with respect to a trend will cancel out. However, price risk is still significant, but lower than if the price is specified as the spot price at the time of delivery or close to delivery. Path-dependent options such as Asian options or lookback options that we studied in Chapter 4 can be used to cover price risk of this sort.

Premiums or discounts with respect to the reference price may also be provided for in the contract. There might be several reasons for such provisions. First, assuming that the quality of the product is the reference quality, the situation of the market might justify either a premium or a discount. Premiums and discounts can provide the incentive to avoid defaults by suppliers and clients. If, for example, prices rise above the fixed contract price, there is a risk that the supplier will default and sell the commodity on the spot market. Providing for a premium, which will give the supplier an incentive not to default, might treat this risk. If, on the contrary, spot prices are lower than the fixed price, the supplier might accept a discount on the reference price in order to secure a client. A second and more important reason for discounts and premiums with respect to the reference price is to compensate for product quality that might be either better or worse than the reference quality. A third reason is to compensate for differences in transport costs when the contract delivery site differs from the reference price delivery site.

Incoterms may be FOB (free on board), meaning that the purchaser is responsible for transportation and delivery, or CIF (cost, insurance, and freight) where freight and insurance are included in the price and the seller is responsible for them. Delivery conditions must also be specified precisely with respect to place and date of delivery, as must conditions of payment, usually through a letter of credit in a given currency and at a given date. A currency that is prevalent on international commodity markets is the US dollar but, whatever the currency being used, there is a currency risk if the currency of one of the parties is not the US dollar. This risk can be hedged using currency derivatives.

Quality is, of course, a very important aspect of a contract. In some cases there is very little leeway for variation. Electrolytic copper, for example, must be very pure with specific electrical conductivity properties. The presence of even small levels of impurity can ruin these properties. For other uses, quality may be less important and specified as optional with price discounts provided for in case of inferior quality and premiums in case of better quality. For instance, wheat contracts often specify optional qualities (American soft wheats of a specified quality, or equivalent EU wheats, which sell at a discount). The same is true of various crude oil grades as well as for fuels such as coal, light fuel oils, and heavy fuel oils with discounts and premiums applying to them, depending on their quality.

Examples   Copper (cathodes, 99.9%); silver refined, at least 99.9%, bars of 1,000 troy oz; Arabian light crude oil; heating oil No. 2 (0.1% sulphur); coal with a minimum heat content of 12,000 Btu/lb, ash 13.5% maximum, sulphur 1%, hardness 41 Hargrove index ...; Wheat, No. 2 soft red ...

Miscellaneous conditions are also important, including notice and penalties in case of cancellation, extent of the responsibility of supplier and penalties in the case of partial or non-delivery, and settlement procedures for conflicts and disputes.

7.5   CONTRACTS ATTRIBUTES, AND RISK SHARING

7.5.1   Treating Risks in Commercial Contracts

Commodity contracts are of course very important with respect to risk. Various types of risks that have already been mentioned are always shared between the supplier and the purchaser:

1. Risk of supply disruption. A purchaser always has to assess the trade-off between the costs of supply disruption and the premium that usually has to be paid to ensure supply security.
2. Risk associated with price variations. Here, a market participant will have to check carefully for delivery dates and for the reference price used in the

contract. Is it a spot price, or a forward or futures price on some commodity exchange?

Negotiating a purchasing contract, especially in the field of raw materials and commodities, needs careful consideration of the various risks. There are indeed several kinds of risks involved in such a contract, for both the buyer and the seller:

1. The *price risk* is the risk attached to price volatility.
2. The *currency risk*, or *exchange rate risk*, is the risk attached to the volatility of the exchange rate applying to the currency of one of the parties with respect to the currency provided for in the contract, if it is different from the national currency of the party in question.
3. The *risk* of *default of the purchaser*, which is the supplier's counterparty risk, is the risk that the buyer is unwilling or unable to pay.
4. The *risk of default of the supplier*, which is the buyer's counterparty risk, is the risk that the seller is unwilling or unable to deliver the commodity.
5. The *quality risk* is the risk that the quality of the product does not comply with the buyer's specifications.
6. A more general risk is the risk of supply disruption or the risk that the supply becomes interrupted or delayed for reasons other than supplier default.
7. Other types of risk include the *risk of accidental damage, the risk of theft*, etc.

The *price risk* is the risk of adverse price variations between the signature of the contract and its completion, that is, the final delivery and payment of the product. Such a risk is, of course, different for the supplier and for the purchaser. Of course, the purchaser is affected by the risk of a price increase, while the supplier is affected, in principle, by the risk of a price decrease. However, the supplier may have to buy the product between the signature of the contract, and the date of delivery. In this case, the supplier is affected by the risk of price increase. As we said, price risks are generally very high for commodities that are internationally traded on competitive markets, but they are generally lower if a system of posted prices exists. However, markets such as these are the exception nowadays. Of course, derivative markets can be used to reduce price risks, but in many cases a good negotiation of the contract can protect the buyer against adverse price variations.

Although forward contracts can be used to protect buyers and sellers against price rises or declines, there may be an important risk associated with actual delivery on one side of the market if the operator is not protected on the other side of the market. For instance, this risk occurs when a seller has concluded a fixed-price contract with a client, but does not hold the product in stock and will be obliged to buy it on spot markets. The seller is protected with respect to his sales price but not with respect to his purchase price. Of course, derivative markets may be used to hedge that risk, but the situation of being protected on one side of the market and not on the other side is clearly particular to trading activities. A trading company that has concluded a fixed-price forward contract with one of its clients which is an industrial end-user for a commodity, but has to get its supply on the spot market at the time of delivery or shortly before delivery is running a significant risk that the price will increase. Conversely, a trading company that has concluded a fixed-price forward contract with one of its suppliers, but has to sell on the spot market at the time of delivery or shortly before delivery is also running a significant risk that the price will decrease. In both cases, our trading company will have to hedge suitably against the risk it is facing on the derivative markets. In the first case, it can purchase a call option or a futures contract. In the second case, it can purchase a put option or sell a futures contract.

Example   Company A has sold 3000 tonnes of electrolytic grade copper to a given electrical equipment company B, on May 20**, for delivery at the end of July 20**, at a fixed price of US$1744/tonne FOB in London, equal to the prevailing London Metal Exchange spot price (US$1744/tonne FOB). There is theoretically no risk (although there are carryover costs) if A has the copper in stock. However, if A does not have the stock, it will have to purchase the copper before it is due to deliver. Waiting until the delivery date and using the spot market is risky. The risk can be offset as we saw in Chapters 2–4 by taking a long position in a futures or forward contract or by purchasing a call option.

In practice, fixed-price contracts are sufficient to take care of the risk only if the price of the product traded is generally stable, which, in the case of basic commodities, has become a rather exceptional situation. Even in the event of a fixed-price forward contract concluded on one side of the market, there still is a remaining risk in terms of opportunity gain on this side of the market. As mentioned in the previous section, this risk may be treated by asking for a premium above the fixed price of US$1744/tonne, with, for example, a fixed price of US$1754.50/tonne, or a premium of about 0.6%. As already noted, the client might find an advantage in agreeing to such a premium, inasmuch as it will give an incentive to the seller not to default.

Another problem encountered with fixed-price contracts is that, while they protect against an adverse price evolution, they do not protect against a favourable evolution. For instance, a trading company may have secured on 30 May 20** a fixed forward price of US$4.55/oz on buying silver, with delivery in two months (end of July 20**). If the price of silver goes up, the company is protected, but it will not benefit from a decrease in silver spot price which is US$4.57 at that time. This point can sometimes be tackled by buying a put but, as we saw in Chapters 3 and 4, options are expensive. For instance, suppose our trader purchases a put with an exercise price of US$4.25/oz for US$0.04/oz. If the spot price stays above until the option's maturity, the all-in cost of the silver is US$4.59, the US$4.55 forward price plus US$0.04, the cost of the option.

Exchange rate risks are usually not addressed in commodity contracts. The US dollar is clearly the international currency used on most international commodity markets and in most international commodity contracts. But, as already noted, there is a currency risk for any party in an international contract if the national currency of this party is not the US dollar. This applies, in particular, to producers, and to industrial end-users of commodities. For instance, an Australian copper mining and smelting company might sell an international trading company a large quantity of copper, say 10,000 tonnes. The risk could be handled by expressing the fixed contract price in Australian dollars, but this would lead to difficulties because the available reference prices, whether the price of the LME or the price of the COMEX in New York, are both expressed in US dollars. What then would be the pertinent rate of exchange applicable to convert the price into Australian dollars? Even if this point were solved, our trading company would still be reluctant to such a provision, because it would mean a supplementary currency risk on top of other already significant risks. Thus, the odds are that the contract will be concluded in US dollars, leaving the Australian party to bear a currency risk. This risk can be hedged away by using the foreign currency derivative markets.[7]

There are also provisions to take care of other risks, such as supplier default risk, purchaser's default, and other risks. This section has been primarily oriented towards risks which are specific to commodity markets and that can be addressed through suitable clauses in the contract. These other risks, include, in particular, counterparty risks, and they are mostly addressed through financial instruments that, although they are usually mentioned in the commercial contract, are so to speak peripheral to it, involving parties other than the seller and the purchaser, such as banks. These risks will be discussed in the next section through the financial instruments that are used to handle them with particular emphasis on the features that are specific to commodity markets.

7.5.2 Risk Saving Instruments in Commercial Commodity Contracts

Bid bonds and performance bonds are financial instruments of the banking sector that are tokens of the ability of the sellers engaged in a commercial contract to fulfil their obligations. They are important and even play a fundamental part in the negotiation that takes place before the conclusion of any commercial commodity contract as well as in the execution of the contract. In particular, when competing for a contract, whether a formal tender has been issued or not, a merchant or trading company will try to obtain a banking guarantee from its bank called a *bid bond* and/or a *performance bond*. From the point of view of the buyer, it addresses the risk of default of the supplier. More precisely, a *bid bond*, or

---

[7] See Clark *et al.* (1993) for an in-depth presentation of the currency derivative markets.

a tender bond in cases where a formal tender has been organised, is a financial instrument aimed at eliminating the risk that a commodity supplier will withdraw from the negotiations after it has been selected or that it will be unable to supply the commodity which is the object of a commercial contract under negotiation. It may be requested at the preliminary phase of the negotiation, in order to ensure that the seller, once chosen by its client, will effectively sign the contract and not withdraw before signature and that, moreover, it has the ability to fulfil its obligations. Once the seller has been selected and has signed the contract, a *performance bond* will usually be requested of this seller by its client. A *performance bond* is a financial instrument aimed at eliminating the risk that a commodity supplier is unable to supply the commodity that is the object of the commercial contract during its execution.

Both bid bonds and performance bonds are issued by the seller's bank. They irrevocably guarantee that the bank will pay the client the value of the bond should the seller not fulfil its obligations either before signing the contract (i.e. withdrawing before signing in spite of an otherwise firm commitment) or after the contract is signed (i.e. being unable to deliver the commodity on time or under the quality provided for).

The value of a bid bond usually ranges between 2 and 5% of the amount of the commercial contract and the value of a performance bond between 2 and 25% of the same amount. If the trading company, or the producer, which is supplying commodities, and taking part in preliminary negotiations is not awarded the contract, the bid bond will vanish immediately. Conversely, if the trading company is awarded the contract, it becomes a performance bond. More precisely, it will be an irrevocable guarantee from the bank to the buyer, whereby the bank is committed to pay to the latter a sum which is stipulated in the guarantee, usually between 2% and 25% of the amount of the contract, if the bank's client, to which the commercial contract has been awarded, does not supply the good provided for in the contract, or does not meet some of the obligations provided for in the contract, or if any other event prevents the execution of the contract.

As mentioned above, another significant risk is *quality risk* or the risk that the supplier does not supply the commodity with the quality mentioned in the contract. The performance bond deals with this risk for the most part but, to avoid any difficulty arising from a subjective appreciation of the quality delivered by the purchaser, *third-party certification* is provided for in the contract. By third-party certification, we mean that a third party which is recognised by both the seller and its client will, at some stage of shipping of the commodity, verify that the quality supplied meets the technical quality specifications which are given in the contract. The buyer usually issues a letter of credit once in possession of the quality certificate and of the seller's performance bond. The party which is certifying the commodity delivered is usually a specialised company, such as SGS, a Swiss company which is one of the largest operators worldwide and specialised in the certification of both qualities and quantities of goods upon shipping or upon delivery. In many important commercial commodity contracts, an SGS certification is a token of security regarding the quality and the quantity in a shipment resulting from a commercial contract. A certification document issued by SGS, or by other similar reputable companies engaged in the business of certification is indispensable for obtaining documentary credit.

While bid bonds and performance bonds are financial instruments aimed at taking care of the counterparty risk from the point of view of the purchaser, *letters of credit*, also called *documentary credits*, are financial instruments that address the counterparty risk from the point of view of the seller, which is the risk of default or non-payment by the purchaser. Here we will discuss the most commonly encountered features of letters of credit.

A letter of credit is issued by the purchaser's bank, also called the *issuing bank*, at the request of the purchaser who has to prove his creditworthiness to that bank. It usually consists in an irrevocable commitment from the bank to pay to the seller, also called the *beneficiary* or the *payee*, the price of the commodity once the bank guarantees that it has been delivered or is safely on its way to being delivered. Irrevocable means that the bank may not cancel or modify the commitment in any way. This guarantee is activated once the bank has received and verified certain authentic documents, such as a commercial invoice, a bill of lading at the port of shipping, or an airbill, along with several others, that guarantee delivery. From this comes the name of documentary credit sometimes given to this financial instrument.[8] The validity of the letter of credit is, however, limited in time. A letter of credit is thus a guarantee of the purchaser's creditworthiness, thereby guaranteeing the sellers they will be paid, provided they have conformed to the terms of the contract and delivered the goods in time and under the quantity and quality provided for in the contract, with suitable documents at the buyer bank's disposal.

A *confirmed letter of credit* (Figure 7.1) is a further guarantee because, in this case, a second bank from the seller's country, called the *advising bank*, is also irrevocably engaged into paying the price of the good once it is on the way towards delivery, even in the event of a default of the purchaser or of its bank. Of course, the issuing bank and the advising bank are both paid by several commissions for their services, which might typically be 2–3% per year all-inclusive, with a variable risk premium. The issuing bank may also ask the advising bank to pay, to accept (an order), to negotiate on documents, or to confirm the letter of credit. Whereas letters of credit are not specific to commodity markets, they are widely used with about 60% of international commodity contracts using letters of credit as terms of payment. Other more complex arrangements with letters of credit are, however, more specific to international commodity markets. First,

---

[8] See, for instance, article 9 of the commercial contract given in Annex 1, which provides for the presentation of nine authentic documents.

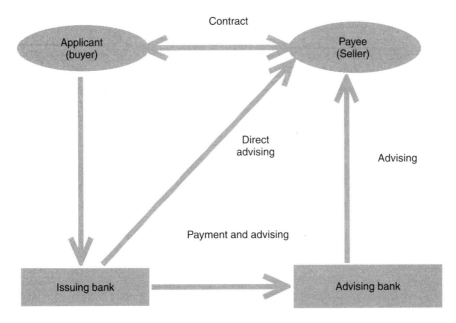

Figure 7.1   General organisation of an irrevocable and confirmed letter of credit

an irrevocable and confirmed letter of credit may also be made *transferable*. The transferable character of the letter of credit, which should be provided for explicitly in the contract, means that the payee may ask the advising bank to transfer part of the credit, or its whole amount, to one or several third parties. This is very useful if the seller has to pay subcontractors or suppliers, provided that the contracts are negotiated with the same provisions in terms of currency, transportation, incoterms, and other conditions. The transferable letter of credit thus extends the guarantee provided by the letter of credit to subcontractors and suppliers. It is, furthermore, well suited to the needs of trading companies and thus to the specificity of international commodity markets.

One of the ways to use the potential of a transferable letter of credit for trading companies on commodity markets is to set up a *back-to-back confirmed and transferable letters of credit*. This is a more complex scheme in which a trading company is both a supplier and a purchaser at the same time and on the same market. Then, the trading company may first arrange a first letter of credit with its client for which it acts as a supplier. It thus is the payee to a first letter of credit, which should be made transferable, and may therefore set up a second independent letter of credit for its supplier, and this second letter of credit will use the first letter of credit as collateral, using the transferable character of the first letter of credit to have its supplier directly paid out of the amount of the first letter of credit (Figure 7.2).

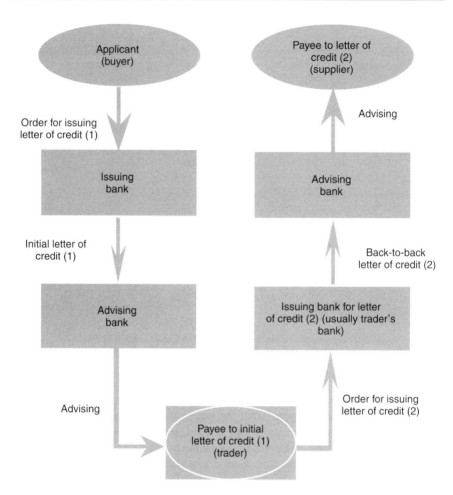

Figure 7.2 Back-to-back letter of credit and its use for trading companies

Finally, another scheme which is well adapted to the specificity of commodity markets and is sometimes used with agricultural commodities which are storable is to arrange a letter of credit with a *green clause* (Youssef, 1998). Under this scheme, the buyer of a commodity for which storage with a warehouse company can be arranged negotiates an irrevocable confirmed letter of credit with a clause saying that a partial advance payment will be provided to the producer against the issue of warehouse receipts for the commodity being stored as collateral. This is well adapted to the needs of small commodity producers, such as farmers in developing countries.

It is indispensable to distinguish between credits, techniques and terms of payment, and the commercial contract in itself. Credits are, by their very nature, distinct from commercial contracts, even though these contracts may be closely linked to them. Banks are not bound in any manner by these contracts, but only by the contracts concerning the financial instruments or by the credits that they issue, even if these are related to commercial contracts. This distinction having been made, an irrevocable letter of credit issued by some reputable bank and confirmed by another reputable bank is strong evidence of the buyer's creditworthiness and of the degree of financial security of a commercial operation.

Of course, other risks are usually not taken into account in the commercial contract itself, but should normally be taken into account in sound management of a commodity trading company as well as in the purchasing management of an industrial firm that is using the commodity as a raw material. The first of these risks is the price risk, which may or may not, as discussed in the previous section, be addressed by suitable pricing clauses, such as fixed prices in a forward operation. In the case of a trading company, it might simply be impossible to address this risk by concluding fixed-price contracts in buying as well as in selling some given quantity of a commodity. Therefore, it is most often addressed on at least one side by a trading company by hedging, using the derivatives instruments as discussed in Chapters 2–4. Taking positions on derivative markets for hedging is usually closely related to the conclusion of commercial contracts, although it might not be performed by the same people in a large trading company, in a large producing firm, or in a large firm purchasing the commodity. While selling or buying physical commodities is usually carried out by the marketing department, trading of derivative instruments is usually carried out by either financial departments or departments or divisions that are specialised in trading on futures and option markets for hedging purposes. Given the risks in handling and misusing derivative instruments, these trading operations should be carefully controlled by the management of the company.

The correct negotiation of a contract does not usually eliminate all price risks and thus the need for adequate covering instruments. If, for instance, prices are fixed in the terms of a contract, this might be held as hedging the buyer against any prices higher than the fixed price provided for. However, this does not take care of the seller's risk, inasmuch as the seller (usually a trading company or a merchant) will usually sell forward a product that will be bought on spot markets shortly before delivery, thus requiring a long hedge. The buyer in this scheme might buy a short hedge, or a suitable put option, in order to benefit from a price smaller than the contract price if the evolution of the markets leads to such a smaller price. Hedging applies not only to the commodity purchased but also to its freight and the London Biffex futures market for freight should take care of this risk. Finally, other physical risks and in particular risks that occur during the transportation and the delivery of the commodity are a matter of conventional insurance, which may be either the seller's or the buyer's responsibility according to the terms of the contract and the incoterms that have been provided for. Finally, whereas many of the attributes of commercial contracts are designed

Table 7.3 Summary of contract and financial instruments addressing various risks on commodity markets

Categories of risks	Instruments used to protect against these risks	Market participants	
		Instruments used for protection against sellers' risks	Instruments used for protection against purchasers' risks
Price risks	Contract instruments	Fixed pricing, forward contract	Fixed pricing, forward contract
	Financial instruments	Short futures, puts, and equivalent OTC instrument	Long futures, calls, and equivalent OTC instruments
	Importance for commodity markets	Fundamental, and characteristic	Fundamental, and characteristic
Currency risks	Contract instruments	Fixed pricing, forward contract in the seller's currency (seldom used)	Fixed pricing, forward contract in the purchaser's currency (seldom used)
	Financial instruments	Short currency futures, puts, and equivalent OTC instruments	Long currency futures, calls, and equivalent OTC instruments
	Importance for commodity markets	Important if the seller's currency is not the US$	Important if the purchaser's currency is not the US$
Counterparty risks	Contract instruments	Obligation of letter of credit	Obligation of bid bond and performance bond
	Financial instruments	Letter of credit	Bid bond and performance bond
	Importance for commodity markets	Fundamental, but not characteristic	Fundamental, but not characteristic
Quality risks	Contract instruments	Optional quality clauses, and third-party certification	Quality specifications, and third-party certification
	Financial instruments	Letter of credit	Bid bond and performance bond
	Importance for commodity markets	Fundamental, and characteristic	Fundamental, and characteristic
Insurable risks	Contract instruments	Obligation of insurance	Obligation of insurance
	Financial instruments	Insurance	Insurance
	Importance for commodity markets	Fundamental, but not characteristic	Fundamental, but not characteristic

to protect both parties entering into the contract, they are not sufficient as such to take care of all of the risks. The very importance of derivative markets for the hedging of industrial commodity producers, users and traders, for instance, and of other financial instruments such as bid bonds, performance bonds, and documentary credits is evidence to the contrary. Table 7.3 above gives a summary of all the contract instruments as well as of the financial instruments used for taking care of the various risks that are encountered by both sellers and purchasers on commodity markets.

7.6 CONCLUSION

The commercial commodity contract, while playing a central part in the physical trading of commodities, is only an element of a complex array of relationships and contracts between the various actors of international commodity markets. Producers, industrial consumers, physical traders, as well as other actors in the financial community, such as banks, brokers on derivative markets, insurance companies, certification and handling companies, etc. are just the main categories of agents that are concerned or that may be concerned with the physical international trading of basic commodities.

Physical contracts are a very important feature of international commodity markets. However, a good discussion of most commodity markets would not be complete if it overlooked the intermediaries on such markets, which are both indispensable and more and more involved on global markets. These intermediaries are trading companies or commodity merchants, and their activity is at the same time very specific and very risky. As such, it has not been the object of any in-depth study since the pathbreaking work of Chalmin (1988). It will be discussed in Chapter 8.

BIBLIOGRAPHY

Ph. Chalmin (1988) *Traders and Merchants*. Harwood Academic Publishers, London.
E. Clark, M. Levasseur and P. Rousseau (1993) *International Finance*, Chapman and Hall, London.
International Chamber of Commerce (Ch. Del Busto) (1993) *ICC Uniform Customs and Practice for Documentary Credits*. ICC Publishing SA, Paris.
International Chamber of Commerce (Ch. Del Busto) (1994) *Documentary Credit Operations for the UCP*, ICC Publishing SA, Paris.
International Chamber of Commerce (1999) *Incoterms 2000. ICC Official Rules for the Interpretation of Trade Terms*. ICC Publishing SA, Paris.
International Chamber of Commerce (1999) *The ICC Model International Sales Contract. Manufactured Goods Intended for Resale*. ICC Publishing SA, Paris.
International Chamber of Commerce (J. Ramberg) (2000) *ICC Guide to Incoterms 2000. Understanding and Practical Guide*. ICC Publishing SA, Paris.

K. J. Shippey (1998) *A Short Course in International Contracts: Drafting the International Sales Contract. For Attorneys and Non-Attorneys*. World Trade Publishers.

UNCTAD (1998) *A Survey of Risk Mangement Instruments*. UNCTAD, Geneva.

H. M. Venedekian and G. A. Warfield (1996) *Export–Import Financing*. Wiley, New York.

J. Woodward (1965) *Industrial Organization: Theory and Practice*. Oxford University Press, London.

F. Youssef (1998) *Finance to Farmers: New Effective Ways to Explore Commodity Trade Finance* in *New Strategies for a Changing Commodity Economy. The Rôle of Modern Financial Instruments*. Selected papers, 'Partners for Development' Summit, Lyons, France. UNCTAD, Geneva.

APPENDIX 7A

Example of a commodity contract

7A.1   Introduction

This is an example of an actual sugar contract with standard specifications and provisions. This should not be considered as a model contract, but rather as a realistic example or case study illustrating the relationships between legal provisions and economic concerns including, in particular, the management of various risks. Model commodity contracts are supplied by a number of organisations, including the International Chamber of Commerce, GAFTA, the American National Grain and Feed Association, the UNCTAD, among others. However, actual contracts adapted to the specific needs of a particular transaction should be, and are most of the time, established by qualified professional lawyers.

7A.2   Analysis of the Terms of the Contract

Let us therefore analyse this contract in relation to the concepts that have been developed above, especially in section 7.5.

The *preamble* to the contract intends to identify the two parties, who state that they are able to fulfil the conditions of the contract and that they commit themselves to do so.

Articles 1–7 define precisely the product, the quantity and quality to be delivered, the price and incoterms (C&F), with the detailed quality specifications defined by Article 21, leaving no option in terms of the quality specifications. An option in terms of the origin (Brazil, or Central or South America) is provided for under Article 2. The number of shipments and the minimum quantity to be shipped, and the documents that should accompany each shipment are defined by Article 5. Article 22 defines packaging.

Article 8 and Article 20 define the terms of payment, and the instruments to be used in order to avoid reciprocal default: an irrevocable, transferable letter of credit to ensure payment of the seller, and a performance bond at 2% to avoid default of the seller. Articles 9 and 10 specify the procedure for the payment, and in particular the documents that are to be presented.

Several articles provide for inspection by SGS, or equivalent certification company or organisation, in order to ensure that the product complies with the specifications. Article 13 states that insurance will be paid by the buyer and under the buyer's responsibility, as this corresponds to the incoterms negotiated. Article 14 deals with force majeure, or events that are beyond the control of the parties.

Other articles define miscellaneous but important items, concerning the execution and validity of the contract, its renewal, and various penalties. Article 16 defines an arbitration procedure.

The contract is signed by two representatives of the two companies, usually senior executive officers. The signatures are to be certified by the notary of each party (in the USA, a notary is a professional lawyer who is independent from the parties and who certifies a contract, in order to ensure that the parties have well understood its terms). In other countries, other professional lawyers are authorised to perform an equivalent certification.

Finally, enclosure 1 to the contract defines shipments and their characteristics, while enclosure 2, also signed by one representative of each party, gives the details of the banks of each party, which is important inasmuch as a letter of credit has been provided for.

Purchase and Sale Agreement

Contract number_____

Buyer _____

Seller _____

Preamble

This contract is made and entered into force this day of_____ 2*** between:

Buyer _____

Hereinafter referred to as the buyer

and

Seller _____

Hereinafter referred to as the seller

Whereas the seller with full authority makes an irrevocable firm commitment to sell and deliver 100,000 (one hundred thousand) metric tonnes (Mts)(+/−5%) of refined cane sugar, and hereby certifies, represents and warrants that it can fulfil the requirements of the agreement and provide the product referred to herein in a timely manner and under the terms agreed upon by the signatories hereafter.

Whereas the buyer makes an irrevocable firm commitment to purchase 100,000 (one hundred thousand) metric tons (+/−5%) of refined cane sugar, cost and freight (CFR incoterms 1990) paid deliverable to any safe port.

Whereas the seller and the buyer now do hereby agree to honour this contract under the following terms and conditions.

Article 1   Product

Refined cane sugar, minimum polarization degree sound and fit for human consumption (see specifications as per article 21) corresponding completely to the EU ASSUC rules as per certificates of SGS or equivalent which shall at the port of loading confirm that the product complies to the specifications.

Article 2   Origin

The origin of the sugar is Brazil, or Central and/or South America at seller's option.

Article 3   Destination

The shipping destination of the sugar is to_____ (see enclosure 1).

Article 4   Basis of Delivery

The basis of delivery and shipment shall be a minimum of either 12,500 Mts (twelve thousand five hundred metric tonnes) and/or 25,000 Mts. (twenty-five thousand metric tonnes) per vessel lift ($+/-5\%$). The 60% (sixty per cent) of the total quantity shall be delivered in vessels of twenty-five thousand metric tons as the port allows and with a shipment frequency to provide adequately for the total quantity purchased to be delivered within a 3 (three) month period. Delivery will commence 30 to 45 days after an acceptable bank instrument is in the seller's bank. The date(s) of the bill(s) of lading shall be considered the date(s) of delivery (see enclosure 1).

Article 5   Shipment Documentation per Lift

The documents to accompany the shipment of the goods are:

1. Full set of clean on board bill of lading, blank endorsed, and marked 'freight prepaid'.
2. Original of certificate of weight and quality issued by a first-class control organisation (SGS or equivalent organisation as accepted by both parties).

3. Certificate of origin.
4. Certificate of weight (two copies).
5. Packing list (three copies).
6. Signed commercial invoice.
7. Health certificate (SGS phytosanitary certificate).
8. Certificate of non-radiation.

Article 6   Quantity

The quantity sold by the seller and purchased by the buyer shall be 100,000 Mts (+/−5% at seller's option), the total delivered and verified by the certificates of weight issued by the inspecting authority and the collective weight results of bill(s) of lading of all shipments that were in effect delivered and shipped to the buyer during the contract period.

Article 7   Product Weight and Quality

The seller guarantees on his account and at the risk of buyer rights of refusal of shipment unless each shipment of sugar shall be provided with an inspection certificate of weight and quality at the same time of loading, and such certificates shall be provided by SGS or similar at seller's expenses and shall be final. The seller is obliged and binds himself to instruct said authority to carry out the inspections in strict accordance with the Refined Sugar Association (RSA) rules, at the source of origin and or point of loading.

The buyer and/or client may, if they so desire at their own option and expenses, provide an additional inspection at port of loading to confirm the inspection certificates issued at loading point. Both parties hereby agree to confirm the inspection certificates issued at point of loading, both parties hereby agree to allow RSA rules to apply and to determine the appointment of an independent and approved arbitrator to hear and pass impartial judgment. Both parties, also agree to be bound and to abide by the arbitrator's decision, whether for or against either buyer and seller.

Article 8   Sale and Payment

The buyer *and* the seller agree to the following quantities, price and method of payment:

A — total quantity :   100,000 Mts (one hundred thousand metric
                                         tonnes)
B — quantity per shipment :   12,500/25,000 Mts (+/−5%)

C — price per metric ton :	US$190/Mts (one hundred and ninety US dollars per metric tonne) C&F.
D — total contract amount :	US$ 19,000,000 (nineteen million US dollars)
E — method of payment	Buyer will open an irrevocable, transferable letter of credit payable 100% at sight against presentation of required documents at loading port, issued by a prime bank (top 10) for 90 (ninety) days. At buyer's option, a revolving letter covering a minimum of 50,000 Mts is acceptable.
F — seller's/buyer's bank coordinates :	See enclosure 2.

Article 9   Financial Instruments and Draws

The seller is allowed to draw against the financial instrument the value of the sugar sold to the buyer only upon presentation of the following documents, in order, to the bank:

1. Commercial invoice.
2. 2/3 original bill of lading 'clean on board' issued to order blank endorsed and marked 'freight prepaid'.
3. Certificate of origin (two-fold).
4. Certificate of weight and quality issued by SGS or similar authority at loading port.
5. Company certificate of sugar fit for human consumption.
6. Packing list.
7. Shipping company statement (two-fold) stating that:

   A. 1/3 original bill of lading and originals of certificate of origin and phyto-sanitary certificate accompanied the shipment.
   B. The vessel's age is not above 20 years.

8. Seller's statement that no commercial invoice accompanies the shipment.
9. Copy of export licence.

Article 10   Procedures

Procedures shall be carried out in the following order:

- Buyer and seller sign the contract.
- Buyer's bank issues the letter of credit for 100% of contract amount, entering into force against receipt of:

A. SGS (or similar) certificate of inspection of product;
B. Seller's bank 2% (two per cent) performance bond.

- Seller executes A & B above, the letter of credit is activated.
- Delivery commences as per contract.

Article 11   Transport Conditions

1. The seller will advise the buyer of the name of the chartered vessel/her flag and position 10 (ten) days before the vessel's arrival at loading port.
2. All supervision charges at loading port are for buyer's account, any taxes or levies at loading port are for buyer's account.
3. On completion of loading, seller's shipping agent shall telex, fax, or cable the buyer of the vessel's sailing date, the name, the flag of the vessel, quantity loaded, any data about buyer's discharge port, not later than 48 hours after completion of loading.
4. Shipment by first-class mechanically self-propelled vessel which must be classified as 100A1 in the Lloyd's register or be of equivalent classification, excluding tankers and vessels which are classified in Lloyd's register as Ore/Oil vessels; chartered vessel must not be older than 20 years.

Article 12   Discharge Terms

1. The vessel master is to advise the buyer agent at the port of discharge the following details: vessel's name, date of arrival, vessel's capacity, number of cargo chamber, quantity loaded per cargo chamber, and the particulars of the vessel's readiness to effect cargo operations.
2. The vessel master shall give 20 days and 7 days provisional notice and 72/36/24 hours final notice of vessel's designate time of arrival at the port of destination to the buyer's agent at the discharge port. Such notices shall be effected during normal business hours and whether in berth or not.
3. If discharge notice is given prior to noon lay time begin from 1:00 PM and from 8:00 AM of the next working day if notice is given after noon. If port is congested, lay time is to commence 24 hours after notice of readiness is given. Buyer is responsible for the commodities.
4. The discharge rate shall be a minimum of one thousand two hundred (1,200) and fifteen hundred (1,500) Mts per weather working day of 24 hours. The times from 17:00 hours on the day preceding to 8:00 hours on the day succeeding any holiday are excluded, even if used.
5. Should the vessel be discharged at a rate greater than average, the buyer shall pay to the seller demurrage as per the rates prescribed in the charter party agreement.

6. Should the vessel be discharged at a rate lesser than average, the seller shall pay to the buyer speed of dispatch as per charter party agreement.
7. It is agreed that these demurrage/dispatch variations will be settled within 5 (five) days from date of receipt of vessel's master invoice and is the buyer's responsibility.
8. All taxes, levies and port dues imposed by the country of destination are for the buyer's account and sole responsibility.

Article 13   Insurance

The buyer is responsible for producing and maintaining in force a policy of marine insurance for the purchased goods subject to this contract in accordance with RSA rules. Any insurance premium is for the buyer's account and sole responsibility.

Article 14   Force Majeure

One of parties will not bear the responsibility for complete or partial default of any responsibilities, if the default will be a consequence of such circumstances as flood, earthquake, and other acts of nature, strike, lockout, riot or civil commotion, war or military actions, and any other cause comprehended in the term 'force majeure', arising after conclusion of contract, as well as governmental decisions, hindering to fulfilment by parties of conditions of contract.

If any of the listed circumstances had directly affected execution of the obligations in time, stipulated in contract, this term in proportion is removed on a time of action of appropriate circumstances.

Article 15   Non-business Days

Saturdays, Sundays and the officially recognised and/or legal holidays of the respective countries shall be non-business days. Should the deadline for doing any act or giving any notice occur on such a non-business day, this deadline shall be changed to be the first business day thereafter. The period for delivery shall not be affected by this clause.

Article 16   Arbitration

By express agreement, the parties agree to attempt to amicably settle any disagreement or dispute. If not possible, they are to submit to the arbitration of the

International Chamber of Commerce. For settlement, the regulations as per ICC 500 are applicable.

Article 17   Authority to Execute this Contract

Each one of the parties represent that it has full authority to execute this agreement and accordingly that the party is bound by the terms and conditions hereof.

Article 18   Execution of the Agreement

This agreement may be executed simultaneously in two counterparts via telefax or facsimile transmission. Written or retyped on the fact of this contract, said, written, or typed alteration shall prevail when acknowledged by both parties.

Article 19   Non-circumvention

The parties accept and agree to provision the International Chamber of Commerce for non-circumvention and non-disclosure with regard to all and every one of the parties involved in this transaction and contract.

Additions, renewals, and third-party assignments with full reciprocation for a period of five years of execution of this contract.

Article 20   Performance Guarantee

A two per cent (2%) performance guarantee against the full value of the unencumbered letter of credit which is applicable on a declining prorata basis on undelivered shipment of sugar.

Article 21   Specification of the Product

International inspection authority (SGS, or similar organisation as approved by both parties) at port shall confirm that the product conforms to the following specifications:

Refined white cane sugar of the crop current at time of delivery, fine free running of regular grain size and fair average of the quality of deliveries made from the declared origin of crop, with minimum polarisation 99.8 degrees, moisture maximum 0.06%, maximum 60 units ICUMSA, colour sparkling white, radiation normal, sound and fit for human consumption, or corresponding completely to the requirements of EU ASSUC Rules, at time of delivery to vessel at port, as per certificate of SGS, or similar, which shall at the port of loading confirm that the product conforms to the specifications.

Article 22   Packaging

Sugar is to be packed in 50 kg net, new poly-lined jute bags of combined tape of 100 grammes each to secure the safety of the commodity during sea transportation. Seller shall supply on each vessel a number of extra empty bags at seller's expense.

Article 23   Revolving Clause

At buyer's option, this contract can be renewed twice under same terms and conditions (except unit price) in order to reach a total quantity of 300,000 Mts.

Buyer to advise seller at least 30 (thirty) days prior expiration of this contract that he is willing to renew it.

Buyer and seller will agree for the new unit price per metric tonne to be applied; this unit price will be adjusted according to the market fluctuations and according to the quantity bought.

Article 24   Penalty Clause

If any party of this contract other that the bank officers representing the buyer and seller should make unauthorized contact with bank of the seller, or the buyer, such contact shall be considered interference with this contract and shall at the option of either the buyer or seller terminate the contract forthwith. The interfering party will be charged with loss of profits on this transaction by the injured parties who will be entitled to file legal proceedings against the interfering party at the International Chamber of Commerce, to recover their losses.

Article 25   Validity

The validity for signing this contract is seven (7) banking days as from the date of this contract.

In witness whereof, the parties hereto have signed below and by doing so accept, approve, and agree to all covenants, terms and conditions herein.

This contract will become null and void if not signed by _____ 2***.

This contract contains 11 pages (including two enclosures).

SELLER'S COMPANY SEAL   BUYER'S COMPANY SEAL
Signature   Signature
Name: _____   Name: _____
Date: _____, 2***   Date: _____, 2***
Witness   Witness
Seller's notary: _____ Buyer's notary: _____
Seal   Seal
Sworn before me on this date: ____   Sworn before me on this date: ____
By the above name: _____ By the above name: _____

Individual of this city of: _____   Individual of this city of: _____
Country: _____   Country: _____
State: _____   State: _____

Contract for purchasing Sugar Enclosure 1 Schedule and Delivery

Product: 100,000 Mts refined canes sugar as per specifications of contract.

	Shipment	Shipment
Quantity/date		
Port		
Consignee		
Address		
	Shipment	Shipment
Quantity/date		
Port		
Consignee		
Address		
	Shipment	Shipment
Quantity/date		
Port		
Consignee		
Address		

Contract for Purchasing Sugar Enclosure 2 Banking Co-ordinates of Seller and Buyer

(Bank to bank telex (KTT) only. If telephone communication is required, it will be arranged by the seller or the buyer)

(A1) buyer's bank name _____

Address: _____

Account name: _____

Account number: _____

Bank officer: _____

Phone No.: _____ Fax No.: _____

Telex: _____ SWIFT: _____

(B2) seller's bank name _____

Address: _____

Account name: _____

Account number: _____

Bank officer: _____

Phone No.: _____ Fax No.: _____

Telex: _____ SWIFT: _____

Buyer, for and on behalf of: _____

Phone No.: _____ Fax No.: _____

Seller, for and on behalf of: _____

Phone No.: _____ Fax No.: _____

Buyer's company seal   Seller's company seal

Signature:_____ Signature: _____

Name: _____ Name: _____

Date: _____ Date: _____

Witness   Witness

APPENDIX 7B

Example of a letter of intent (loi)

We _____ (seller's name) hereby certify, under the penalties of perjury, that we are ready and willing and able to sell refined cane sugar according to the following terms and conditions:

*Product: Grade A refined white cane sugar

*Origin: South/Central America

*Quality:

	Polarization	99.8% Min.
	Moisture	0.04% Max
	ASH Content	0.04% Max
	Granulation	fine to medium
	Solubility	100% free flowing
	Incumsa RBU	45 RBU
	Radiation	Normal
	Colour	White

*Packaging: 50 kg net new poly-lined jute bags

*Quantity: six hundred thousand/600,000/metric tons

*Cargo size: Approximately 12,500 metric tons vessel to be used

*Shipping shipments to begin within 30 to 55 days after receipt and confirmation of buyer's letter of credit (L/C).

*Delivery: As per contract to be determined. First delivery starts 45/forty-five/days after establishment of buyer's L/C.

*Term: 12/twelve/months from start of deliveries.

*Price basis: C&F any safe world port (ASWP)

*Funding: An irrevocable, confirmable, transferable, designable, revolving letter of credit.

8
The actors of commodity trading

8.1 INTRODUCTION

As already noted and discussed under various angles, the high volatility of commodity prices has become a fundamental characteristic of the markets at least since 1973. It has led to an important role for international commodity trading companies as intermediaries on physical markets and as operators and intermediaries through brokerage subsidiaries on the derivative markets. Based on the discussion in Chapter 7, the role of trading companies is essentially one of an intermediary that contributes to adjusting the supply originating with the commodity producers to the demand emanating from industrial end-users. Inasmuch as markets are global, these companies operate worldwide. The activity of international commodity trading companies thus fundamentally aims at ensuring physical transfers for basic commodities between one place and another worldwide. More precisely, this implies:

1. Pre-transportation of the product between its production site and the shipping port or airport at which they should be made available.
2. Storing the product before shipment and further short-term storage of the product in the course of its shipping, subject to transportation conditions and to transhipments, whenever authorised and/or necessary.
3. Conditioning and/or other industrial transformations of the product.
4. International transportation of the product.
5. Other post-shipping operations.

Trading companies are by no means the only actors on commodity markets. The above activities may be carried out by either the trading company itself or through specialised subcontractors. The activity of an international trading company can therefore go far beyond the scope of its core activity of trading to include tasks that require industrial facilities adapted to the nature of the commodities being processed. Thus, a trading company will often be present in the industry of basic commodities itself. Conversely, producers and industrial end-users of commodities can also maintain trading subsidiaries and trading divisions. Finally, production, trading and industrial consumption of commodities are often closely related. In any case, commodity trading must be flexible and adapted to interactions with a number of other operators. These other operators are essential. They ensure that both the supply and demand sides do adjust to each other on these markets worldwide. Actions leading to this adjustment are risky. To manage the risk, operators can either use insurance or, more generally, transfer it to other parties. This means using the services of the financial community and in particular those of banks and insurance companies. Clearly, bankers and insurers are major actors in terms of the effectiveness of operations at an acceptable level of risk on international commodity markets.

An analysis of the major activities involved in the international trade of commodities will enable us to establish a classification and a characterisation of the various actors that are encountered in the chain that links the producer of commodities to the final end-user. Thus, this chapter will be organised as follows. In the next section we will examine the role of all these actors as well as the risks they encounter in their various activities. In section 8.3 we focus on commodity trading companies and their growth strategies where it will become clear that these companies do bear a significant part of the risks that are inherent in international commodity trading. We have seen that one of the main risks is price risk. Traders and other direct market participants are therefore always either net buyers or net sellers on physical markets because of temporary mismatches between supply and demand. Consequently, they are always subject to some net exposure to price risk. The financial instruments discussed in Chapters 2, 3, 4 and 6, aimed at hedging against these risks, are therefore of great importance to these operators. Other risks are those discussed in Chapter 7 from the angle of optimal contract provisions and other financial techniques, such as the letter of credit.

Trading companies specialising in basic commodities have had difficulties in the recent past that have caused some of them to disappear. This has often occurred through mergers and acquisitions and a number of smaller trading companies have been obliged to merge with larger companies or companies with more appropriate strategies. There is, in the commodity trading industry as in many others, a scale effect in favour of large actors. In the area of international commodity trading, it might be said that 'God is on the side of big battalions'. Finally, at the end of the third section, we will present a representative panorama of the largest and most active trading companies. The volatile nature of international commodity trading is such that dominant positions can be very fragile and, consequently, this panorama will not attempt to give any significant ranking of the companies.

8.2 THE ACTORS OF INTERNATIONAL TRADE IN COMMODITIES

8.2.1 The Actors of International Trade in Commodities: An Overview

The complete process of an operation in the international trade of basic commodities is complex and the role of the various actors varies according to the commodities being traded. Whoever is responsible for such an operation, whether it is a trading company or the trading division of a producer or an industrial end-user, the tasks to be completed are many and varied. They can imply the participation of shipowners, shipbrokers, forwarding agents, companies specialised in control, physical management and transportation of raw materials as well as banks and insurance companies, which are in charge of the financial and physical security of operations. All these actors are specialised in functions that are fundamental to an optimal execution of commercial commodity contracts. The actual number of agents and intermediaries varies according to the commodity in question:

1. In the case of energy commodities, secondary energies, such as refined petroleum products and coal are end-user products which may directly be used by end-consumers and distributed by retailers. Here, there are a small number of intermediaries (trading companies, and wholesalers only, and no transformation industry for these products).
2. There usually is a small number of intermediaries in the case of agricultural commodities for which stockkeeping and conditioning are the most important steps of the commercial sequence of operations.
3. A larger number of intermediaries is required in the case of metals, for which transformation steps into a final consumption good are more complex. This means that there may be a number of intermediaries on these markets, including large trading companies, secondary merchants, wholesalers, and brokers.

Besides the trading companies, the brokerage companies and their clients, other actors on physical markets that are neither commodity suppliers nor commodity purchasers are also important. We will discuss them and their role in the following section. Table 8.1 summarises the main actors of international trade in commodities. Figure 8.1 also gives a simplified picture of the roles of these various actors.

8.2.2 Direct Market Participants: Producers, Traders, and Industrial End-users

We define direct participants as the main economic agents that effectively participate in commodity markets in terms of supply and demand. We can exclude from our discussion downstream wholesalers and retailers that sell distribution services of either industrial products or, in some cases, basic commodities (but on

Table 8.1   A classification of the main operators on international (physical and derivative) commodity markets

Main classes of commodities		
Energy products	Metals	Agricultural products
Operators that are present on both physical markets and (if any) on derivative markets		
Oil and gas companies, coal mining	Mining companies	Large farmers and farming companies
Oil refiners	Smelters and refiners	Elevator companies and other stockists
Electricity production companies	Rolling and extrusion companies	Basic food industries, textile industries, and other related industries
Electricity distribution companies	Secondary smelters and refiners	Secondary food industries textile industries, and other related industries
Gas distribution companies	Metal industries	Other transformation industries
Large traders and merchants in oil products, natural gas, LPG, and coal	Large traders and merchants in steel products, common non-ferrous metals, other non-ferrous metals, and precious metals	Large traders and merchants in agricultural products (grains, sugar, coffee, cocoa, tea, textiles and other products)
Secondary traders or merchants	Secondary traders or merchants	Secondary traders or merchants
Stockists/distributors	Stockists/distributors	Distributors
Financial operators that are present on derivative markets (including both organised futures and option exchanges and over-the-counter markets)		
Banks	Banks	Banks
Other financial intermediaries, including brokerage companies	Other financial intermediaries, including brokerage companies	Other financial intermediaries, including brokerage companies
Investment funds and pension funds	Investment funds and pension funds	Investment funds and pension funds
Speculators (hedge funds and public speculators)	Speculators (hedge funds and public speculators)	Speculators (hedge funds and public speculators)

a comparatively small scale). Stockists and warehouse agents are often integrated with either producers, or traders. Considering the sequence of operations presented in Figure 8.1, we are thus led to focus our discussion on three main categories of market participants: producers, trading companies, and industrial end-users. These three categories of participants are, however, closely interlinked. We will see that producers are in many cases vertically integrated and maintain both

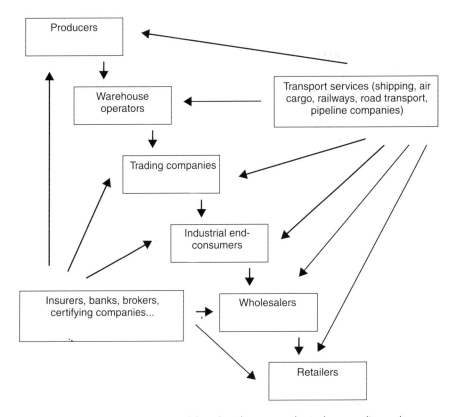

Figure 8.1   A simplified presentation of the roles of actors on physical commodity markets

trading and industrial subsidiaries. Trading companies and industrial end-users of commodities are integrated as well. It is therefore difficult to discuss these three categories of direct market participants separately, except perhaps that the central role of trading companies justifies a separate and more in-depth discussion. As far as industrial end-users are concerned, they are very diverse and often disconnected from basic commodity markets. We thus propose to devote this section mainly to producers, which are directly related to international commodity markets and to some cases of industrial end-users that are significantly present on these markets.

Throughout the 1990s, international commodity markets were characterised by a strong movement towards deregulation and privatisation. Deregulation in a broad sense has also included the removal of many public guarantee systems, the agricultural sector being the general exception. This evolution has thus favoured the development of derivative markets and private insurance schemes for managing price volatility to the detriment of public or state-operated price guarantee systems. However, the situation of commodity producers can be quite different depending on the commodity or the commodity group, such as energy commodities, mineral commodities, and agricultural commodities. Even within a particular commodity group, situations in terms of pricing mechanisms and market structure are quite diverse. These situations are subject to a number of factors — natural, economic, historical, and political. Although it is impossible to describe all of the existing situations, it would be interesting to give a few examples that illustrate some of the most frequently encountered situations.

In the energy commodity industries, the market network is comparatively quite simple because there are only one or two steps of transformation between the producer and the final end-user. This is true of the oil and gas industry. It is well known that crude oil is available as a primary commodity in many places of the world (North America, Central and South America, Europe and the Russian Federation, Asia, the Middle East, and Africa). However, crude oil is not directly usable for an end-consumer. It must be refined to obtain the various end-user products (liquefied petroleum gas (LPG), jet fuel or kerosene, gasoline, heating oil and diesel oil and fuel oil, in particular). Thus, the production side of the oil industry comprises the upstream crude oil production and exploration and the oil refining industry. It is usually closely related to the production of natural gas. There are a number of oil and natural gas companies that are present in upstream production of both oil and natural gas. Global oil and gas companies, which are the largest ones, are fully integrated in most cases. They are an example of what we said at the beginning of this subsection about the close links that often exist between production, trading, and industrial end consumption. These companies are usually present in the upstream crude oil and natural gas production, in the oil refining industry, in the physical trading business (of crude oil, natural gas and refined products), as well as in the retailing of all refined products.

Table 8.2 gives a list of oil and natural gas companies that are present in the production of oil and gas and/or of refined petroleum products. All these companies are present on the supply side on international markets for crude oil and natural gas. Inasmuch as they operate refineries, they are also present on both the supply and demand side on markets for refined oil products. There are also a number of large companies that are specialised in natural gas production, such as British Gas, Gazprom, Gasunie in Europe. These companies may also be involved in gas distribution.

Some large oil companies are horizontally integrated, which means that they are present in the production of primary energy commodities other than crude oil, such as natural gas, and, less frequently, coal. The production of coal is usually in the hands of specialised companies that operate coal mines. These specialised companies are thus on the supply side of international coal markets and can be in the physical trading side as well. An example of a coal company that is owned by a large oil company is Exxon Coal, a subsidiary of Exxon. BP Amoco and Shell are also present in coal production. Other coal companies may

Table 8.2 Examples of large oil and gas companies involved in the upstream production of crude oil and natural gas, and/or in the downstream activities of oil refining and petrochemistry

Oil and gas companies and their characteristics	
Name of companies	Characteristics
Global companies	
ARCO, BP–Amoco, Chevron, Exxon–Mobil, Shell Group, Texaco, Total Fina–ELF	These companies are operating worldwide, and are usually vertically integrated, so that they are involved in upstream oil and gas production, oil refining, petrochemistry and downstream chemistry, the physical trading of crude oil and oil refined products, operating fleets of tankers and pipeline networks, gas distribution, and retailing of oil refined products
National or regional companies	
Abu Dhabi National Oil Company, BHP (Broken Hill Proprietary) Petroleum, Kuwait National Oil Company, National Iranian Oil Company, Lukoil, Norsk Hydro ASA, PEMEX, Qatar General Petroleum Corporation, Pertamina, Rossneft, Saudi ARAMCO, Sonatrach, Statoil, Petroleos de Venezuela SA (PDVSA)	These companies are operating in specific producing countries or regions of the world, and are usually, but not always vertically integrated, so that they are involved in upstream oil and gas production, oil refining, petrochemistry and downstream chemistry, and in the physical trading of crude oil and oil refined products worldwide, in gas distribution, and retailing of oil refined products in the country or region in which they are operating

be subsidiaries of mineral commodity companies. An example is BHP Coal, a subsidiary of the Australian company BHP (Broken Hill Proprietary Ltd). BHP is involved in a number of metal commodities such as steel, major non-ferrous metals such as copper, lead, nickel, and zinc, precious metals such as gold and silver, as well as in crude oil. Billiton, a British metal and mining company, also has coal subsidiaries in Australia. A number of other coal producers are present in the various production areas (Australia, Canada, China, Poland, the USA, and South Africa being the main exporters). Among these, Amcoal, Anaconda Minerals, Gencor, Peabody Coal, Pittston and Weglokoks are some of the best known. Most of these companies are specialised in coal production and hence are suppliers and possibly purchasers through trading subsidiaries on international coal markets. Some of them, including Gencor, have activities in a wide range of commodities.

note Gencor not Glencor

As we pointed out in Chapter 1, electricity used to be produced by local, national or regional companies, usually in a monopolistic environment. Electricity markets are, however, becoming more and more competitive in Europe, North America, and Australia, with a move towards deregulation and privatisation and the development of active spot and derivative markets. Electricity-producing companies are quite numerous throughout the world as suppliers on the existing national, regional, and international electricity markets. An important feature of electricity is that it cannot easily be stocked and, generally speaking, in a given geographical area its supply must be equal to its demand. The demand for electricity is, however, very volatile. Increased deregulation and competition are leading to the emergence of electricity trading companies whose activities aim at equating supply with demand. These trading companies are often subsidiaries of electricity producers, which traditionally have been vertically integrated, controlling distribution as well as production. However, the situation is changing rapidly. In the new competitive electricity markets, trading and distribution of electricity are becoming independent activities, which may or may not be controlled by electricity producers.

Ferrous and non-ferrous metal products constitute the most important non-energy mineral commodities. Steel products are, of course, among the most important metal commodities, although in the developed world, steel intensity, i.e. the quantity of steel consumed per unit of GDP, is on a decreasing trend owing to substitution by other materials such as aluminium and plastics. There are active spot markets for a number of steel products, in Europe, in the USA, and in Japan, but no derivative markets, although the recent development of internet markets might lead to informal derivative markets. The most important producers are Bethlehem Steel (USA), Nippon Steel (Japan), Posco (Korea), and, in Europe, British Steel, Usinor (France), ARBED (Luxembourg), and Thyssen (Germany) among others. In Latin America, Siderbras (Brazil) is an important emerging producer.

Non-ferrous metals can be divided into three broad classes:

1. *Common non-ferrous metals*, that include the six metals quoted on the LME: aluminium, copper, lead, nickel, tin, and zinc.
2. *Minor non-ferrous metals*, such as antimony, bismuth, cadmium, chromium, cobalt, lithium, magnesium, mercury, molybdenum, titanium, tungsten, uranium, vanadium and zirconium, and the rare earth metals.
3. *Precious metals*, which include gold, silver, and the platinum group metals (PGM), including platinum, palladium, ruthenium, rhodium, osmium, and iridium.

Aluminium is among the most important of the common non-ferrous metals. It is one of the most abundant metals within the earth's crust and is an element of many minerals, such as common clay, but the only aluminium ore of economic interest is bauxite. Aluminium production based on bauxite is an electricity-intensive and comparatively expensive process compared with steel products. However, since aluminium is a relatively light metal, it has become a strong competitor for steel.

Aluminium is produced in a variety of regions and countries of the world, including countries of the OECD area, emerging countries, as well as countries with economies in transition such as Russia. The main producers of aluminium are Alcoa (USA), with a production capacity of some 15% of world supply, Alcan (Canada), Péchiney (France), Norsk Hydro (Norway), Krasnoyarsk and Novokuznetsk (Russia), and Venalum (Venezuela).

As mentioned in Chapter 1, the leading spot and futures market for aluminium is the London Metal Exchange (LME), but the NYMEX/COMEX in New York has recently developed aluminium futures. Spot and futures LME prices are often used as reference prices in commercial contracts.

Copper is another common and very important non-ferrous metal. Its uses stem from its physical properties and in particular from the fact that it is a good conductor of electricity — at least under its refined form often referred to as cathodic grade copper which is 99.99% pure copper. It is therefore widely used for electrical wiring and electrical appliances. In alloys, it is also used as a material for a number of other manufactured goods.

Like aluminium, copper is produced in a many countries. There are copper producers in the OECD area (Australia, Canada, etc.), in the transition countries such as Russia, in the emerging economies of Latin America such as Chile and Mexico and the poor countries of Africa, including Zambia. Chile, Zambia, and Canada are the dominant exporters. The market is more competitive than the aluminium market and there are many producers. The most important of these producers are companies such as Codelco (Chile), Rio Tinto Zinc (UK), Broken Hill Proprietary (BHP) (Australia), Zambia Copper (Zambia), Phelps Dodge (USA), and Inco (Canada). The main spot reference prices concern refined copper.[1]

Copper is also a metal with a comparatively complex production process. There are several kinds of ores produced in a first stage as blistered copper, a comparatively impure form. Blistered copper has to be processed to obtain refined cathodic grade copper used for electricity conduction. Copper is also used as an alloy. The price of copper is quite volatile and copper derivative markets are very active.[2]

Other common non-ferrous metals are lead, nickel, tin, and zinc. Although they are essential for some industries, they are comparatively less important than aluminium and copper. Whereas aluminium is a substitute for steel products and copper is used in many different applications, nickel, tin and zinc are metals

---

[1] As shown in Chapter 1, reference spot prices for copper are LME cash prices, and American producers' prices.
[2] Including, as mentioned in Chapter 1, the LME, and the NYMEX/COMEX in New York.

that are used as either additives in alloys or as coatings for flat products. These metals are thus complements to steel products and other materials, so that their markets are related to the markets for these materials. Lead has a specific use in automobile batteries, for which it has no substitute, at least under the present technological conditions. Its other uses in the fields of piping and plumbing are decreasing because of its toxicity. These four metals are quoted on the LME, which supplies universally recognised reference spot prices and is their leading futures market. In the case of tin, however, a leading physical market that also supplies reference prices is the Kuala Lumpur spot market in Malaysia.

Important nickel producers are the Norilsk complex in Russia, Inco and Falconbridge in Canada, Western Mining in Australia, Eramet-SLN in New Caledonia, and several Japanese producers. Producers from Far Eastern countries such as Malaysia, Indonesia, and China dominate the market for tin. Other major producers are Bolivia and Brazil. The main producing companies are Malaysia Mining Cy, Indonesian and Chinese companies, Paranapanama (Brazil), and Comibom in Bolivia. OECD countries with a strong mining industry, such as Australia and Canada, are less present on this market than in the markets for other non-ferrous metals. Australian and Canadian producers are much more present, even dominant, on the international zinc market. These producers include Cominco and CEZ in Canada, Pasminco Ltd in Australia, and historical European producers, such as Vieille Montagne in Belgium, Metallgesellschaft in Germany, Asturiana de Zinc in Spain. A major historical producer is Rio Tinto Zinc.[3]

Lead is a metal with mines all over the world and fairly competitive markets. Its production is dominated by Australian, Canadian and American producers, although Chinese producers are of increasing importance. The main actors are Pasminco Ltd in Australia, also involved in zinc, Asarco and Doe Run in the USA, Cominco in Canada, also involved in zinc, some traditional European producers, such as Union Minière in Belgium, and some Latin American companies.

There are numerous minor non-ferrous metals.[4] As a rule, their markets are small and often less competitive than those for the common non-ferrous metals. Some of their markets are dominated by groups that can be on niche markets, but are usually diversified into other metals or minerals. Industrial networks are comparatively simple because many of these metals have only very specific uses. There are cases of markets dominated by monopolies or oligopolies with a few end-users as well. For instance, cobalt is still a market with a dominant producer. This producer is Gecamines in the Republic of Congo and one of the reference prices is Gecamines' producer prices. A situation with a dominant producer should normally contribute to a comparatively stable price. In the case of

---

[3] RTZ, a British company that historically was established in the now exhausted Spanish Rio Tinto mines, is a major international company, involved in zinc and other non-ferrous metals in Australia and in the UK.

[4] The word 'minor' is misleading here. Many of these metals are certainly not minor in terms of price, because they are rare and under strong demand because of specific uses for which there may be few or no substitutes.

cobalt, however, political instability in the Congo and emerging competition from Zambia Copper, Inco and Falconbridge in Canada, and from Russian producers make this metal very volatile and highly speculative.

In the case of other metals, prices may be more stable than is the case for most commodities with little imbalance between supply and demand and therefore a less important role for trading companies. This is the case for metals with markets that are still dominated by state producers, such as tungsten. The spot prices of other metals can be very volatile and sometimes subject to manipulation by traders, which can seriously upset markets in the absence of organised derivative markets.

Examples of strategic metals available for special alloying are chromium, manganese, molybdenum, which are complements to steel products. Magnesium and titanium are light metals, and titanium is a substitute for aluminium in some strategic uses. Examples of diversified groups involved in minor metals are Phelps Dodge (involved in copper, but also in molybdenum through its subsidiary Climax), Cominco Ltd. in Canada (involved in copper, and in a number of minor metals and elements, such as bismuth, cadmium, germanium, indium, molybdenum, etc.). These minor metals have reference spot pricing systems that are often producers' prices, but no organised derivative markets.[5]

[Precious metals include silver, gold, and the six platinum group metals: ruthenium, rhodium, palladium, osmium, iridium, and platinum, the most important of which are platinum and palladium. Silver and gold were metals that formerly were used as monetary metals and have thus traditionally been financial assets as well as metals used in jewellery. Whereas the role of silver as a monetary metal almost completely disappeared at the end of the nineteenth century, gold played a monetary role with a controlled price until 1971. This price was US$20.67/oz throughout the nineteenth century until 1933, and US$35/oz between 1933 and 1969. In 1933, the hoarding of gold coins, and the holding of any private speculative gold stocks was prohibited in the USA but authorised in many other countries, and there were active spot markets in London, Zurich, Paris, and elsewhere. On these markets, however, until 1968, prices were always close to the guaranteed price of US$35/oz. At the end of 1974, the ban on individual stocks of gold in the USA was removed. Since that date, gold has evolved into what might be called a commodity. First, its market has become more and more competitive. By the end of 1974, gold production was dominated by South African producers and in particular by Anglo-American Corporation (AAC, now Anglo-American PLC after a merger of AAC and Minorco in 1999). This was because the controlled valuation of gold had not kept up with costs and had made most mines outside of South Africa unprofitable. Things changed significantly as the price for deregulated gold went up sharply, and many mining companies were able to produce

---

[5] But, as seen in Chapter 1, there is a spot market in London for antimony, bismuth, cadmium, chromium, cobalt, titanium sponge, ferro-manganese, ferro-molybdenum, mercury, selenium, and tungsten.

gold competitively in Canada (Echo Bay, Placer Dome, Barrick Gold), the USA (Homestake Newmont), and Australia (Western Mining). Furthermore, the financial role of gold is declining, as more and more central banks no longer consider gold as an essential asset. Conversely, the industrial role of gold has increased but, due to increases in supply and selling of speculative stocks, the price of gold has continuously decreased since the historical high price of US$870/oz in 1980.[6]

Silver is a metal that is increasingly an industrial metal (with about 50% of its demand related to photography) rather than a financial asset. Major producers are Latin American, such as Grupo Industrial Minera Mexico, and Centromin in Peru, Canadian (Noranda Mines, Cominco), and Australian, including BHP. The recycling of spent photographic material is playing an increasingly important role.

Platinum and palladium and other platinum group metals are also becoming increasingly important as industrial metals and less important in their traditional uses, such as jewellery. This is due to their properties as catalysts, which have been of interest in the oil refining and in the chemical industries for a long time. But the demand for platinum and palladium, which is a good substitute for platinum in its uses as a catalyst, has steadily increased since catalytic exhausts were required in cars because of environmental regulations in the European Union, the USA, and Japan. Here, South African producers dominate the market. A leading actor is Anglo-American PLC. AAC used to control three major platinum producers: Rustenburg Platinum Holdings, Lebowa Platinum Mines, and Potgieterrerust Platinums. All three of these companies are now subsidiaries of Anglo-American Platinum (AMPLATS), the world leader in platinum group metals, itself a subsidiary of Anglo-American PLC. Other South African producers are Gencor, with PGM interests in IMPLATS, Lonrho, and Northam. These South African producers currently control about 70% of the market for platinum. Russian producers follow with a company known as NMCC, present in the Norilsk mines under the Arctic circle, with the participation of Finnish and Australian investors. These Russian producers also dominate the market for palladium and are thus a major competitor for South African platinum producers. Emerging producers are ZIMPLATS, in Zimbabwe, which is controlled by the Australian BHP, and Stillwater, in the USA, with facilities in Stillwater, Montana. Inco and Falconbridge, in Canada, also produce platinum and palladium. The market is becoming more and more competitive and it is very volatile due to uncertainties and political problems in Russia. However, there are active derivative markets for both platinum and palladium. Among other platinum group metals, rhodium is the most important. It is a very rare metal, produced by the same producers and used as an additive for catalysts. Its spot price is very volatile, but no futures markets are available for hedging.

---

[6] A typical price of gold in the year 2000 would have been US$275/oz.

Precious metals and some other base metals, including minor but strategic non-ferrous metals, are also useful for their chemical compounds and salts or in special or elaborate physical forms. Examples of such downstream products are compounds of gold and platinum that are used in medical applications, platinum and palladium catalysts for the chemical industries, the oil industries, and catalytic exhausts in cars. All these high-technology and very elaborate products are manufactured by specialised companies that are often partially integrated with some trading activity in precious metals. An example of these specialised companies is the British company, Johnson Matthey. This company manufactures gold, silver, and PGM elaborate products such as catalysts and chemical compounds of these precious metals in the UK and in the USA. Johnson Matthey is also very active in the trading and in the assaying of precious metals. The US company Engelhard and its French subsidiary Engelhard-CLAL have similar activities. These companies are therefore involved in the trading of precious metals as well as other base metals and supply products and compounds of precious metals. They are also diversified in supplying compounds of some other non-ferrous metals, such as titanium. All these products are characterised by high technologies and high value-added. The partial vertical integration of companies such as Johnson Matthey and Engelhard is therefore effective in managing the risks related to being present on international markets for precious and other non-ferrous metals.

Globally, we can highlight several points that describe the most prominent features of metal producers. A first point is that the markets for metallic commodities are evolving towards more competitive structures. This, in turn, is driving the trend towards mergers. The aluminium markets are a case in point. Up until about 1980, ALCOA was the dominant producer. Then, due in large part to technical innovations that drove down costs, a number of other comparatively smaller producers became able to compete with ALCOA. However, these bauxite-based technological advances have come to an end and the electrolytic process has now almost reached its physical maximum. Combined with the trend to competitive markets, this means that survival depends on cost-cutting and the only way to cut costs has become external growth through take-overs leading to economies of scale. A number of recent take-overs and attempted take-overs have indeed been observed in recent years in the aluminium industry. Kaiser and Alumax have been taken over by Alcoa and Alcan, Algroup (ex-Alusuisse) and Péchiney have applied to merge, although it is likely that, due to European Commission opposition, only the merging of Alcan and Algroup will be allowed. Many other mergers or take-overs have been observed in other areas of the metal and mining industries and, as we saw in the special cases of Johnson Matthey and Engelhard, there are also cases of partial downstream vertical integration. These companies are not fully integrated, but they are specialised in precious metals. They have also been involved in recent take-overs and mergers. For instance, Engelhard merged with the French company CLAL in 1998.

A second point stems from the fact that, unlike refined oil products, metallic commodities are far from end-consumer goods. Most metal commodities, which usually are refined metals, require several steps of industrial transformation before they are incorporated into such end-consumer goods. This means that few of the actors of the mining and metal industries are fully vertically integrated from the raw material to the retail market stage. There are some exceptions. The large aluminium producers are vertically integrated, and the most fully integrated is Alcoa, which is involved in traditional aluminium upstream products, such as rolled products, but also in semi-finished goods and in finished products (for housing, in particular). The French producer Péchiney is also vertically integrated, although perhaps less so than Alcoa, being present in aluminium and in its application in packaging and also in the physical trading of aluminium and the brokerage activities related to aluminium derivative markets. Such vertical integration usually goes along with specialisation. For instance, both Alcoa and Péchiney are involved almost exclusively in aluminium.[7]

The third point is a logical consequence of the second point with respect to the principle of diversification. Few metal companies are vertically integrated and specialised in one product. This is because, except perhaps for very large companies that can cope with the risks inherent in a non-diversified position and the smaller niche-market companies, other companies find better opportunities in external growth through diversification.[8] It appears indeed that many mining and metal companies are involved in several metal commodities as well as in other mineral and energy commodities. Clearly, such diversification relates strategic complementarities and cost reductions coming from scale effects to a straight-forward Markowitz portfolio management. A number of large mining and metal companies stand as examples of such diversification (see Table 8.3 below).

This is the case of BHP in Australia, which has activities in steel, petroleum, coal, diamonds, and in many metals, including copper, lead, zinc, titanium, gold, and silver. As mentioned above, it recently diversified into platinum through a take-over in Zimbabwe. Anglo-American PLC is another example of a large company which is diversified in energy, steel and a number of metals, including precious metals. But Anglo-American PLC is also present in coal (through Anglo Coal), in base non-ferrous metals (in particular, copper, zinc and nickel), in chromium and manganese (through a joint venture with Billiton), in forestry products, in several downstream industries, and in financial services. A third global company is RTZ, which is diversified in a number of activities in metals

---

[7] Besides aluminium, Alcoa is involved in plastic packaging (vinyl packaging), while Péchiney is involved in ferro-alloys.

[8] It could be argued that if markets are efficient and shareholders can diversify on their own, the argument for diversification falls down. But a commodity company that invests (often in a period of high profits due to high commodity prices) in a diversified portfolio of commodity producers can achieve, in addition to the usual benefits of diversification, savings in fixed costs and the usual value creation resulting from successful take-overs, thus creating more value than an ordinary investor in a diversified portfolio of commodity companies.

and various upstream minerals and ores, including aluminium, borates, copper, gold, iron ore, lead, nickel, salt, silver, talc, titanium, and zinc, and in energy commodities, such as coal and uranium. As a final example, we mention the Canadian company Cominco Ltd, which is diversified in a number of common non-ferrous metals, such as copper, precious metals such as gold and silver, and some rare strategic metals, such as bismuth, cadmium, germanium, indium, and molybdenum. Cominco is also involved in the production of compounds of these metals.

We end this subsection with a discussion of market participants on agricultural commodity markets. In contrast with what is observed for energy commodities and other mineral commodities and metals, where dominant producers are most often huge global companies, most basic agricultural commodities are still produced by small producers, which might not even be registered companies. In the case of most agricultural commodities produced in the OECD area, the family farm is still by far the dominant model, although its size is steadily

Table 8.3 Examples of mining and metal producing companies that are specialised, and/or vertically integrated, or diversified, and/or horizontally integrated

Metal and mining companies and their characteristics	
Name of companies	Characteristics
Specialised, and/or vertically integrated companies	
Usinor, CORUS, ARBED, Alcoa, Alcan, Péchiney, De Beers, Stillwater, Johnson Matthey, Engelhard, and Engelhard-CLAL etc.	These companies are specialised in specific mineral commodities with little diversification, and are usually vertically integrated, so that they are involved in mining, smelting and refining, and/or in some downstream products, and/or in physical trading. Most of them are large global companies, often involved in take-overs, but some are comparatively smaller companies that operate on niche markets
Diversified, and/or vertically integrated companies	
BHP (Broken Hill Proprietary), Anglo-American PLC, Rio Tinto Zinc, Cominco Ltd, Phelps-Dodge, etc.	These companies are diversified and are usually vertically integrated in a number of mineral commodities, including energy commodities, ores, metals and other minerals, they are involved in mining, smelting and refining, sometimes in trading and other downstream industrial operations. Most of them are large global companies, often involved in take-overs.

increasing throughout the world. Outside the OECD area, small or very small farmers also exist side by side with comparatively large producers. This is the case for tropical commodities, for example. Furthermore, in spite of a movement towards deregulation and less protection, in many countries and for many products, prices are still controlled or subject to public guarantee schemes that aim at protecting farmers against price fluctuations. This means that in many cases, producers of agricultural commodities are not directly exposed to international markets and do not sell their production directly on these markets. The usual scheme is that they sell their output to stockists and warehouse operators, which can be co-operative structures in continental Europe or elevator companies in the USA and in Canada. Consequently, in many cases, producers of agricultural commodities are not direct actors on international markets and there is little to say concerning them within the framework of this section. Neither are they direct actors of derivative markets, except perhaps for (usually large) farms in countries such as the USA, Canada, and especially Australia and New Zealand, inasmuch as in these two latter countries all subsidies and guaranteed price schemes have been eliminated.

In the emerging economies of the tropical world, the evolution towards deregulation and the removal of controlled prices or price guarantees is also a strong trend. In the case of tropical agricultural commodities, farmers or producers are often not direct actors on international markets and their supply is frequently channelled through other actors, such as warehouse operators. However, the emergence of efficient markets for warehouse receipts and/or new derivative markets for some agricultural commodities, such as the emerging futures market for pepper in India (UNCTAD, 2000) may have beneficial consequences for small farmers from developing countries (Matringe, 1998).

There are, however, a few basic agricultural commodities that are produced by larger actors, whenever they are the result of some industrial transformation of agricultural commodities supplied directly by farming. This is the case of sugar (whether raw sugar or white refined sugar). Sugar may be produced by crushing and processing either sugar cane or beet and this is usually an industrial operation which is in the hands of large companies, such as Tate and Lyle in Europe (Chalmin, 1990). These companies are usually vertically integrated and present in the trading and sometimes in the distribution and retailing of sugar, so that we will come back to them when discussing industrial end-users and trading. Other significant industrial end-users of agricultural commodities are large food companies. These companies are very diverse and numerous and they are purchasers of agricultural commodities. An example of these companies is the Swiss company Nestlé, which purchases a number of basic agricultural commodities (sugar, coffee, cocoa, etc.) on world markets. Another example is the French company Eridania-Beghin-Say (controlled by the Italian Montedison) which is also very active in the trading and purchasing of agricultural commodities such as sugar, oilseeds and edible oil, and spices.

8.2.3   Other Actors on the Commodity Markets

In this section we are going to discuss a number of actors on the commodity markets that are neither traders nor producers, but are either directly or indirectly involved in the physical trading of commodities. Those directly involved are stockists or warehouse operators, shippers and other transporters as well as industrial end-users. Those indirectly involved include certain intermediaries, brokers, and suppliers of various services, including insurers and banks. The trading companies will be analysed in the next section.

Stockists and warehouse operators indeed play a fundamental role on international commodity markets. Elsewhere in this book, we have discussed the importance of stocks in the economics of commodities. Stocks are clearly essential for the regulation of commodity markets and several types of agents hold stocks. Most large trading companies that are present on the international markets for grains, such as Farmland and Cargill, also operate grain elevators. Holding inventories, of course, has a cost, called the cost of carry that includes the storage costs and the opportunity cost of capital (see Chapter 2). This cost is effectively charged to the client on international markets and, as discussed in Chapter 2, is an important element of futures price formation. Holding physical stocks dampens price fluctuations related to crop variations caused by the weather and other natural hazards such as disease and pests. It is thus important for large traders in agricultural commodities to hold stocks.

In the case of metals, there is also much stockpiling and, for base non-ferrous metals, the LME has a network of approved warehouses all over the world. In addition to running futures and option markets for these metals, the LME also runs a spot market, which is, in effect, a market for warehouse receipts. Thus, in addition to hedging services and supplying reference prices, the LME also provides a service which is equivalent to running warehouses for industrialists involved in these base non-ferrous metals. However, many other agents, such as trading companies, producers, and industrial end-users, also hold stocks and there are even companies that are more or less specialised in managing warehouses. In all cases, the existence of efficient futures markets with the possibility of physical delivery ensure the competitiveness of the activity of managing stocks, because of the possible arbitrage between commodities stored in the warehouses of organised futures markets and commodities stored in other private warehouses.

In the case of minor non-ferrous metals, there are no organised futures markets and the existence of physical speculative stocks contributes to the regulation of the market, but under less competitive and less transparent conditions. This situation adds to the high price volatility of these metals.

Precious metals are partly financial assets, so that there are enormous stocks of these metals available. Some of these stocks are in the hands of private persons, because of the traditional hoarding of gold and silver. Financial agents, such as banks, specialised funds, various investors, and some pension funds hold other stocks. For instance, the well-known American investor Warren Buffet made investments in silver totalling 129.7 million ounces between 1997 and 1999.

In the case of oil and oil products, stocks are usually in the hands of vertically integrated large oil companies, independent oil refiners, and pipeline companies.

Commodity carriers also play a fundamental role on international commodity markets. On these markets, physical transportation is essential for delivering the commodities where they are needed. It is dominated by seaborne trade. In some particular cases, however, other means of transportation are used, such as pipelines for natural gas and crude oil, and air cargo in the case of very expensive commodities, such as precious metals. Trucking and railway transportation are less prevalent in international trade and are reserved for comparatively smaller shipments and distances.

Seaborne transport is subject to several international agreements, such as the Brussels and the Hamburg conventions. These conventions are applicable in a large number of countries and are concerned with liabilities due to loss, damage, and delay. The main problem for sea carriers is to deliver the commodity in good condition, at the destination and on the date specified in the contract. The date of delivery may sometimes be guaranteed, especially in the case of an industry working under a 'just in time' scheme.

Where the seaborne transport of basic commodities is concerned, operations are quite complex, inasmuch as they require a number of intermediaries with specific responsibilities. In case of problems and disputes, the commercial contract is very important and it is necessary to be able to refer to some legal support that may help solving these problems.

Transport is one of the most significant costs for either a trading company or an industrial end-user of commodities. It is not always easy to manage and, as we saw in Chapter 7, it implies a number of risks and logistical problems that must also be kept under control. There are a number of actors in the transport business, including shipowners, shipbrokers, transport agents, and forwarding agents.

Shipowners and shipbrokers are, of course, fundamental, as they are responsible for the shipping proper. Several possibilities are available for shipping:

1. *Regular shipping lines*, which is a well-organised form of shipping, with posted prices. More than 95% of this traffic is container traffic.
2. *Tramping*, which is an OTC market, on which the shipowner and the charterer negotiate a charter for the use of a ship.

On regular shipping lines, a shipowner, or often a group of shipowners, price the freight after a discussion with shippers or their representatives, which represent the freight users (in the case of commodities, producers or trading companies). Pricing is established on a posted price basis, and is available from groups of shipowners as a fixed price, except for the variable costs related to fuels and to exchange rates. For these variable costs, a bunker adjustment factor and a currency adjustment factor (BAF–CAF) are usually applied. However, in this segment of the market for freight, outsiders can offer freight rates which are significantly lower, often by 20–30%, but there is a risk that the quality of their services will not be equivalent.

Besides regular shipping lines, there is an OTC market for freight, on which shipowners and user-charterers negotiate the conditions of freight services. This market involves specialised ships, such as bulk carriers, ore carriers, other dry cargo ships, and also oil and methane tankers of all tonnage. Because of the specific characteristics of the ships, it is a technical market, which might require a shipbroker as an intermediary. On this market, the ship is usually chartered through a contract, called the charterparty, which defines the conditions of transportation (duration, if the charter is concluded for a limited time, starting date for the charter, points of departure and of arrival).

As shown in the sugar contract in Annex 1 of Chapter 7, the duration of calls in ports (which is distinct from the time of shipping) is carefully negotiated in terms of the quantity to be unloaded from the ship. In particular, this contract provides for a minimum quantity to be discharged (1200 tonnes/day) in order to avoid a costly immobilisation of the ship, which implies being able to provide for discharge from barges if the harbour is congested. This may be achieved through WIBON (whether in berth or not) or WIFPON (whether in port or not) clauses. Strikes and labour disputes on the harbour can in this case lead to significant overcosts. If discharge is over schedule, there are costs, called surrestaries. Conversely, if it is completed ahead of time, a premium, called dispatch money, is provided.

As noted in Chapter 1, this OTC market for tramping may itself be considered as a commodity and it is quite volatile. As also noted previously, a futures market related to a freight index (BIFFEX)[9] is available for hedging against this risk, especially with the new BIFFEX contract opened in 1998 on the LIFFE in London. This OTC market for freight is important for basic commodities with a comparatively low price that are the object of large commercial contracts, such as fertilisers (urea, the price of which is about US$175/tonne CFR; raw or refined sugar; cereals; ores, etc). These commodities require ships with a tonnage of between 25,000 and 50,000 registered tons.

The volume of basic commodities using tramping services is estimated as 1.3 billion tonnes/year worldwide, excluding oil. Shipowners specialised in oil tankers are often subsidiaries of major oil companies, such as Exxon, Chevron, Petrobras, BP-AMOCO, and Shell, but there are oil tanker companies that are independent of oil companies, such as Trodos in Greece, World Line in Hong Kong, and Japan Line in Japan.

Shipbrokers are intermediaries that are necessary to both sellers and buyers of commodities, because the market for tramping is both complex and technical.

---

[9] Baltic Index for Freight Futures Exchanges; more precisely, an index called Baltic Panamax Index, related to the BIFFEX index, is the index that serves as reference for the LIFFE contract.

These brokers have detailed information about shipowners and their fleet (condition and availability of ships, etc.) and on market trends. BIFFEX quotations are ex post results of shipbrokers' actions. Shipbrokers may therefore advise either buyers or sellers in the charterparty to be concluded with shipowners. They are very useful as intermediaries between the parties with commodity buyers or sellers on one side and shipowners on the other side. Negotiations on freight rates and on the conditions of transport are often conducted by two shipbrokers, each of which is representing one of the parties. A charterparty is signed between the two parties after preparation of the negotiation with the support of shipbrokers. In the case of a tender for delivery of a large quantity of a commodity, a shipbroker may be asked to study the cost of transportation in order to help a company that wants to submit a bid to quote a price.

Large trading companies may, however, have specialised services that are able to evaluate the cost of freight themselves. These trading companies negotiate directly with the shipowners with whom they usually work. However, in the case of agricultural and food commodities, for instance, shipping often depends upon weather conditions, the destination and the availability of ships. Under these conditions, it may sometimes be difficult, even for a large trading company, to identify in advance the shipowner that will be able to answer a given tender, such as a demand for delivery of 40,000 tonnes of rice at New Orleans in a delay of 20 days, knowing that this might require two or three ships. On the other hand, in the case of regular deliveries, an ongoing contract may be signed between the two parties. Where industrial raw materials are concerned, there might be fewer fluctuations in the traffic and ongoing contracts may also be concluded. This might be true, for example, of the steel industry which has a good deal of control over its output and which must have regular supplies of coke and iron ore. Similarly, an aluminium maker such as Péchiney must have regular supplies of bauxite.

The market for the services of shipbrokers is dominated by large companies, such as R. S. Platou in Norway. R. S. Platou, founded in 1936, is an example of a shipbroking company involved in a variety of commodities (oil and oil products, agricultural and food commodities, as well as mineral and metal commodities). In London, Clarkson is one of the largest shipbroking companies, which, of course, is in line with the size of the port of London's traffic. In other countries, such as France, there are smaller shipbrokers, such as Barry-Rodgliano-Salles, a specialist in the chartering of oil tankers and dry cargo ships (for instance, for the shipping of cereals such as rice) as well as in the outright buying and selling of entire ships. Lerbret is another smaller French shipbroking company that is specialised in agricultural and food commodities. The relationships between shipowners, shipbrokers, and commodity market participants are founded on mutual trust, technical skills, and in-depth knowledge of the markets.

Air transportation and other means of transport deserve a few words. Air freight is of interest for comparatively expensive commodities, such as precious metals. It is regulated internationally by the Warsaw Convention, which defines, in particular, the carrier's minimal liability. As in the case of shipping, there are carriers that offer cargo or freight services on regular scheduled flights on a posted price basis. Most regular carriers have signed international IATA agreements that apply to freight. Just as in the case of shipping, there are also charterers and outsiders who practise lower prices on an OTC basis.

Commodities that use air cargo services are usually very expensive and they are often in quantities that are too small to justify chartering a whole aircraft. Consequently, regular airlines and specific outsiders are prevalent in the freight for expensive commodities. Compared to shipping, it has a number of advantages. It is much faster than shipping. A cargo of fine Australian wines, or of refined Australian gold can be made available in London in less than three days, instead of two or three months by shipping. This can be an important consideration since it eliminates most of the price risk during transport (but not between the order and the effective delivery). Air freight is also much less risky, and, consequently, insurance is much cheaper than in the case of shipping. Furthermore, regular air carriers systematically include insurance in their prices and only a comparatively cheap residual insurance may be required by the market operator. Documents such as the airway bill, the equivalent of the bill of lading in shipping, also lend themselves to payment techniques such as the letter of credit. Finally, air freight is simpler than in the case of shipping with less need for intermediaries other than forwarding and transport agents.

Road and railway are also indispensable in the transport of commodities, usually for smaller distances between the production areas and the port or the airport of delivery and between the port or the airport of delivery and the facilities of the industrial end-user.

Commodity market operators also use the services of other intermediaries, such as forwarding agents and transport agents. These intermediaries are useful for both shipping and air freight. Forwarding agents act as representatives of market participants. Their role is to communicate their instructions to subcontractors and to act as customs clearing agents, representing market participants for custom clearance of their goods. However, the activity of these intermediaries is changing and broadening, and many global forwarding service companies are now diversified into logistics and transport agent companies, which propose organising a global transport service tailored to the needs of a particular market participant. This includes acting as agents for a full range of services, such as warehousing, insurance, packaging, obtaining customs and sanitary clearance, and, finally, acting as shipping or air brokers. The logistics services community is now developing sophisticated computerised electronic data interchange (EDI) systems, which aim at both managing transactions (orders, transport documents, billing, etc.) and at ensuring the control of information and the tracing of goods.

A leading forwarding company offering broadened and diversified services is Panalpina, originally a Swiss company. It is now present all over the world with a turnover of about 5.5 billion Swiss francs in 1999. Panalpina has developed an integrated forwarding concept which goes beyond traditional forwarding and customs clearance services, including all the services of the transportation sequence as well as air and sea brokerage services through its subsidiary, Sea and Air Broker. Panalpina works with key commodity industries, such as the energy and oil industry, and the mining industries, especially in the transport of equipment for these industries.

Insurance companies and *insurance brokers* provide other services that are indispensable to commodity market participants. Insurance brokers are intermediaries between insurance companies and market participants. They also have close relationships with banks and shipowners. As a rule, insurance brokers involved in commodities deal with all sorts of commodities, in order to diversify their client portfolio. They are essential because any commodity, whatever its nature, is subject to so many heavy risks during its physical transportation that trading companies cannot realistically assume them. We saw in Chapter 7 that these risks include transportation and warehousing risks, other physical risks, political risks, and credit or counterparty risks. All these risks can be covered through a suitable insurance policy. Such insurance policies may be offered by large international insurers, such as Lloyd's, Allianz, CMA, Axa, ACE, Generali, and many others, and they are generally managed by specialised insurance brokers. Examples of insurance brokers that are involved in maritime insurance are Marsh McLennan, a world leader in this area. Other important brokers are AON, Willis Cooron (all three being American), and JLT/SIACI (an Anglo-French group).

Insurance policies are usually comprehensive marine and war risk insurance, including war risks and similar risks, such as 'strikes, riots, civil commotions and mine risks' (see e.g. the example of a sugar contract given in Annex 7A of Chapter 7). These policies are compatible with the minimal requirements of FOB, CIF, and C&F incoterms, but do not usually cover quality risks. An uninsured market participant is only covered by guarantees provided for by international conventions, whereby the liability of the carrier is very limited. A number of clauses in the international conventions, such as force majeure, defect or inadequacy of packaging, can even exonerate the carrier of any liability. Insurance brokers develop a specific and often personal relationship with trading companies involved in commodities. As noted previously, this relationship is founded on mutual trust and professional expertise.

Although limited in scope, the services of *verification, testing* and *certification* companies, that we denote, for the sake of brevity, as certification companies, are very important for commodity market participants. The business of these companies on international commodity markets is to test and verify shipments of commodities and then issue a certificate whereby:

1. The quality of a commodity shipment is certified to comply with the quality norms provided for in the commercial contract.

2. The quantity of commodities involved in a cargo, and the nature of packaging (which should be such that the quality of the shipment should not suffer at sea, at least under usual navigation conditions), are also certified.

The certification is usually valid only if no transhipment occurs. SGS whose headquarters are in Geneva, Switzerland, is one of the world leaders in certification and it is heavily involved, among other activities, in testing and certifying commodities. Its turnover was 2.092 billion Swiss francs in 1999, of which about 40% corresponds to its European activities, about 25% to its activities in Asia, and another 25% to its activities in the USA. Other important certification organisations are Bureau Veritas in France, Inspectorate and ITS in the UK, Cotecna in Switzerland, and Saybold in the Netherlands. The Lloyd's Register group is also involved in verification and certification activities. In the field of metal commodities, and especially in the case of precious metals, certification has traditionally been the business of assayers, whose activity is closely associated with refining. This activity has benefited from technological advances in methods of non-destructive chemical analysis, such as atomic emission spectroscopy, which is able to detect very low quantities of impurities in a metal sample. In London, for example, Alex Stewart (Assayers) are first-class metal assayers with subsidiaries all over the world. They have diversified their activities into testing and certifying most other commodities, including oil and oil products, coal, and agricultural commodities. As far as gold and silver are concerned, evidence that a refiner approved by the London Bullion Market Association (LBMA) has produced the metal may be required of traders. Many of these approved refiners are also active in the physical trading of precious metals. LBMA approved refiners of gold include, for instance, Johnson Matthey PLC in the UK, Engelhard Inc. in the USA, or its French subsidiary Engelhard-CLAL in France, who are all active in the trading of precious metals.

The services of *banks* and of other financial institutions, such as *brokers or intermediaries on organised (or OTC) derivative markets*, are also essential to commodity market participants. As emphasised elsewhere, there are time lags in commodity market operations. In particular, the purchase and resale of a commodity by a trader as well as delivery and payment are usually not simultaneous. Under these conditions, in addition to hedging, market operators will obviously need the credit services of a bank. As discussed in Chapter 7, the irrevocable letter of credit is a useful banking technique that is available for providing a cash advance to a seller, while removing the seller's counterparty risk, i.e. default by the purchaser.[10] Another useful banking technique is the performance bond, which addresses the buyer's counterparty risk, i.e. default by the seller. Longer-term credit techniques, which involve commodity-related collateral, such

---

[10] Or, for a more complete guarantee, the irrevocable, transferable, and confirmed letter of credit.

as asset-backed financing, have also been discussed in Chapter 6. It is therefore clear that banking services, and especially the services of internationally oriented banks, are essential to international commodity trading, especially in the case of trading companies.

Another service that is essential to the commodity trading community is *hedging* because of the problem of price volatility that is a characteristic of commodity markets. Hedging can be effected by using futures and options on organised derivative markets. On these markets, trading has to be conducted through the services of an approved intermediary. In the USA, the Commodity Futures Trading Commission (CFTC) has the regulatory task of supervising the conduct of brokers, while in the UK this regulatory task is performed by the Financial Services Authority (FSA). There are several levels and several categories of intermediaries, whose names may differ in various countries and on various exchanges. Banks and specialised brokerage firms alike may act as intermediaries and many of them are members of organised exchanges, which are allowed to trade on these markets either for their own account or on behalf of clients. In the USA, professionals qualified to act fully as brokers on futures markets are called futures commission merchants (FCMs). FCMs are allowed to receive funds from their clients for margin deposits. Another category of professionals is introducing brokers, which may not receive funds from their clients and must therefore act through an FCM. There are also floor brokers, who trade on the exchange floor, usually as employees of FCMs, and floor traders that trade for their own account and must use the services of an FCM. On the CBOT, floor traders and floor brokers have to be individual members of the exchange. Individual membership requires a recommendation by two members of the board, a successful personal qualification exam, and the purchase or rental of a seat. Seats are sold on an ongoing basis through an auction process. Firm membership requires some different criteria, particularly in terms of creditworthiness and net worth.

In the UK, there are also specialised brokerage firms and financial institutions that accept trading for clients on futures markets. These firms may also become members of recognised exchanges if they pass the relevant expertise, creditworthiness, and net worth criteria.

Futures commission merchants in the USA, or intermediaries with various names in other countries, which might be brokerage firms or banks, act as intermediaries for the hedging purposes of physical commodity market participants. As shown by Table 8.4, in the cases of three major commodity futures exchanges, such as CBOT, LIFFE, and LME, these brokerage firms may either be subsidiaries or specialised divisions of major international banks, or subsidiaries of physical market participants, including producers, end-consumers, and traders. We can see that brokers can be either banks or specialised subsidiaries of banks. This is the dominant category in the case of exchanges such as the CBOT and the LIFFE, which are heavily involved in financial futures. Brokers can also be trading

Table 8.4 Commodity futures brokers (on CBOT, agricultural commodities; on LIFFE; on LME; examples for the CBOT and the LIFFE; full list for the LME)

Origins of commodity brokers on futures markets	
Chicago board of trade (agricultural contract FCMs)	
Banks or subsidiaries of banks	Physical market participants, or their subsidiaries
ABN AMRO Inc., Barclays Capital Inc., Crédit Suisse First Boston, Deutsche Bank Securities Inc., J. P. Morgan Futures Inc., Lehman Brothers Inc., Merril Lynch Futures Inc., Morgan Stanley and Co. Inc., Nomura Securities International Inc.	Cargill Investor Services Inc., Farmers Commodity Corporation, Gulf Trading Corporation, Hagerty Grain Co. Inc., Iowa Grain Co., Lakes Trading Group Inc.
LIFFE members	
Banks or subsidiaries of banks	Physical market participants, or their subsidiaries
ABN AMRO Equities (UK) Ltd, Bank of Nova Scotia, BNP-Paribas SA, Barclays Capital Inv. Bank, Chase Manhattan International Ltd, Crédit Lyonnais Rouse Ltd, Crédit Suisse First Boston (Europe) Ltd, Deutsche Bank AG, Dresdner Bank AG, J. P. Morgan Securities Ltd, Lehman Brothers International Europe, Merril Lynch International, Morgan Stanley and Co. International Ltd, Nomura International PLC, Société Générale	Cargill Investor Services Ltd, Mars UK Ltd,[a] Nestlé UK Ltd,[a] SA Sucre Export— Suiker Export NV,[a] Tate and Lyle Industries[a]
LME (Members, Ring Dealing Members, and Associate Broker Clearing Members)	
Banks or subsidiaries of banks	Physical market participants, or their subsidiaries
Category 1: Ring dealing members: Barclays Bank PLC, Bank of Nova Scotia, Crédit Lyonnais Rouse Ltd, Fimat International Banque SA	Category 1: Ring dealing members: Metallgesellschaft Ltd, Sogemin Metals Ltd, Amalgamated Metal Trading Ltd, ED&F Man International Ltd, Trilands Metal Ltd
Category 2: Associate broker clearing members: Deutsche Bank AG, Dresdner Bank AG, Macquarie Bank Ltd, Chase Manhattan International Ltd, Goldman Sachs International	Category 2: Associate broker clearing members: Cargill Investor Services Ltd, Engelhard International Ltd, Mitsui Bussan, Koch Metals Trading Ltd

[a] Indicates non-public order member.

companies, or their subsidiaries. Quite logically, this is the dominant category in the case of the LME, which is exclusively a commodity derivative market.

In addition to hedging instruments traded on organised derivative markets, there are also OTC derivatives. These OTC derivatives are supplied by the same financial actors. They are very useful to physical market participants if there is no organised derivative market. They are also useful when the products offered by organised markets are not adapted to the needs of these participants, as discussed in Chapter 4.

We can conclude that the services of financial actors, including banks and financial brokers, are invaluable to physical commodity market participants. They contribute to offset the counterparty and price risk that otherwise would be unbearable and would heavily hamper international commodity trading. In addition, banks provide their usual services of short-term cash advances, cash husbandry and long-term loans that are indispensable to the development of the activities of these physical market participants.

8.3 INTERNATIONAL TRADING COMPANIES

8.3.1 Overview

International commodity trading companies have a long history and have existed at least since the beginning of the seventeenth century. Clearly, some large companies specialised in overseas trading with shares outstanding in the general public did exist long before the Industrial Revolution. At that time, large overseas trading companies were already closely related to the financial community. These companies were indeed among the first companies to be quoted on stock exchanges. For instance, the Amsterdam Bourse started in 1611 by exchanging shares of the Dutch East Indies Company (in Dutch, Vereenigde Oostindische Compagnie), founded in 1602.[11] Another example is the *Compagnie d'Occident*, also called the Mississipi Company, in France, whose stocks were quoted at the emerging Paris Bourse and gave rise to an episode of dramatic speculation followed by a crash and bankruptcy of the company in 1720.

A new generation of commodity traders emerged during the nineteenth century after the Industrial Revolution. In particular, two of the leading trading companies of today date back to that time. Louis Dreyfus was founded in 1851 by Léopold Louis Dreyfus in France and started in wheat trading while Cargill was founded in 1865 as a wheat elevator company in the US Middle West by William Wallace Cargill. Interestingly enough, both companies started as family businesses and they are still private, family companies. We will come back to these companies in more detail later.

---

[11] At that time, Amsterdam was an innovative financial centre, as the Renaissance Italian cities, such as Venice, had been one century earlier.

The role of trading companies was renewed after the 'oil shocks' of 1973–74 and of 1979–80, which led to strong price movements on the international commodity markets. At the same time, as noted above, dramatic currency fluctuations followed the removal of a fixed gold price. Exchange rates that since 1945 had been defined under a fixed parity system with the US dollar became much more volatile under a floating rate regime. Since the early 1970s the already existing trading companies, such as Louis Dreyfus and Cargill, the oldest ones, have developed at a fast pace. This was also the case of some other more recent trading companies, such as Sucden, ED&F. Man and Czarnikov.

The world of commodity trading is quite heterogeneous, because there are a number of very different commodities and very different commodity markets. Besides a few very large traders, there are also a number of smaller companies, whose activity is limited to specific products and to specific geographic areas, often in a particular market niche. There are also traditional trading companies in some countries, such as the *sogo shosha* in Japan. As emphasised throughout this book, commodity traders have a risky activity. To manage the risks inherent in their activity, traders have several distinct long-term strategies. Some of them are vertically integrated with upstream and downstream industrial activities. In this case, the relative importance of individual commodities in their overall activities, and hence their corporate risks, are decreased and diversified. Other traders specialise in trading as such, often diversifying their activities into a number of commodities and financial services. In the following subsection, we are going to identify, within this heterogeneous world, the mechanisms of trading activities, and in a second subsection, the long-term corporate strategy of large trading companies. A third subsection will illustrate these considerations and analyse some significant examples of trading companies.

8.3.2 The Mechanisms of International Trading

As discussed earlier, the activity of trading companies is at the very heart of international commodity markets and it is an essential link within the sequence of activities that develops between producers and final end-users. Whatever their size, whether they are small companies or large international companies, in their core activity, which is trading as such, they are subject to the same requirements. These requirements entail having full and continuous access to market information and developing a network of ongoing relationships between a team of traders on both physical and derivative markets and all other market participants.

More specifically, trading requires immediate and ongoing access to the evolution of physical markets. It also means permanent relationships with potential clients, with other trading companies, with derivative markets, and with banks. In other words, it means being plugged into the market network. Information and its processing stem from the co-ordinated activities of marketing and other operational departments, on the one hand, and, on the other hand, of the trading rooms. Trading rooms are staffed by men and women, usually not yet out of their thirties, with various backgrounds, who have received on-the-spot practical training. Trading room participants are in permanent contact with other market participants by phone and internally with their own marketing department. They continuously analyse market trends by using the various techniques that we presented in Chapter 5. They attempt to assess the trends relating to supply and demand as a support service for the marketing and trading teams. The information that they supply helps the physical traders in marketing departments to quote prices to their clients, often with an immediate feedback to the trading room whenever a contract is concluded. In this case, the trading room will have to take an appropriate hedging position on the derivative markets.

Thus, the activity of trading rooms is based on the capacity and the experience of their staff, who frequently apply the judgmental approaches to the markets as discussed in Chapter 5. Staff reactions must be rapid if not instantaneous. Moreover, teamwork is often a central element in the performance of a trading company. All market operations conducted in trading rooms are handled by telephone and may imply agreements that are binding for both parties. Thus, there is a non-written code of conduct that is characteristic of many spot and futures markets. For instance, most transactions concluded on the Rotterdam oil spot market, on which large oil trading companies play a central role, are OTC telephone transactions. The information supplied by the market room is therefore central for two types of activities:

1. Physical trading activities with purchasing and reselling of commodities and, of course, physical delivery implying the mastery of logistics that we discussed above.
2. Simultaneous hedging on various derivative markets.

Traders seldom use brokers on physical markets. However, for completing large shipments, such as finding 2,000 tonnes of wheat to complete a cargo of 25,000 tonnes of which 23,000 tonnes have already been secured, brokers are sometimes useful to standard trading companies. Consequently, there are comparatively few physical brokerage companies and they are usually specialised. Examples of such brokers are Procom in the Netherlands, specialised in cereals, and Pasternak in the USA, specialised in soya bean and soya bean meal. Beyond these considerations, the internal organisation of trading companies may differ widely in various companies, depending on their market specialisation, their development strategies, and their size. But whatever their products and the volume of their operations, trading companies must be aware at all times of their risks on physical markets, their logistic risks, and their financial risks as a whole, including risks inherent in the derivative markets themselves, even if used for hedging purposes only (see e.g. Chapter 6).

8.3.3 Large Trading Companies and their Development Strategies

Many trading companies are incorporated as private companies and are therefore not quoted companies. Consequently, they are not subject to disclosure constraints. This situation helps to preserve confidentiality which is indispensable in trading operations on international markets. A number of these companies are still family-owned companies that were initially founded and developed by some historical entrepreneur whose image is still strong in the corporate culture of these trading firms. This is the case with Léopold Louis Dreyfus, William Wallace Cargill, and Marc Varsano, the founder of Sucre et Denrées. These companies initially counted on the commercial skills of their founders and were established with comparatively small amounts of capital. However, transformation into large trading firms required significant amounts of capital, especially when they diversified out of trading proper in order to vertically integrate with upstream or downstream industrial activities.

As significant examples, we are going to analyse the development of the three largest trading companies in terms of turnover: Cargill, Glencore, and Louis Dreyfus.

Cargill (USA) Cargill is still a private, family company, owned by the Cargill and MacMillan families. It was founded, as noted above, in 1865, just after the Civil War, by William Wallace Cargill in Minnesota. It started with traditional farming activities in wheat and other grains with facilities for the storage of crops. The development of the company was based on this agricultural activity but it was soon oriented towards developing and managing a network of elevators in the neighbourhood of navigable waterways and harbours, especially along the Mississippi. In the first stage of development, perhaps until the 1930s, Cargill's activities were mainly American with offices in Argentina and in Europe.

The international expansion of Cargill's activities can be traced to the creation of an export department in 1929, which came along with growing international trading activities. At that time, Cargill based a representative in Genoa (Italy) for the sale of grain shipments that were loaded and transported FOB from Minneapolis. As early as 1930, Cargill became established in various strategic places — Winnipeg, Rotterdam, Buenos Aires — and continuously developed its facilities, including research laboratories, elevators, terminals in ports, etc. After the Second World War, and especially since the 1970s, Cargill's external growth continued with a number of take-overs. These included take-overs of trading companies in cotton (Hohenberg Bros.), in sugar (a joint venture with Taiwan Sugar Corp.), in flour and in milling (Burrus Mills), in the steel industry (North Star Steel) and in the processing and trading of meats (MBPXL Corporation). Cargill also diversified into malt, salt, orange juice, and cocoa (through the take-over, in 1987, of General Cocoa Holland BV and of Gerkens Cocoa products). During that period, Cargill established subsidiaries throughout the world. For instance, as a joint venture with Chinese partners in 1988, it built a cotton-processing complex in China. Other take-overs include Continental Grain in 1999, which was just behind Cargill in the trading of grains, and which brought to Cargill huge storage facilities estimated at 170 million bushels in the USA, Argentina and Europe. However, the application of American antitrust laws in 2000 obliged Cargill to sell its subsidiary, Cargill Saci, producing pet food in Saladillo (Argentina) to the Swiss Nestlé group. It was also obliged to sell four export terminals on the Mississippi with elevators and wharves.

Cargill's activities are vertically integrated from upstream production, including seeds, to warehousing, including industrial transformation (fruit and grain grinding) and shipping with the support of a complete fleet and harbour facilities. Before the 1970s, all their activities were concentrated on agricultural and food commodities. But, as early as 1970, Cargill diversified its activities into the steel and oil industries. At the moment (2000), Cargill's turnover in food and agricultural commodities is the third largest in the USA, after Philip Morris and Conagra. It should also be noted that Cargill has recently invested in e-trading with the establishment of an electronic exchange for cotton. This electronic exchange was initially developed with Louis Dreyfus and Plains Cotton Co-operative and some other market participants that joined later.

Cargill's industrial activities have become very large and they now represent 70% of its consolidated turnover. This having been said, activities concerning various commodity groups are managed as separate activities and are treated as independent profit centres. Consolidated results published by the Cargill group show that the group's turnover averaged about US$50 billion between 1995 and 1999 with a small profit margin of between 1% and 2%, which is usual in trading activities (see Table 8.5 below).

Glencore At least in its present status, Glencore is a comparatively young company, founded in 1994 through a management buyout of the Swiss Marc Rich trading company, itself founded only in 1974. Its turnover of about US$40 billion is currently the second largest in the world, coming just after Cargill. At its beginning, Glencore was purely involved in trading and the core of its activities is still in pure trading. Its headquarters are located at Baar, in the Zug canton of Switzerland and it is the largest private company in Switzerland. Glencore is involved in practically all categories of commodities: energy commodities (oil

Table 8.5 Evolution of Cargill's consolidated turnover and profits (1995–99)

Years	1995	1996	1997	1998	1999
Turnover (billions of US$)	50.9	55.9	55.6	51.4	45.7
Profit (millions of US$)	671	902	814	468	597
Profit/turnover (%)	1.21	1.61	1.46	0.91	1.30

and oil products, coal, natural gas), practically all minerals and metals and most agricultural commodities.

In agricultural commodities, Glencore is involved in pure trading, especially in Eastern Europe. However, in energy and metal commodities, it has had a strategy of vertical integration and diversification through a number of international take-overs on all continents.

Louis Dreyfus   Like Cargill and Glencore, the French company Louis Dreyfus (LD), is private. However, some of its subsidiaries are quoted public companies. In particular, Louis Dreyfus Natural Gas, a company involved in the trading of natural gas in North America, is quoted on the New York Stock Exchange. Another company, Louis Dreyfus Citrus SA, involved in the trading of citrus fruit worldwide, is quoted on the Paris Bourse. In both cases, the parent company holds a majority of the capital. Louis Dreyfus is a little older than Cargill, as it was founded in 1851 by the French trader Léopold Louis Dreyfus. Very early on, by the 1870s, Louis Dreyfus was truly involved in the international trading of a number of commodities, such as wheat imported from Russia and guano imported from Peru. By 1905, Louis Dreyfus was already established in a number of countries in South America, South Africa, Asia, Europe, and Australia, with 114 offices alone in Russia.

The consolidated turnover of Louis Dreyfus in 1999 is estimated as US$25 billion. Louis Dreyfus is the third largest trading company worldwide after Cargill and Glencore. It is just as diversified as Cargill, being involved in the trading of a number of commodities, including cereals, oilseeds and edible oils, cotton, sugar, rice, feeds for cattle, meats, dairy products, cocoa, coffee, forestry products, ethyl alcohol, oil and oil products, natural gas, and electricity. It is also diversified into various upstream and downstream industrial activities, including industrial transformation processing of a number of agricultural commodities (grains, soybeans and other oilseeds, rice, etc), oil and gas exploration, production and refining, shipping, real estate and finance. It recently established a new subsidiary (LD Com) involved in telecommunication services.

Louis Dreyfus has established subsidiaries throughout the world. In the USA, the Louis Dreyfus Corporation is involved in agricultural commodities with important interests in rice and its processing. Louis Dreyfus Natural Gas, based in Oklahoma City, is one of the largest independent natural crude oil and gas operators in the USA with production facilities in Oklahoma, Texas, the Gulf of Mexico and New Mexico. In Germany, Louis Dreyfus operates an oil-refining subsidiary in Wilhelmshafen. In Latin America, its subsidiary in Argentina, SACEIF, is operating grain and oilseed crushing, storage, harbour, and shipping facilities. Coinbra, one of its subsidiaries in Brazil, is also involved in grain and oilseed crushing. Louis Dreyfus Citrus operates orange groves and orange processing facilities in Brazil and in Florida. In Brazil, Louis Dreyfus also operates, through one of its subsidiaries, an integrated industrial complex involving lumber and forestry products and furniture production facilities. Louis Dreyfus is now developing again in Russia and in other former Soviet republics, such as the Ukraine, Georgia, and Azerbaidjan, especially in grains and oilseeds. It is also a large shipowner through its subsidiary Louis Dreyfus Armateurs and other associated companies with a fleet of 45 ships and capacities in dry cargo, chemicals and natural gas, which serve the needs of the group, but which can also be chartered.

In terms of emerging new commodities, Louis Dreyfus is involved in the trading of electricity. It has become one of the leaders in the trading of electricity in the deregulated environment that prevails in the USA. In Europe, where deregulation of electricity markets is also gaining momentum, it has established a joint venture with Electricité de France in London (EDF Trading Ltd, in which EDF holds 66.7% and Louis Dreyfus has a minority stake of 33.3%) which will develop electricity spot and futures trading activities. Finally, Louis Dreyfus is involved in real estate in the USA. It is also present in financial activities through a French investment bank, Aurel SA, but with a minority stake. Aurel SA is the successor to Louis Dreyfus Finance, which was completely owned by Louis Dreyfus, so that the company is perhaps less involved in pure finance than it used to be.

Other trading companies   Besides Cargill, Glencore and Louis Dreyfus, there are a number of other large commodity trading companies that may be mentioned. The Argentinian group Bunge y Born is a large trading company that was often mentioned as one of the largest trading companies (Chalmin, 1988; Chalmin *et al.* 1990). Its consolidated turnover is equivalent to that of Glencore, but this group is now less and less involved in trading. Tradigrain, the trading subsidiary of the co-operative group Farmland Industries in the USA, which is an integrated group in the field of agricultural commodities and food industries, is strong in the trading of grains. There are a number of other, smaller trading companies, which might be specialised in specific commodities and/or on a niche market in a particular country. For instance, Soltraco AG, with headquarters in Basle (Switzerland), a subsidiary of the Belgian Solvay Company, is one of the world leaders in the trading of urea.

The Japanese *shogo shosha* constitute a very special type of trading company. These companies are involved in general trading of commodities and industrial goods on international markets as well as the Japanese markets. Some of these companies are very large and they are involved in commodity trading. For instance, Mitsui, the largest of these companies, is involved in all kinds of commodities (iron and steel products, non-ferrous metals, and agricultural commodities, etc). Mitsui's turnover is impressive at US$118.5 billion in 1999. This makes Mitsui one of the largest international companies with a turnover almost equal to that of General Motors. However, this turnover is not comparable to those of the other large trading companies we have discussed, because a large part of it stems from non-commodity goods. Another example of *shogo shosha* company is Itochu, also involved in the international trading of most commodities.

The picture of the market for commodity trading is changing rapidly. Trading is a risky business. Except perhaps for very large established companies, such as Cargill, Glencore, and Louis Dreyfus, and subsidiaries of very large oil companies or of very large metal and mining companies, the position of a trading company is often fragile and often threatened. Consequently, the failure of even the large trading companies is a quite common event. Chalmin (1988) mentions, for instance, the failure of the Cook company. Other companies disappear because of take-overs and mergers. Table 8.6, which gives a panorama of current trading companies, is thus a currently valid picture that is given for the sake of illustration, but might change significantly in the medium to long term.

8.4 CONCLUSIONS

The diversity and the specific characteristics of the actors on international commodity markets are related to the complexity and the global scope of these markets. This complexity results in a number of risks that occur throughout the sequence of market operations. One of the most important risks is the price volatility, due to short-term market imbalances that occur on these markets. These market imbalances are strongly related to the dynamics of stocks.

Among market participants, trading companies play a central role and their activity is quite risky. We have seen that, as a rule, to reduce their risks, trading companies orient their corporate strategies into three main directions. The first direction is diversifying their trading activities into several commodity markets. This first type of strategy is a traditional Markowitz portfolio diversification, but it is generally not sufficient. In particular, many commodity markets tend to be correlated with each other. This reduces the covariance effect and the diversification benefits that could be expected of such a strategy. A second direction in the strategy of trading companies is thus vertical integration with upstream and downstream industrial activities. The integration of these industrial activities reduces the covariance effect and actually contributes to better risk management. This second strategic direction is not incompatible with the first. We have seen that the most successful trading companies, such as the 'big three', Cargill, Glencore, and Dreyfus, have diversified the commodities in which they are involved and integrated upstream and downstream into industrial activities. In the same manner, we have seen that many commodity producers, especially in the oil industry, are completely integrated from their oil wells to the retailing of gasoline and other end-user refined oil products, including, naturally, trading activities. Some trading companies are even getting away from trading or at least reducing the importance of trading in their activities. But

Table 8.6 Significant examples of trading companies involved in various classes of commodities (non-exhaustive list; source: field survey)

Agricultural products

Cereals	Cargill (USA), Bunge y Born (Argentina), Louis Dreyfus (France), André (Switzerland), Soufflet (France), Toppfer (Germany), Tradigrain (USA), Glencore (Switzerland), Archer Daniels Midland (USA), Conagra (USA)
Oilseeds	Cargill (USA), Louis Dreyfus (France), Toppfer (Germany), Bunge y Born (Argentina), Tradigrain (USA)
Cotton	Dunavant (USA) (US cotton), Louis Dreyfus (all cottons), Cargill (all cottons), Uzagroimpex (Uzbekistan) (Central Asian cotton), Chinatex (China), Copaco (France) (African cottons), Paul Reinhart (Switzerland)
Meats	SOCOPA (France), Amiga (Israel), Louis Dreyfus (France), Cargill (USA)
Dairy products	Francexpa (France), Louis Dreyfus (France)
Coffee	Neuman (Germany), Volcafé (France), Cargill (USA),
Cocoa	Cargill (USA), Phibro (USA), Tardivat (France), Albrecht und Dill (Germany), ED&F Man (UK), Continental BV (Netherlands)
Natural rubber	Metallgesellschaft (Germany), Lee Rubber (USA), Phibro (USA), Safic Alcan SA (France, Metallgesellschaft Group)
Pepper and other spices	McCormick (USA), Burns Phil (Australia), Man Producten (Netherlands)
Sugar	Cargill (USA), Louis Dreyfus (France), ED&F Man (UK), Tradigrain (USA), Tate and Lyle (UK), Glencore (Switzerland), Sucre et Denrées (France), Safic Alcan (France)

Metals

Base metals (Other than precious metals)	Billiton (UK), Metallgesellschaft (Germany), Phelps-Dodge (USA), Noranda (Canada), Glencore (Switzerland), Metal Resources Group (UK), Péchiney World Trade (France)
Precious metals (Gold, silver, PGM metals)	Engelhard (USA) and Engelhard-CLAL (USA-France), Johnson Matthey (UK), Platinum Guild (USA)
Diamond	De Beers (South Africa)

Energy

Oil and gas	Shell Trading (UK), ELF Trading (France), Glencore (Switzerland), Phibro (USA), Louis Dreyfus (France)
Coal	Billiton (UK), Peabody Coal Trade (USA), Glencore (Switzerland), Co Trading (UK)
Electricity	Cargill (USA), Louis Dreyfus (France) and EDF Trading (France-UK)

a third strategic direction that is prevalent in the world of trading is external growth through take-overs and mergers. We have observed this strategic direction in several of the cases that we discussed. It leads to fixed cost reduction due to scale economies as well as to risk reduction. In the case, for instance, of Glencore, this third strategic direction is obvious, but it is also present in the two other large trading companies that we mentioned, Cargill and Louis Dreyfus.

It should be stressed that the industry of international commodity trading is one of the less static industries. In the world of commodity trading, positions may never be taken for granted and change may be rapid. A number of examples prove that successful trading companies have been thrown into situations of great fragility, and even into bankruptcy, practically overnight. Some of the examples given in Chapter 6 show that this has often been due to the mismanagement of hedging tools, such as futures markets, or to speculative positions taken on these markets. The case of Cook Industries (Chalmin, 1988) is an obvious case in which speculation on futures led a firm to bankruptcy in a few months.

It therefore seems that, nowadays, most trading companies reduce the price risk through short-term hedging strategies, long-term diversification, vertical integration, and external growth strategies.

It should be noted that the evolution of trading companies is strongly influenced by the wave of globalisation that started at the end of the twentieth century. In many ways, this wave of globalisation is a return to the previous wave of globalisation at the beginning of the twentieth century. As noted by Labys and Lesourd (1988a and b, 1989), in the case of coal, the development of the international coal market that occurred during the 1970s and the 1980s led to a revival of the international coal market. This revival was in some ways a return to a situation that was observed just before the First World War.

But this second wave of globalisation of the twentieth century has occurred in a completely different technological environment that will no doubt significantly transform international commodity markets. In particular, the development of e-commerce will probably change the structure and the efficiency of commodity markets. For instance, a growing number of internet trading sites appear for commodities that were hitherto only traded on OTC markets with no organised spot or futures markets available. The emergence of these markets, which are akin to organised markets but with fewer rigidities, is likely to accelerate the 'commoditisation' of many products. The recent development of a number of internet trading sites for products that previously were not fully commodities is impressive. Trading sites for steel products, chemicals, some energy products, emission certificates, etc. have, for instance, recently developed. The prices observed on these internet markets become reference prices, or, so to speak, 'the market's compass' for the specific commodities that are traded on them. This is no doubt a revolution on commodity markets. In particular, informal futures markets have already developed on these internet markets. This spontaneous evolution, interestingly enough, recalls the evolution that occurred on commodity markets such as the Chicago Board of Trade at the end of the nineteenth century, during the previous wave of globalisation. At that time, markets such as the CBOT, which were forward markets for warehouse receipts, evolved spontaneously into futures markets. The development of electronic futures will no doubt have important consequences on the evolution of commodity markets. If this evolution goes on, the distinction between OTC derivatives and traded derivatives with electronic quotations, and even the duality between spot and futures markets, will vanish. The development of e-commerce is therefore both a challenge and an opportunity to international commodity market participants. E-commerce may also lead to more transparent markets. Thanks to its development, commodity market operators will have at their disposal faster and more reactive tools that will help them to manage the many and varied risks associated with commodities and commodity trading.

BIBLIOGRAPHY

W. G. Broehl, Jr. (1992) *Cargill: Trading the World's Grain*. University Press of New England, Hanover, NH.

W. G. Broehl, Jr. (1998) *Cargill: Going Global*. University Press of New England, Hanover, NH.

Ph. Chalmin (1988) *Traders and Merchants*. Harwood Academic Publishers, London.

Ph. Chalmin (1990) *The Making of a Sugar Giant: Tate and Lyle 1859–1989*. Harwood Academic Publishers, London.

Ph. Chalmin, J. L. Gombeaud and Ch. Prager (1990) *The Global Markets*. Harwood Academic Publishers, London.

G. Jones (1998) *The Multinational Traders*. Routledge, London.

B. Kneen (1995) *Invisible Giant: Cargill and its Transnational Strategies*. Pluto Press, New York.

W. Labys and J. B. Lesourd (1988a) *Factors Underlying Price Determination on the International Coal Market*. Working Paper ECA 1988-22, ESIPSOI, Marseilles, June.

W. C. Labys and J. B. Lesourd (1988b) The new energy markets, Chapter 2 in J. K. Jacques, J. B. Lesourd and J. M. Ruiz (eds), *Modern Applied Energy Conservation. New Directions in Energy Conservation Management*. Ellis Horwood/Halsted Press—Wiley, Chichester/New York, 37–83.

W. C. Labys and J. B. Lesourd (1989) Facteurs explicatifs des ajustements de prix sur le marché international du charbon, *Revue de l'Energie*, **416**, December, 1035–1045.

O. Matringe (1988) Will the use of market-based instruments turn next millennium's producers into entrepreneurs?, in *New Strategies for a Changing Commodity Economy. The Rôle of Modern Financial Instruments*. Selected papers, 'Partners for Development' Summit, Lyons, France. UNCTAD, Geneva.

UNCTAD (General ed.: Ph. Chalmin; ed.: Ch. Prager, UNCTAD Secretariat; Co-ordinators: O. Matringe and L. Rutten) (2000) *World Commodity Survey 1999–2000. Markets, Trends and the World Economic Environment*. United Nations, Geneva.

9
Conclusion: International commodity trading — problems and prospects

In conclusion, we wish to stress the main points that stem from our analyses of international commodity markets. We also intend to tentatively identify the possible oncoming evolutions of international commodity markets and of international commodity trading.

International commodity markets have been shown throughout this book to be characterised by three main features. *They are markets for basic commodities with standardised qualities; they are global markets; and they are traders' markets.* All three features are interrelated. This conclusion aims at analysing the key characteristics of international commodity markets and trading along these lines. It also discusses their future trends and evolution.

As shown in several chapters of our book, basic commodities are fundamentally simple products. They are characterised by a comparatively simple bundle of quality attributes. For example, metals are mainly characterised by their purity. More complex sets of quality attributes are present in the case of agricultural and energy commodities. In all cases, however, these quality attributes are simple enough to be recognised all over the world as constituting a standard quality for a given commodity. This characteristic is welcome in a globalised market.

One of the developments that has been discussed here and there in our book is that an increasing number of goods have reached commodity status. Indeed, it seems that goods with more and more complex quality attributes, and with more and more abstract characteristics reach the status of a commodity. Coal, electricity, telecommunication time, weather, and environmental surroundings have reached commodity status or are in the process of reaching it. This raises an important question for the coming years: will this tendency continue, so that other goods, in a broad sense, either complete their evolution towards commodity status or tend to commodity status? New or existing products such as weather derivatives, emission permits, insurance products, telecommunication services, among others, are obvious candidates at reaching full commodity status. Other basic commodities which are now characterised by inefficient and local markets, such as many rare and strategic metals, may also be touched by such a development. This implies some international recognition of standard quality attributes for all these goods and services. Other goods and services which have not yet undergone any evolution in their status may well, in the future, become at least partly commoditised.

The second characteristic feature of commodity markets is their global character. It seems, as has just been discussed, that standardisation is a necessary, but not a sufficient condition, for them to be traded on global markets. Globalisation means more than mere standardisation. In particular, it rests on intense competition between producers and sellers all over the world. Here, the oncoming evolution seems to lead to mixed blessings. Of course, a large number of commodity markets have become increasingly competitive in the past, and this trend continues. However, another movement in the opposite direction, towards concentration through mergers and take-overs, has also been observed in more recent years. For instance, in the oil and gas industry, recent mergers and take-overs have been a steady trend. In the USA, these mergers even seem to go against a century of antitrust actions. Were not Exxon and Mobil, that recently merged together, two companies historically separated from the Rockefeller empire in 1911 on the basis of the 1896 antitrust law? This movement can, however, be an adaptation to global and hence larger markets that, very logically, require larger companies because of scale effects. It can also have adverse effects against the competitive character of our global markets and lend itself to the constitution of dominant positions and of cartels.

A third feature of global commodity markets is the role of traders, defined as companies which buy physical commodities intending to resell them at a profit. The importance of trading is clearly a consequence of the existence of global commodity markets. Global markets imply some kind of a Ricardian international division of labour. This means that producers are often located in geographical areas which are not consuming all of the commodity they produce. Moreover, the global economy is a complex system in which imbalance between supply and demand on commodity markets is a prevailing phenomenon. Hence the importance of trading companies and the price risks they face. These risks have given rise to the fast development of derivative markets that is closely related to trading and to the development of global commodity markets. Several questions for oncoming years can be raised in relation to trading and to derivative markets. A first question is the evolution of trading itself. As discussed in Chapter 8, trading is subject to a steady evolution towards concentration through take-overs and mergers. Will this evolution go on, with the possible effect that it can weaken the competitive character of markets? At the moment, this is a question that is difficult to assess, because take-overs and mergers in the trading industries come along with another strong movement towards vertical integration. Vertical integration of trading companies is a logical movement because, along with the use of derivative products, it tends to improve the risk-return pattern of trading industries. This movement is therefore likely to go on. What about the concomitant growth of derivative markets, which has been very rapid during the 1990s? Derivatives are useful for two main categories of agents: hedgers and speculators, the latter being defined as investors with a particular risk-return profile. It is clear that the development of commodity markets will also lead to some steady growth in the use of commodity derivatives for hedging purposes. Global and diversified investment requires assets with particular return-risk profiles and in particular assets whose returns are weakly correlated with those of traditional financial assets, such as equities and bonds. This can also lead to rapid growth in demand for derivatives that will be independent of the demand for hedging.

Finally, one last question remains. The prices of most commodities have been declining in real terms in the very long run, especially due to technical progress. This has led to more and more efficient production and use of all these commodities that is reflected in their prices. Despite several 'oil shocks', crude oil is cheaper, in real terms, than what it was a century ago. This is also true of many metals, such as aluminium. Despite the fact that it went up from a nominal value of \$35/oz between 1933 and 1968 to a higher nominal value of about \$275/oz, the price of gold is, in real terms, smaller than it used to be 50 years ago. This decline of real prices is also true of the prices of a number of agricultural goods. Will this technological trend go on? Is it compatible with the preservation of our environment, and what will its implications be on the structure and evolution of international commodity markets?

Index